F

Sloane's New Bicycle Maintenance Manual

Eugene A. Sloane

A FIRESIDE BOOK

Published by Simon & Schuster

New York   London   Toronto   Sydney   Tokyo   Singapore

Fireside

Simon & Schuster Building
Rockefeller Center
1230 Avenue of the Americas
New York, New York 10020

First Fireside Edition 1981

FIRESIDE and colophon are registered trademarks
of Simon & Schuster Inc.

Designed by Chris Welch
Manufactured in the United States of America

1 3 5 7 9 10 8 6 4 2

Library of Congress Cataloging in Publication Data
Sloane, Eugene A.
[New bicycle maintenance manual]
Sloane's new bicycle maintenance manual / Eugene A. Sloane.—1st
fireside ed.
p.   cm.
"A fireside book."
Includes index.
1. Bicycles—Maintenance and repair—Handbooks, manuals, etc.
I. Title.
TL430.S59 1991   91-14699
629.28'772—dc20   CIP

ISBN 0-671-61947-0

Grateful acknowledgment is made for permission to reprint
from the following articles:

"Frame Repairing and Refinishing," by Otis Childress, from *Bike World*
(October 1977, Volume 6, Number 10).

"Tips to Inexpensive Frame Painting," by Otis Childress, from *Bike
World* (January/February 1979, Volume 8, Number 1).

Contents

Introduction

If you can handle a screwdriver, a wrench, and a few other simple tools, you can learn to keep your bicycle in tip-top working condition. I will explain how to adjust the brakes for safe, reliable, stopping power. You will see how to keep the over 100 ball bearings in the working parts of your bicycle clean and the bearing surfaces correctly adjusted for smoother, easier pedaling and longer component life. And you will find that the chain can, when properly maintained or replaced, withstand the stress of uphill climbs without breaking.

Best of all will be the knowledge that once you have overhauled your bicycle, nothing can go wrong (short of a broken frame) that will hold you up for very long on a camping trip, a spin through the park, or a commute to work.

In this book we will concentrate primarily on all aspects of keeping your bicycle safe and in good repair. For details on the prevention of injury, for evaluation of bicycles and their parts, tips on safe riding, commuting and bike tripping, racing and bike history and lore, please refer to my expanded volume, *The Complete Book of Bicycling*.

I am grateful to the folks at Shimano, SunTour, Campagnolo, and a host of other component manufacturers for their help in providing technical details, drawings, and photos on their latest products. Performance Bicycle Shop, the bike catalog and retail outlet people, were most helpful, as were Park Tools and the tool catalog organization, The Third Hand.

1

How to Keep Your Brakes in Safe Condition

..... **B**e *sure* you can stop your bicycle in time to avoid an accident. Use the braking methods below, and follow the brake adjustment instructions shown here to get maximum stopping power from your brakes.

BRAKING TECHNIQUE

Before we get into brake maintenance, here's a brief review of safe brake operation. First, remember that your *front* brake provides 90 percent of the total braking power of *both* brakes combined. Let me illustrate. Place a book on the table, with one end against your hand. Think of that hand as the front brake. Now, with the other hand, push the book. You will see that the brake hand stops the book, but the rear of the book rises up off the table. That is what happens when you apply the brakes. The rear wheel tends to rise in the air and lose contact with the ground. Obviously, the less contact, the less braking power. If for some reason your rear brake is not working (for all the reasons I cite below in the brake adjustment section), the front wheel may lock up. When that happens you could be pitched forward off the bike and get hurt. Which is a good reason to make darned sure *both* your brakes are in good working order.

Always apply both brakes at the same time, never the front one alone. If you apply only the front brake you risk an "endo" or a pitch over the handlebars. Another reason for the poor performance of the rear brake is its much longer cable. Just the part of the cable that goes through the spaghetti tubing measures 9 inches on the front and some 30 inches on the rear brake on a typical all-terrain bicycle. The extra 21 inches of cable tubing means a lot more friction at the brake lever. It takes more hand pressure to apply the rear brake than the front one. The longer rear cable also stretches far more than the shorter front cable.

If you're going downhill fast, keep your weight as far back as possible for maximum braking ability. If you have to make an emergency stop on the flats, shift your bottom as far back on the saddle as possible as you brake. That way you put more weight over the rear wheel for safer braking.

Brake before you corner! If you brake *as* you corner the bike could skid out from under you. Slow down *before* you come to a sharp turn. Keep the inboard pedal upright for maximum pedal-to-ground clearance.

The U.S. Consumer Products Safety Commission requires that a rider of 150 pounds going at 15 mph on a flat, smooth, dry surface (such as a concrete roadway) with the wind velocity less than 7 mph (direction not specified) be able to stop within 15 feet of initial brake application (both brakes). As a practical matter, the heavier you are the longer it's going to take you to stop. Conversely, the lighter you are the sooner you can stop, so muscular heavyweights should anticipate braking needs for a safe, controlled stop. Practice braking on a variety of surfaces such as sand, gravel, or cement until you become familiar with how the brakes work, and how you and the bike react to them. Be especially careful on slippery surfaces, such as sand, snow, mud, or ice. Avoid braking so hard that you lock up one or both wheels. Check your brakes every 500 miles or every two months of *riding* time (not calendar time). Here's how. On a dry, hard-surfaced, traffic-free street, chalk a length of 15 feet. If you have a speedometer on your bike, fine. If not, just get going at a good clip, to an estimated 15 mph—which is a lot faster than you may realize on a bike. Most of us, if we don't know, almost always think we're going faster than we are. Once up to speed, apply both brakes, carefully at first. If you overshoot and can't stop within 15 feet, make several tries. Apply the brakes harder each time. If you always overshoot, your brakes are defective.

Wet weather cuts braking power substantially! Be aware that you will likely travel *60 feet* on the flats at 5 mph before you come to a stop in wet weather. Slow down and apply brakes sooner when it's raining. If your bike has steel rims, remember that brakes don't grip as well on steel as they do on aluminum, especially in wet weather.

Brake shoes harden with age, especially near the ocean where ozone seems to accelerate hardening of brake shoe compound. As brake shoes harden and wear, you lose braking power. You may be able to come to a gradual, *anticipated* stop, even with hardened brake shoes. But rocklike brake shoes won't stop you in an emergency, when you need full braking power. If you have had your bike for over two years, I recommend you replace all four brake shoes, even if they *look* okay. Please see brake shoe replacement instructions below. When you do buy new brake shoes, take the old ones to the bike shop for an exact make replacement.

Also be aware of the insidious nature of brake cable stretch. These cables stretch with use. You can even stretch brake cables on a brand-new bike. First, look at how far brakes are from the rim. Then grip the brake levers as hard as you can. Do this three times. Now look at the brake shoes. You will see they are farther away from the rim because the cables have stretched. They will stretch even more as you ride. Brake cable stretch cuts your braking power two ways. First, as the cable stretches, brake shoes have to travel farther before they begin to grip the wheel rim, which cuts braking response time. Second, if brake shoes get too far from the rim, brake levers may travel all the way to the handlebars and still not stop you in time to avoid an accident.

Here's a warning about BMX bikes. Some of these bikes have a special front brake arrangement so brakes work through a 360-degree twist of the handlebars. This design is dangerous for at least two reasons. First, children can brake for controlled trick riding, even with the handlebars reversed. The danger here is that kids can ride with the fork reversed. A reversed fork means that steering becomes very quick and very unforgiving, which can easily lead to loss of control. Second, the front brake cable follows a tortuous route through a kind of clutch gadget, which when neglected makes the front brake lever hard to apply. The longer cable also stretches. The danger is exacerbated by kids' neglect of things mechanical. I recall one bike accident case on which I was an expert witness. In this case both brakes had become inoperable, the front one because of the poor design, and both because of cable stretch. When the brakes ceased working, this lad simply dragged his foot on the ground to slow down. On one sharp turn with his foot drag-braking, his foot was trapped between the front wheel and the bike frame, and he suffered considerable injury. The moral here is don't buy your child a bike with this design brake, and keep close tabs on the bike's mechanical condition. Do not rely on your child to bring mechanical defects to your attention.

A Note About El Cheapo Bikes. I was going to be nice about this and refrain from any pejorative overtones about the relationship between the cost of a bike and the safety of that bike, but the truth is that inexpensive bicycles have inexpensive parts that may contribute to accidents and bodily injury. Cheap bikes are also often poorly assembled. Quality control is too often low. For example, brakes on these bikes are not nearly as effective, in my opinion and experience, as the brakes on better bikes. Cheap brakes can have a lot of stretch in working parts, such as brake arms, because they are cheaply made of inferior metals. I am amazed that these bikes pass Consumer Products Safety Commission standards. I have found these bikes, brand-new ones, with misaligned wheels which have loose or uneven spoke tension. Frames can be misaligned. Wheel bearings can be loose. I have even found headset bearings missing, and headsets dangerously loose. All of these conditions, misaligned wheels and frames, loose or unevenly tensioned spokes, loose headset bearings, can, individually and/or collectively, cause uncontrollable front-wheel shimmy, which almost instantly causes loss of control and an accident. True, these conditions, if they exist on a more expensive bike, can also lead to front-wheel shimmy and an accident. Here is how to keep *your* good bike in safe operating condition, starting with the brakes.

Tools You Will Need

You need the right tools to work on your brakes. The bicycle industry has yet to standardize the sizes of nuts and bolts used in its many parts. Such lack of uniformity is, in a way, understandable since bicycles and bicycle components sold in the U.S. are made in the U.S.A., Japan, Taiwan, South Korea, France, Germany, Italy, Great Britain, and other countries.

For example, some brakes need a 19-mm wrench to equalize spring tension to keep brake shoes evenly spaced from the rim. Other makes of brakes use a 2-mm Allen wrench for the same purpose. The tool list below may include more tools than you need for the brakes you have, but the overrun will be small and inexpensive. If your bike shop does not carry a particular tool, let me refer you to The Third Hand. This outfit carries every bike tool known to man, and some unknown ones, until today. Their catalog is enough to make a bike mechanic swoon. To reach The Third Hand, phone them at 916-926-2600, FAX them at 916-926-2663, or write them at P.O. Box 212, Mt. Shasta, CA 96067. They are a boon to cycling folk.

Before we start, please study Fig. 1-1 so you can become familiar with the name and location of all parts of the bicycle. That way we will both speak the same bicycle language. *Here's the list of tools.*

1. *Torque wrench:* You can buy a simple beam-type torque wrench (Fig. 1-2), calibrated in inch/pounds, for about $48 from Sears Roebuck. Ask for catalog No. 9HT445125.00. I give torque specifications for each part of your bicycle throughout this book. Use a torque wrench and the

Fig. 1-1: Study this photo to become acquainted with the names of bicycle components and frame members: 1. Chainwheel; 2. Pedal with toe strap and toe clip; 3. Chain; 4. Rear derailleur; 5. Front derailleur; 6. Front brake; 7. Brake lever; 8. Brake cable; 9. Handlebars; 10. Stem; 11. Saddle; 12. Seat post; 13. Front-wheel dropout and quick-release; 14. Bottom bracket; 15. Derailleur cable guide on down tube; 16. Freewheel; 17. Wheel rim; 18. Spokes; 19. Tube valve; 20. Tire; 21. Wheel hub; 22. Chain stay; 23. Frame lug; 24. Fender; 25. Fork crown; 26. Fork blade, showing fork rake; 27. Hub flange; 28. Seat-tube cluster; 29. Seat stay; 30. Seat tube; 31. Steering tube; 32. Rear derailleur idler pulley; 33. Top tube; 34. Fender stay; 35. Down tube; 36. Crank; 37. Rear-wheel dropout.

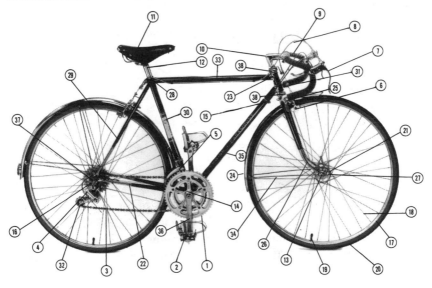

Fig. 1-2: Beam-type torque wrench is inexpensive, easy to use.

appropriate torque specification to make sure each part of your bicycle is safely tightened. Now, here's a word about torque.

Torque is the force required to produce a twisting motion around an axis, as when you turn a nut or bolt to tighten or loosen it. You need a torque wrench to insure that the bolts and nuts on a bicycle are safely tight. Bicycle component manufacturers specify tightness in inch/pounds. Buy a torque wrench calibrated in inch/pounds. You could use a torque wrench calibrated in foot/pounds, but that would be like using a hammer where a feather would do. If you use a foot/pound torque wrench, first translate the inch/pound specification into foot/pounds by dividing by 12. For example, if you need to tighten a nut to 36 inch/pounds but use a foot/pound torque wrench, divide 36 by 12 to obtain the correct torque of 3 foot/pounds. Bicycle component manufacturers located outside the U.S. commonly use metric measurements instead of inch/pounds or foot/pounds as their torque specifications. Use Table 1-1 to change metric torques to inch/pounds or foot/pounds.

Table 1-1 METRIC TO INCH/POUNDS OR FOOT/POUNDS CONVERSION

cm/kg = inch/pounds × 1.15
cm/kg = foot/pounds × 13.8
m/kgs = foot/pounds × .1383
foot/pounds = m/kgs × 7.2329
foot/pounds × 12 = inch/pounds
inch/pounds ÷ 12 = foot/pounds

Take it easy if you use a foot/pound wrench, because that monster can snap off a bike bolt with just a slight over-torque.

Use a torque wrench to tighten or to check the tightness of a bolt or nut. Turn the torque wrench *clockwise* (tightening direction) to *test* the tightness of a nut or bolt. If you turn the torque wrench in the loosening direction (counterclockwise) you will find that the "break-away" measurement is a lot less than the torque you applied when you tightened the nut (clockwise). For example, I tightened a nut to 150 inch/pounds (clockwise). Then I turned the torque wrench counterclockwise to loosen this nut. The nut turned (broke-away) at 100 inch/pounds, which of course did not accurately reflect my original tightening torque of 150 inch/pounds.

To repeat, use a torque wrench to *check how tight* a bolt or nut is by turning the nut or bolt with the torque wrench in the tightening direction. As you apply pressure on the wrench, watch the nut or bolt carefully. Stop the instant it starts moving. The reading on the torque wrench is the tightness of the bolt or nut. Use a torque wrench to tighten a nut or bolt. Watch the indicator as you turn the wrench. Stop the instant the indicator reaches the torque setting you want.

There are three types of torque wrenches. The beam-type torque wrench (Fig. 1-2) is not as accurate as the click type or the dial type. However, it is accurate enough for the home workshop. If you want the ultimate in torque wrench accuracy, use the click type, made by Proto Tools. It costs about $160. The easiest to use is the accurate dial type, also made by Proto. It costs about $173. I recommend the dial type for use by bike shops or bicycle clubs or wherever a lot of bicycle repair and maintenance is performed. All of these torque wrenches come with understandable instructions.

Use Table 1-2 below as a general guide to safe tightness of brake parts. These torque specifications are from brake manufacturer's technical literature.

Table 1-2 TORQUE SPECIFICATIONS FOR BRAKES

Part	Tightness in Inch/Pounds
Brake shoe in brake arm	50–80
Cable carrier binder bolt	50–75
Round cable carrier binder bolt	35–50
Cross-over cable binder bolt, in brake arm	50–75
Sidepull brake cable binder bolt	50–75
Brake arm mounting bolt	50–75
Brake lever mounting bolt	50–65
Brake lever clamp bolt (replacing extension levers)	13–22

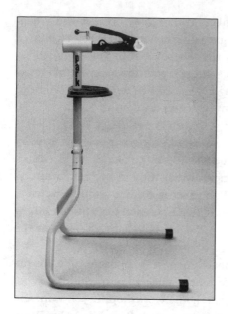

Fig. 1-3: Park workstand has leg that folds for storage.

2. *Workstand.* To work on your bike you need some way to hold it up off the floor at a convenient height. You could hang your bike by padded hooks from the ceiling, but the bike won't hold still that way. The best solution is a bike workstand, such as the Park stand which collapses compactly when not in use (Fig. 1-3).

3. *A set of Allen (hex) wrenches* in 2-, 2.5-, 3-, 4-, 5-, and 6-mm sizes.

4. *Wrenches* in 8-, 9-, 10-, and 11-mm sizes.

5. *A 19-mm thin cone-type open-end wrench* if you use SunTour XCD brakes so you can adjust spring tension to keep brake shoes evenly spaced on each side of the wheel rim.

6. *Cable cutter.* Optional, but snips off brake and derailleur cables neatly, so ends don't unravel before you can solder them closed. This tool is made by SunTour and does work very well.

7. *Soldering iron and solder.* Optional, but a neat and easy way to solder cut ends of cables to keep them from unraveling. This also makes it easy to remove cables for servicing components, and to reinstall the same cable.

8. *A Park third hand* (Fig. 1-4) or a NSH strap-type third hand, to hold the brake shoes tightly against the rim while you adjust the cable. You could use a pedal toe strap, but the third hands shown here are far easier to use. If you have cantilever brakes use the special Park third-hand tool that spreads wide apart for these brakes.

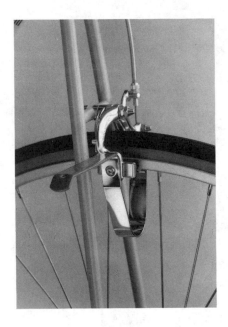

Fig. 1-4: Park third hand tool for road-bike sidepull and centerpull brakes holds brake shoes against the wheel rim so you can adjust brake shoes or change a brake cable.

Fig. 1-5: Park fourth hand tool holds cable taut while you tighten cable binder bolt and nut.

9. *A Park fourth hand* (Fig. 1-5). Holds the cable taut while you tighten the cable binder bolt.

10. *No. 282 LocTite* (the kind that does not harden to ironlike consistency but does keep nuts and bolts from rattling loose). Use LocTite on all bolts and nuts *except* hubs, bottom brackets, pedal bearings, and headsets. Keep it away from brake shoes and rims!

BASIC BRAKE INSPECTION, WHAT TO CHECK FOR

There are four types of brakes used on bicycles. All-terrain bicycles use cantilever brakes (Fig. 1-6), U-brakes (Fig. 1-7), or cam brakes (Fig. 1-8). Road bikes use centerpull brakes (Fig. 1-9) or sidepull brakes (Fig. 1-10). Find which type of brake is on your bike and refer to that section of this chapter for brake maintenance instructions. First, a few words of caution.

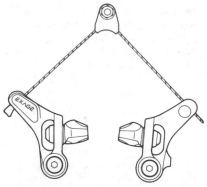

Fig. 1-6: *Cantilever brake.*

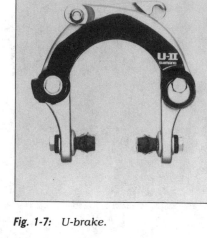

Fig. 1-7: *U-brake.*

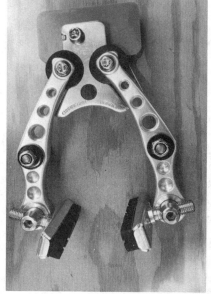

Fig. 1-8: *Cam action brake.*

Fig. 1-9: *Centerpull brake. "A," lock-nut; "B," Adjuster barrel for removing minor cable stretch; "C," Binder bolt nut on cable carrier.*

Fig. 1-10: Sidepull brakes. Arrows point to adjuster barrel and locknut on the brake arm.

Fig. 1-11: Cable binder bolt and nut. Fourth hand tool holds cable taut.

1. *Bolts and nuts: A loose bolt or nut on a brake can spell disaster!* On my very first ride on a brand-new ATB, the main front brake cable slipped right out of the cable carrier (arrow, Fig. 1-11). This left me with just the rear brake to stop with. Fortunately I was going slowly, on a traffic-free road. I know, I know, I should have squeezed the brake lever hard first, to make sure the cable binder bolts were tight. That's the danger of making assumptions; you could be wrong. Assuming effective quality control can be hazardous to your health! On cantilever and centerpull brakes the crossover cable end, where it's held by the binder bolt in the brake arm (Fig. 1-12), may also slip if that bolt is not tight enough. The crossover cable is the short cable that rides in the cable carrier. One end of the crossover cable has a lead tab (Fig. 1-13) that can be pulled out of the brake arm when the brake shoes are squeezed together, to

Fig. 1-12: Crossover cable is held by the binder bolt in cantilever brake arm.

Fig. 1-13: The other end of the crossover cable in Fig. 1-12 has a leaded tab end which fits into the brake arm. To remove a wheel, squeeze brakes together, pull out the brake tab. Now brake arms will spread far apart so the fat tire can be removed on this all-terrain bike. (Note: Road-bike brakes have a quick-release lever to spread brakes apart for wheel removal.)

let the tire fit past the brake shoes when you remove and replace the wheel. The other end of the crossover cable is held in the brake arm by a binder bolt (Fig. 1-12). Check all brake nuts and bolts at least every six months to the safe torque tightness as in Table 1-2 above.

Loose brake-shoe binder bolts and nuts: If the nut that holds the brake shoe in the brake arm (Fig. 1-14) works loose, *the brake shoe can dodge down under the rim.* If that happens, no brake. Or, as has happened on three road-bike accident cases on which I was an expert witness in the ensuing litigation, a loose brake-shoe binder bolt permitted the brake shoe to pop up so it rubbed on the tire wall. Fig. 1-15 shows a

Fig. 1-14: *To remove or adjust a brake shoe on an all-terrain bike, use the Allen wrench to hold the brake shoe in place and a 10-mm wrench to loosen or tighten the brake-shoe binder nut.*

bike where this happened. You can see that the brake shoe is tilted upward so there is rubber-to-rubber contact between the brake shoe and the tire sidewall. This contact brings the brake shoe even closer to the tire than it was to the rim, because the tire is fatter than the rim (ATB fat tires are more vulnerable to such wheel lockup). When the front wheel locks up, all the forward momentum of the rider and the bike is concentrated on the front wheel axle. This instantaneous transference

Fig. 1-15: *Here is what happens when a brake shoe is not safely tight in the brake arm. In this case the brake shoe gradually worked upward until it touched the tire. When the front brake was applied, the brake shoe tipped up and grabbed the tire sidewall. The front wheel locked up. Weight of the rider and the bike combined to bend the fork blades as shown. Let this be a lesson to make sure brake-shoe binder bolts and nuts are safely tight. See Table 1-2.*

of force or energy is absorbed by the fork blades as the bicycle comes to a screaming halt and propels the rider off the bike, over the handlebars, or to one side or the other. In the three accidents I noted above, the fork blades were bent backward in an identical S-shaped pattern (Fig. 1-15). Two of the bike accidents occurred in the Midwest, the other in the Northwest—thousands of miles and three or four years apart. These accidents resulted in serious injury to the rider. They each happened on a mild day on smooth, dry concrete.

There are two possible scenarios that contributed to these accidents. When the rider applied the brakes, one or both brake shoes popped up and grabbed the tire. Instant lockup. The scenario is that the brake-shoe binder bolts were loose enough, or became loose because of vibration, to permit the shoes to work their way upward and grab the fatter tire. Instant lockup. Yet another reason for brake-shoe pop-up and rim grab is lack of toe-in. Toe-in is where the front of the brake shoe contacts the rim first, as described later in this chapter. If the *rear* of the brake shoe contacts the rim first, the shoe may dig into the rim and be forced upward, where it will grab the tire and cause instant wheel lockup and an accident, as described above. A combination of no toe-in plus insufficiently tightened brake-shoe binder bolts can make brake-shoe tire-grab quite likely. Please see the brake-shoe adjustment section of this chapter for toe-in instructions.

Exposed springs: The springs on some older cantilever brakes are exposed and could pop out from behind the stub that holds them in tension (arrow, Fig. 1-16). If you have such a brake, make sure the spring is in proper position, at full tension, especially if you have worked on the brake. Check the spring from time to time to make sure it is in place, especially if you have transported your bike.

Handlebar height adjustment: If you have moved the handlebars up or down on your ATB, you *must* readjust the front brake shoe rim clearance. If you *raised* the handlebars, the brake shoes move *closer* to the rim, so close you may have wheel lockup. If you *lowered* the handlebars, the brake shoes will be *farther* from the rim. If you lowered the handlebars a lot, you may have little or no front brake.

About Cable Stretch

Brake cables stretch over time, sometimes over a very short time, such as during your very first ride. When cables stretch, brake shoes get farther away from the rim. If brake shoes get too far away, the brake

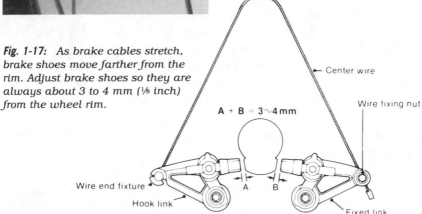

Fig. 1-16: *A brake spring can pop out if hit by a branch or from impacts with the ground, leaving you with zero braking from that brake. Make sure exposed brake springs like this one are always securely in place behind their retainer tab.*

Cable carrier

Center wire

Wire fixing nut

A + B = 3∼4mm

Wire end fixture

A   B

Hook link

Fixed link

Fig. 1-17: *As brake cables stretch, brake shoes move farther from the rim. Adjust brake shoes so they are always about 3 to 4 mm (⅛ inch) from the wheel rim.*

lever may bottom out on the handlebars and still not stop you. In addition, as brake shoes get farther away from the rim, braking response time, and stopping power, are reduced. I'd like to see you go right out to the garage, now, and check your bike for brake cable stretch. Pull on each brake lever as hard as you can and hold them tight. Do they bottom out on the handlebars? When you push the bike while gripping the levers closed, will one or both wheels turn? Let go of the brake levers. Look at the brake shoes. Are they more than ⅛ inch (3–4 mm) away from the wheel rim (Fig. 1-17)? If so, your brakes are unsafe. You can remove minor cable stretch at the brake levers. Major cable stretch requires more work. Let's start with minor cable stretch. These instructions apply to all types of bicycle brakes.

BRAKE ADJUSTMENTS ON ALL-TERRAIN BICYCLES

Cable stretch: If brake cables have not stretched too far, you can remove this minor cable stretch with a simple adjustment at the brake lever. Both front and rear brake levers have a cable adjuster barrel (Fig. 1-18) to remove minor cable stretch. This barrel has two parts, a locknut ("A" in Fig. 1-18) and the barrel body ("B" in Fig. 1-18) which is threaded into the brake lever itself.

Here's how to remove minor cable stretch with the adjusting barrel:

1. Hold the adjuster barrel ("B" in Fig. 1-18) with one hand while you turn the adjuster barrel locknut ("A" in Fig. 1-18) a few turns counterclockwise to loosen it.

2. Hold the barrel locknut while you turn the barrel counterclockwise (Fig. 1-19) until brake shoes are about ⅛ inch from the wheel rim. Tighten the barrel locknut against the brake lever body.

3. Readjust as above until brakes shoes are ⅛ inch from the wheel rim. *Note:* This adjustment will be easier if you hold the brake shoes against the rim. Use a strap or third hand brake tool.

Comment: I prefer more than the ¹⁄₁₆-inch brake shoe-to-rim clearance specified by brake manufacturers for two reasons:

a. If the brake shoes are within the specified 2-mm clearance (that's a tad over ¹⁄₁₆ inch) from the rim, and you grab the brake levers, you have little choice but to have the brake shoes pressed hard against the rim, or not at all. I prefer a ⅛ inch clearance, so I can modulate brake

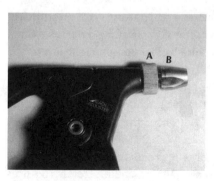

Fig. 1-18: Cable-stretch adjuster barrel on an all-terrain bike brake. "A" is the adjuster barrel locknut, "B" the adjuster barrel.

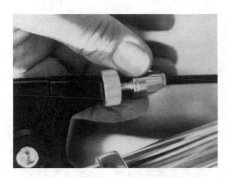

Fig. 1-19: Remove cable slack by turning the adjuster barrel counter-clockwise.

pressure more accurately. Remember, with only a ¹⁄₁₆-inch shoe-to-rim clearance the brake lever does not have to travel far to achieve wheel lock-up. At the ¹⁄₁₆-inch shoe-to-rim clearance, any misalignment in the wheel will likely cause one of the brake shoes to drag on the rim, at least until the wheel is re-trued. The tendency is to turn the cable adjuster (see below) at the brake lever to move the brake shoe farther away. Do not do this! All you will do is decrease braking power and response time. Instead, true the wheel (see Chapter 11).

b. If you cannot bring brake shoes ⅛ inch from the rim with these minor adjustments, major cable stretch has occurred and your bike is unsafe to ride until it is removed. Here is how to do it.

Removing Major Cable Stretch, All-Terrain Bicycles

1. Turn the brake-barrel locknut clockwise until it is almost flush against the brake lever adjusting barrel.

2. Turn the brake lever adjuster barrel clockwise as far as possible. Now the adjuster barrel is in position for fine-tuning out later minor cable stretch, but brake shoes will be very far from the wheel rim, much too far for safety. Turn the locknut counterclockwise until it is tight against the brake lever body. Now you are ready to remove major cable stretch.

3. Hold shoes against the rim with a third hand tool.

4. Hold the main brake-cable binder bolt in the cross-over cable carrier (Fig. 1-20) with an 8- or 9-mm wrench (depending on manufacturer). Loosen the binder nut (Fig. 1-20) with a 9- or 10-mm wrench.

5. Remove cable slack by pulling on the main brake cable with a pair of needle-nose pliers (or use a fourth hand tool, Fig. 1-20).

6. Hold cable tension on the main brake cable and pull out cable stretch. Tighten the cable-carrier fixing bolt.

Fig. 1-20: To loosen or tighten the cable carrier locknut and bolt (cable binder bolt) use two wrenches as shown, one to hold the bolt, the other to turn the nut.

7. Hold the binder bolt (Fig. 1-20) with one wrench, while you tighten its nut to 50 to 75 inch/pounds. Remove the fourth hand and the third hand tools if you use them. Check the tightness of the cable fixing bolt by squeezing the appropriate brake lever closed as hard as you can. If the cable slips out of the cable carrier binder bolt, repeat the steps above, until the main brake cable will not slip. This tightness check is important, because if the cable slips, that brake is inoperative, and you could have an accident if you need to stop and can't. Proceed with the fine-tune brake shoe-to-rim clearance as shown in the minor stretch–removal section above.

Round Cable Carriers Require Special Treatment

Some brakes use a two-piece, flat-shaped cable unit (Fig. 1-21) instead of a cable carrier with a channel (Fig. 1-22). As Fig. 1-21 shows, the main brake cable, "A," is clamped in the carrier, "B." The *end* of the main brake cable is held by a binder bolt in the brake arm. A separate, shorter cable has two lead tab ends. The single tab end fits into mating holes in the carrier. One of the two lead tabs fits into a slot in the brake arm. The remaining tab is a pull tab, so this shorter cable can be removed from the brake arm to spread brake shoes apart in order that the wheel can be removed. To spread brakes apart, squeeze brake shoes together, then pull the tab end of the cable out of the brake arm. For this type of cable carrier, remove major cable stretch this way:

1. Follow Steps 1 to 3 above to readjust the adjuster barrel and clamp brake shoes against the wheel rim.

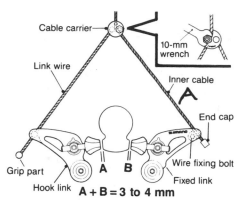

Cable carrier

10-mm wrench

Link wire

Inner cable

A

End cap

Grip part

A   B

Wire fixing bolt

Hook link   A + B = 3 to 4 mm

Fixed link

Fig. 1-21: *A round-type cable carrier. Link wire hooks into the carrier and into the brake arm (link). The other wire (inner cable) is held in the cable carrier by the binder bolt which squeezes the carrier plates together. The other end of the inner or main cable is held by a binder bolt in the brake arm. Adjust the carrier so both cables are the same length.*

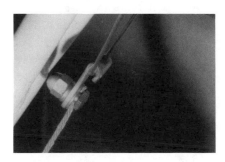

Fig. 1-22: *A conventional channel-type cable carrier used on cantilever, cam action, U-type and sidepull brakes.*

2. Hold the cable carrier binder bolt with an Allen wrench and turn the binder bolt nut ("B" in Fig. 1-21) counterclockwise two or three turns, or just enough so the main brake cable is loose in the carrier.

3. Turn the main cable binder bolt on the brake arm (Fig. 1-21) with a wrench counterclockwise two or three turns, just enough so you can pull the main brake carrier slack through it (and through the cable carrier, too). Use pliers to pull the cable, if necessary.

4. Tighten the cable binder bolt on the brake arm to 50 to 75 inch/ pounds.

5. Push the cable carrier up *so the main brake cable and the shorter cable are the same length.* This is important. Both brake shoes can only be pressed evenly against the wheel rim when both cables are the same length. Otherwise one brake shoe can drag or the other one can be too far from the rim for effective, safe braking.

6. Tighten the cable carrier binder bolt to 50–75 inch/pounds.

7. Check cable binder bolt tightness by squeezing the brake lever hard. Retighten binder bolts if cable slips.

8. Use the brake lever adjuster barrel as shown above to remove any remaining cable slack and to bring the brake shoes ⅛ inch from the rim.

Other Brake Shoe Adjustments

1. *Brake shoes should also be about* $^1/_{32}$ *of an inch, no more than that, from the rim top* (left in Fig. 1-23). Shoes should also be parallel to the rim (center, Fig. 1-23). To make these two adjustments:

2. Hold the brake-shoe binder bolt with one wrench (an Allen or open-end wrench, depending on brake make) while you loosen the binder bolt nut with another wrench, as shown in Fig. 1-24. Move the brake shoe up or down until it is $^1/_{32}$ inch below and parallel to the rim top.

3. *Brake shoes should toe-in,* as shown in Fig. 1-25. On some brakes this toe-in can be made by rotating an eccentric washer at the brake binder bolt (Figs. 1-25 and 1-26). Toe-in permits the rear of the brake shoe to contact the rim last. Toe-in also helps reduce squeaking when you apply the brakes hard. Leave about $^1/_{32}$ inch at the trailing (rear) end of the brake block. Loosen the brake shoe mounting as in Step 2

Fig. 1-23: *Adjust brake shoes so they are about* $^1/_{32}$ *inch below the tire. Shoes* must not touch the tire.

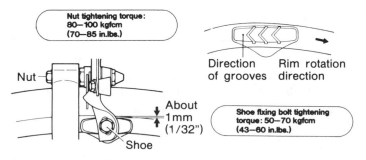

Fig. 1-24: Brake shoes should toe-in
slightly. Modern brakes have an eccentric washer that can be adjusted
to toe-in the brake shoe. Here a
SunTour brake shoe is being loosened so washer can be adjusted.

Fig. 1-25: Shimano brakes have an eccentric control washer to adjust toe-in.
Toe-in is correct when the rear end of the brake shoe is a bit farther from the
wheel rim than the front part of the brake shoe. Toe-in prevents brake
screech.

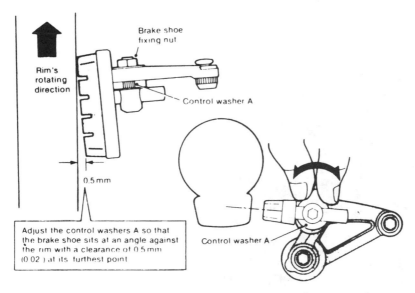

above, twist the eccentric washer to adjust toe-in, and retighten the
brake-shoe mounting bolt. If brakes do not have a toe-in washer, gently
twist each brake arm as shown in Fig. 1-27.

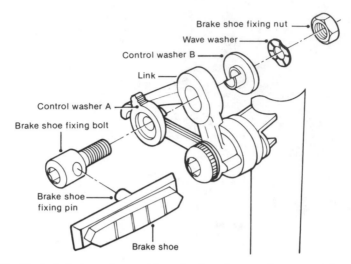

Brake shoe fixing nut

Wave washer

Control washer B

Link

Control washer A

Brake shoe fixing bolt

Brake shoe
fixing pin

Brake shoe

Fig. 1-26: *Exploded view of a cantilever brake, showing location of the control (eccentric) washer "A."*

Fig. 1-27: *Use a wrench or this special Park tool to toe-in brakes without an eccentric washer.*

4. *After making all the adjustments above, both brake shoes should be equidistant from the wheel rim.* Depending on the make of the brake, there are several ways to equalize brake-shoe distance on both sides of the rim. First, however, check the wheel to make sure brake-shoe drag is not caused by an out-of-line wheel rim. Spin the wheel. Watch where the rim passes a brake shoe. If the rim comes closer to, then farther away from, the shoe, realign the rim before more adjustments. Please see Chapter 11 for wheel truing instructions.

Brake Shoe Equidistance Adjustments, ATB Brakes

Keep brake shoes the same distance from the rim (assuming you have made all the adjustments above) by adjusting brake arm spring tension. Some brakes have a spring force adjuster which can be turned with a 2-mm Allen wrench (arrow, Fig. 1-28). The SunTour XCD brake requires a 19-mm wrench to adjust spring tension. You could also use an adjustable crescent wrench to turn this spring tension nut (Fig. 1-29).

1. *Replace brake shoes* when they wear past the tread and/or become age-hardened or coated with aluminum oxide which has scraped off an aluminum rim. To replace a shoe, loosen the brake-shoe binder bolt.

Fig. 1-28: Arrow points to a tiny 2-mm bolt that controls spring tension on this cantilever brake. Adjust this bolt to keep brake shoes equidistant from the wheel rim.

Fig. 1-29: On SunTour XCD brakes, use a 19-mm or open-end wrench as shown to adjust brake spring tension.

Twist the shoe up so you can pull it out of the brake arm. Replace with a new shoe. Some brake shoes have a directional arrow (Fig. 1-30). Make sure this arrow points in the direction of rim rotation. Years ago some cantilever brake shoes came with one end open (Fig. 1-31). The reason for one end of the shoe being open is so just the brake-shoe rubber could be replaced by pushing it out the open end and pushing in a new one. However, if the brake shoe open end faced toward the front of the bike, the brake shoe block would pop right out of its holder on the first brake application, with loss of braking from that brake. Replace such a brake shoe with a modern one-piece shoe. Readjust brake shoes as shown above, installing new ones. I recommend installing all four brake shoes rather than just one, for safer, more even braking. Tighten brake-shoe binder bolts (mounting bolts) to 50 to 80 inch/pounds. When you replace brake shoes, check the tightness of the brake-shoe binder bolt by twisting the brake shoe firmly. If the shoe moves, retighten the binder bolt so it is held very firmly in the brake arm for safety.

2. This is a good time to check the brake mounting bolt tightness, which should be 50 to 80 inch/pounds.

Fig. 1-30: *If brake shoes have a directional arrow, make sure it points in the direction of wheel rotation.*

Fig. 1-31: *Older-model brake shoes have one end open. This end* must *face toward rear of the bike. Otherwise the brake shoe could be forced out of its holder when it contacts the rim.*

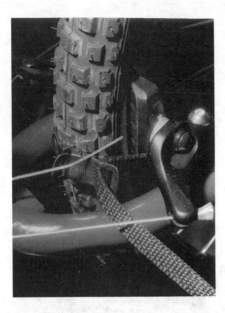

Fig. 1-32: Use a strap to hold brake shoes against the rim when making adjustments, if you do not have a third hand tool.

Brake Cable Installation

Brake cables will eventually fray, wear out, and require replacement. Here's how to do it:

1. Hold brake shoes against the rim with a third hand tool or a strap (Fig. 1-32).
2. Loosen the cable carrier binder nut (Figs. 1-20, 1-21, and 1-22). Pull the cable out of the carrier. If your bike has a round cable carrier, see instructions on these carriers above, and loosen the main brake cable at the brake arm so you can remove this cable for replacement with a new one.
3. Align the brake-lever adjusting barrel so the groove matches the groove in the brake lever (Fig. 1-33). Screw the adjusting barrel all the way in, toward the brake lever. In some newer brake lever designs, you must push the cable end out of the cable clip (Fig. 1-34).
4. Lift the brake cable upward and pull the lead tab end out the brake lever. If there is a tiny cable end adapter in the brake lever slot where the cable end fits, save it and use it with the new cable.
5. Pull the old cable out of its spaghetti tubing, shove a new cable in the tubing, and reverse the above stops. Realign the brake shoes as shown earlier in this chapter.

Fig. 1-33: To remove a cantilever brake cable, align the grooves in the adjuster barrel and the brake body so the cable can be pulled up and out of the brake lever.

Fig. 1-34: Newer brake levers have a cable grip that holds the lead tab end of the brake cable.

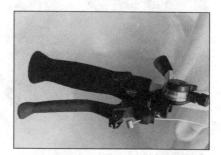

Note: Only a leaded end no bigger than 7 mm will fit into the new Shimano SLR brake levers. For a replacement that fits, take your old cable to the bike shop for an exact duplicate.)

About U-Brakes

U-brakes require a few separate adjustments beyond those outlined above, although they also require those, such as brake shoe-to-rim clearance, shoe alignment, toe-in, etc. Use them, along with the few special precautions below:

1. If your ATB has a U-brake installed at the chain-stay level and its brake shoes wear down, a brake arm may contact and rub on the chainwheel (left, Fig. 1-35). The solution here is simple. Move the toe-in adjusting washer to the inside of the brake arm (right, Fig. 1-35).

2. Note that there is a brake-spring tension equalizer bolt on the brake arm which is adjusted with a 2-mm Allen wrench, to bring brake shoes equidistant to the rim.

Fig. 1-35: When U-brake cables stretch or brake shoes wear, and the brake is mounted low, on the chain stays, the brake arm may rub on the chainwheel, as shown at left. A solution is to move the adjuster washer from the outside to the inside of the brake arm, as shown at right.

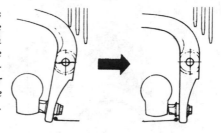

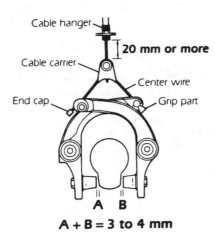

A + B = 3 to 4 mm

Fig. 1-36: On U-brakes, make sure there is at least 20 mm (a tad over ¾ inch) of cable between the cable carrier and the cable hanger. This prevents the carrier from hitting the hanger when the brake is applied. If it hits the hanger, braking power is lost.

3. The distance between the bottom of the cable hanger (where the main brake cable spaghetti tubing is held) and the cable carrier should be at least 20 mm (¾ inch or more), as shown in Fig. 1-36.

4. The distance from the centerline of the cable-carrier binder bolt and the centerline of the brake-arm binder bolt (which holds the brake arm in the bike frame) should be 90 mm (3½ inches), as shown in Fig. 1-37.

Cam Brakes

Cam brakes also require a few special adjustments, which are:

1. To remove a wheel, squeeze the brake shoes against the rim and pull the cam plate out from between the brake arms (Fig. 1-38).

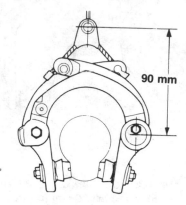

Fig. 1-37: *On U-brakes,* make sure *there is at least 90 mm (a tad less than 3⁹/₁₆ inch)* distance between the centerline of the cable carrier bolt and the centerline of the brake-arm mounting bolt.

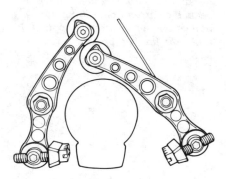

Fig. 1-38: *To remove a wheel from a bike equipped with cam action brakes, squeeze the brakes together and pull out the cam carrier from between the brake arms.*

2. To keep brake shoes equidistant from the rim, use a 15-mm wrench on the adjusting bushing of the brake arm (Fig. 1-39). Turn the bushing clockwise to increase spring tension, counterclockwise to decrease spring tension.

A Word About Brake Levers and Brake-Shoe Clearance

Some brake levers have a reach adjuster that moves the lever closer to or farther away from the handlebars, depending on your finger length. You can find this adjuster by looking for the words REACH ADJUSTER on the brake lever body. Depending on the make, use a screwdriver or a 2-mm Allen wrench to make this adjustment. On dual-shift levers on index shifters, you will have to hold the shift lever out of the way to get at the reach adjuster.

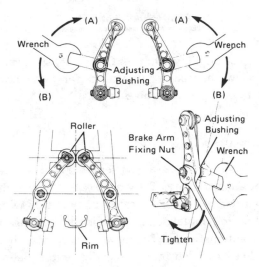

Fig. 1-39: To keep cam action brake shoes equidistant from the rim, turn each brake-arm adjusting screw with a wrench until shoes are equalized.

Brake Lever Position

Loosen the brake-lever clamp bolt (Fig. 1-40) and move the brake lever on the handlebars to a position most comfortable for you. On the new dual-lever shifter and brake combination, hold the shift lever out of the way so you can use a 5-mm Allen wrench on the combination lever. Tighten this bolt to 50 to 70 inch/pounds.

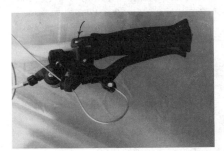

Fig. 1-40: Adjust position of an ATB brake lever on the flat handlebar by loosening the brake lever clamp (arrow), moving brake lever to the desired position, and retightening the clamp bolt.

ALL ABOUT ROAD-BIKE BRAKES

Some road bikes use cantilever brakes (Fig. 1-25) similar to ATB bikes. If so, simply follow the above instructions for these brakes. Here is maintenance data on other road bike brakes.

The Hazard of Extension Levers

Extension brake levers, a.k.a. "safety" levers (Fig. 1-41), lull you into a false sense of braking security. They are easier to reach than the main brake levers, particularly if, like most of us, you ride with your hands on top of downturned handlebars. In a panic stop you may reach for the extension levers automatically. This is why they are so dangerous.

If your bike has extension brake levers, go out, squeeze them hard, and watch how close they come to the handlebars. Unless your brakes are perfectly adjusted, you will very likely find that these levers can be squeezed all the way, or very close to the handlebars. Still holding them closed, now look at the main brake levers. You will see that they still have more room to travel. In fact, you can probably hold one extension lever closed and still be able to push the bike so that the wheel turns. Yet the main brake lever will lock up that wheel so it will skid along the floor if you push the bike. There are two reasons why extension levers are much less effective than main brake levers. First, extension levers inherently have a shorter distance of travel than the main levers, so they are very likely not going to stop you in an emergency, even though you can squeeze them all the way down to the handlebars. Second, brake-cable stretch and brake-shoe wear allow brake shoes to rest

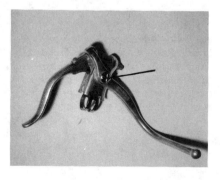

Fig. 1-41: Remove the lever axle bolt (arrow) counterclockwise to remove dangerous extension levers (see text).

farther from the rim, so that extension levers become even less effective. In fact, I have checked dozens of brand-new bikes, right on the sales floor (mostly in discount stores, to be sure), and found extension levers squeezable down to the handlebars with at least an inch of travel left in the main brake levers. These bikes are an accident waiting to happen. Even if your brakes are perfectly adjusted so that the extension levers will stop you safely, they won't always do so. As I noted, brake cables stretch, brake shoes wear, and so your brakes slowly get out of adjustment until the extension levers are virtually useless.

When I mentioned the dangers of extension levers to the bicycle buyer of a major multi-store sporting goods firm, he sent a memo to the bicycle section manager in each store to remove these levers from every bike in stock. He then went to his bicycle supplier and ordered them removed from bikes on order.

Removing Extension Levers

Follow these steps to remove extension levers:

1. With a screwdriver, turn the extension lever clamp bolt counter-clockwise all the way (Fig. 1-41).
2. Remove the extension lever (Fig. 1-42).
3. Remove the lever axle (Fig. 1-43) and replace it with a shorter one you can buy from your bike store. Take the old one in for a replacement that fits. You need shorter axles because the old ones will stick out like nails and cause pain if you wrap your hands around them.

Fig. 1-42: *Replace the longer extension-lever axle with a shorter one after removing the lever (see text).*

Fig. 1-43: *An extension-lever axle (center) is removed from the brake body by an Allen wrench, as shown.*

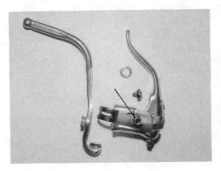

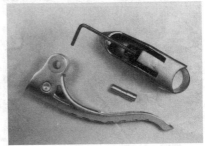

Road-Bike Brake Adjustments

The instructions that follow apply to the bike centerpull and sidepull brakes. As with ATB bike brakes, road-bike brakes gradually become dangerously ineffective with cable stretch, brake-shoe wear, and brake-shoe hardening. Adjustment specifications for road-bike brakes are the same as for ATB bike brakes. These include: brake-shoe clearance from the rim, brake-shoe alignment on the rim, brake-shoe toe-in, brake-shoe replacement. Please review these specifications, above, before proceeding with adjustments on your road-bike brakes.

Road-Bike Centerpull and Sidepull Brakes, Cable Stretch Removal

Before removing cable stretch on centerpull brakes and sidepull brakes:

1. Make sure the tire release lever is in the closed position. This is the lever that spreads the brake shoes apart so you can remove the wheel. On centerpull brakes the tire release lever may be on the brake lever (Fig. 1-44) or on the cable guide (Fig. 1-45). On sidepull brakes, the tire release lever may be on the brake lever or on the brake arm (Fig. 1-10).

Minor Road-Bike Cable Stretch

1. Use the cable slack adjuster barrel to remove cable stretch. On centerpull brakes these adjusters may be on the cable guide (Fig. 1-

Fig. 1-44: Brake release lever on a road-bike brake lever. Turn the release lever to spread brake shoes apart for wheel removal.

Fig. 1-45: *Brake release lever, "C," is on the cable carrier; "A" is the cable stretch adjuster barrel; "B" is the adjuster barrel locknut; "D" is the cable carrier binder bolt.*

45). On sidepull brakes they may be on the brake arm (Fig. 1-10). On both types of brakes the adjusting barrel may also be on the top of the brake levers. In either location they work the same way. Each adjuster has a locknut and an adjusting barrel.

2. Turn the locknut counterclockwise a half turn or so.

3. Turn the adjusting barrel counterclockwise until brake shoes are within ⅛ inch from the wheel rim.

4. Tighten the locknut, clockwise, as far as possible. This will keep the adjusting barrel from moving under vibration.

Major Road-Bike Cable Stretch

1. Turn the adjusting barrel locknut counterclockwise as far as possible.

2. Close the barrel clockwise, as far as possible.

3. Follow the steps in the all-terrain bike section above on pulling excess cable slack through the cable binder bolt on the brake carrier (centerpull) or the brake arm (sidepull).

Road-Bike Brake-Shoe Alignment

Follow the same steps in aligning brake shoes on the rim as for all-terrain bike brakes above. Follow the same procedure for toe-in, with one exception. If your brakes do not have an eccentric washer (see ATB brake section above) then *carefully* pry the brake arm to adjust toe-in (Fig. 1-27). Use an adjustable wrench or a special brake tool to make this adjustment.

Sidepull and Centerpull Brake-Shoe Equidistance Adjustment

As with ATB bicycles, road bike brake shoes should be equidistant from the wheel rim. If a brake shoe rubs on one side of the rim, first check wheel alignment (see Chapter 11). On centerpull or sidepull brakes:

1. Loosen the brake mounting bolt (Fig. 1-46).
2. Move the brake until both brake shoes are the same distance from the rim. Hold the brake arms while you tighten the brake shoe mounting bolt.

Fig. 1-46: *Keep sidepull brake shoes equidistant from the wheel rim by loosening brake mounting bolt, moving brake so shoes are equidistant, and tightening the brake mounting bolt nut. Use two wrenches as shown. The 12-mm wrench simply holds the brake in position while you tighten the mounting bolt nut.*

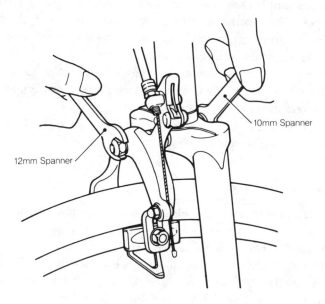

10mm Spanner

12mm Spanner

Cable Replacement, Road-Bike Centerpull and Sidepull Brakes

1. First, bring your old, your frayed, your worn-out cables to the bike shop (in your car) for an exact replacement. Some modern brakes are awfully finicky about cable end sizes and cable thickness. I recommend you also replace the outer sheath (spaghetti tubing) with an exact replacement.

2. If your brakes have the cable coming out the top of the brake lever, thread the cable through the hanger from the front of the brake and up and out of the top.

3. If your brake cable runs underneath the handlebar tape, thread the cable end the same way except run the cable out the back instead of the top of the brake lever. Cut the cable guide the length of the handlebars and tape it to the handlebars. From here on out follow the cable replacement instructions and brake-shoe alignment instructions above.

Road-Bike Brake-Lever Location

If the brake levers on your road bike are uncomfortable to reach, you can move them on the downturned handlebars. Just loosen the brake-lever clamp bolt, usually with a 5-mm Allen wrench (Fig. 1-47), position the brake lever to the new position, and retighten the clamp bolt. See Torque Table 1-2 for correct tightening torque. Note that Park Tools has three new brake tools. Fig. 1-48 shows a third hand tool which replaces the one shown in Fig. 1-4 and which fits *all* bike brakes; Fig.

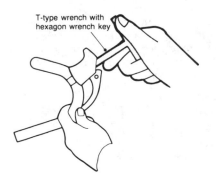

T-type wrench with hexagon wrench key

Fig. 1-47: Reposition road-bike brake levers on downturned handlebars to suit your reach by loosening the brake clamp bolt, moving brake lever, and retightening the clamp bolt.

1-49 shows a fourth hand tool replacing the tool shown in Fig. 1-20; and Fig. 1-50 shows a wrench, with one end for 14-mm centering nuts and the other end for centering sidepull and centerpull brake springs. The next chapter will cover derailleur adjustments, so necessary to keep your bicycle shifting smoothly, accurately, and safely.

Fig. 1-48: A new Park third hand brake tool holds any brake shoe against the rim. Knob at right locks sliding arm to fit all brakes.

Fig. 1-49: A new Park fourth hand tool has a ratchet permitting brake cables to be pulled up tightly before tightening the cable binder bolt.

Fig. 1-50: Park wrench for centering brake shoes over wheel rim. One end of this wrench fits over springs to center them. The other end is 14 mm for brake centering nuts.

2
Derailleur Adjustment and Maintenance

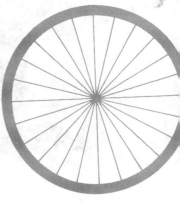

he word "derailleur" is French. It means a device that derails or moves something from one position to another. On your bike, the moving action is on the chain. When you shift, the derailleur nudges the chain from one gear to the next.

Two types of derailleur systems are now on the market. One is the conventional *friction* shift system that has been the mainstay of gear selectors for at least the past fifty years. If your bike was made before 1987, it probably has friction shifters. Index shifters were introduced in that year. This system moves the chain very precisely from one gear to the next. Most index shifters move with a click as you shift from gear to gear, eliminating the need for feeling your way with the shift levers to move the chain to the gear you have selected. Index shifting lets you concentrate on where you are going, without looking back and down to check the gear you're in. It should be a positive contribution to safe cycling. A new variation of index shifting uses dual shift levers (Fig. 2-1), one lever for shifting to a lower gear, the other lever to shift to a higher gear. Fig. 2-2 shows the dual index shifters on combination brake and shift levers for road-bike downturned handlebars. Both types of index systems work pretty much alike. One difference is that in the single-shift lever index system you have the choice of switching back to a conventional friction shifting system (Fig. 2-3) if something goes wrong with the index system. The dual lever system does not provide this

Fig. 2-1: Dual-lever index shift/brake lever combination on an all-terrain bicycle. "A," removable cover for derailleur cable replacement; "B," cable tip; "C," long-shift lever for shifting from a small to a larger freewheel cog or chainwheel; "D," small-shift lever for shifting from a larger to a smaller cog or chainwheel; "E," cable slack adjuster to remove minor cable stretch.

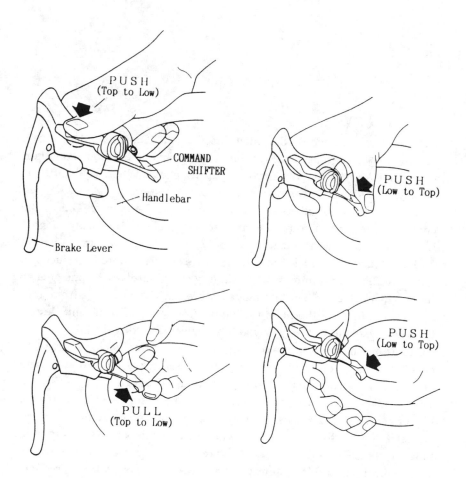

Fig. 2-2: Dual-index shifters on a road bike, on downturned handlebars. Courtesy SunTour.

option. In the words of one such system manufacturer's technician, if something goes wrong, such as chain stretch, so you cannot shift to a lower gear, you'll have to get real creative. My suggestion is to study the adjustments required by the dual lever system so you can do that, if necessary, when you're far from a bike shop. For example, if the derailleur cable stretches so you can't shift to a lower, hill-climbing gear, you need to know how to remove this cable stretch.

One problem I see with single or dual lever index systems has nothing to do with them, directly. This is where the bicycle manufacturer routes the cables through the inside, rather than the outside, of the frame. Index systems need clean, smoothly working cables to work properly. The bends where cables enter and leave the frame tubes may create cable friction.

SHIFTING TECHNIQUES FOR BOTH FRICTION AND INDEX SHIFTERS

You need to know how and when to shift gears on your bicycle. There may be nothing wrong with your equipment, but a lot wrong in how you use it. If you know how to shift, then anything else that goes wrong with your derailleurs is a mechanical problem. For example, on both a friction or an index shifting system, it is possible to shift so you get a grinding noise from the chain. If you shift correctly, the chain stays happy and quiet. There are mechanical reasons for chain noise as well. Let's start with shifting techniques before we get into solving mechanical problems.

Here's a quick review of how to shift from one gear to another. Derailleur manufacturers claim you can shift while straining on the pedals going up a steep hill. Perhaps. I prefer not to risk a pedal slip and resultant groin contact with the top tube. My advice is always to anticipate shifting needs. Shift to a higher, hill-climbing gear *before* you hit a hill. Shifting while you muscle uphill is not always possible. If you can't shift, stop, lift the rear wheel off the ground, twirl the pedals and shift to a bigger rear cog and/or a smaller front chainwheel. Turn the bike at an angle to the trail to reduce the gradient. Straddle the bike, and put one foot on a pedal at the twelve o'clock position. Push that pedal down hard. As you do, hoist yourself up on the saddle, put your other foot on the other pedal, and clomp down on it. If you still can't get going, the hill is too steep, or you're inexperienced at this maneuver (don't do it on a road; this is strictly an off-road, trail technique). Let's say the hill is too steep. I suggest you walk up the steep section until it levels out a bit. Nothing to be ashamed of, unless you're an Olympic-class rider.

If the chain makes noise after you shift, you most likely haven't moved the chain all the way onto the rear cogs. Move the rear shift lever slightly one way or the other until the noise is gone. If the chain rubs on the front derailleur cage *after* you have shifted the rear derailleur, turn the front shift lever slightly one way or the other until the noise is gone. This type of chain rub is caused by the chain assuming a different angle after a rear derailleur shift, so now it rubs on the front derailleur cage. You will have to make these minor shift adjustments even with any of the new index shifting systems. Perfect they aren't. I strongly recommend you practice shifting through all the gears while pedaling on a safe surface, such as a vacant school parking lot. Once you get used to shifting it will be instinctual, just like with a manual auto shift system. You should not have to look down and/or back to check which gear you're on. All that matters is how you feel. Is the gear comfortable?

Single-lever index shifters operate just like friction shifters, but you do not have to feel your way onto a gear. When you move the shift lever, the chain falls accurately on the gear you have selected, *if* the system is correctly adjusted.

Dual-lever index shifters, on the other hand, do take a bit of explaining. First, it's very easy to inadvertently touch the small shift lever ("C" in Fig. 2-1), which then clicks the rear derailleur to a higher gear. This is especially true on the all-terrain bike handlebar-mounted version (Fig. 2-1). When you are straining uphill, an accidental and unforeseeable shift to a higher, less advantageous gear is not the best thing that could happen to you. At worst such an accidental shift could cause a spill. So watch where you place those fingers when riding with dual shifters.

How to Shift Dual-Lever Index Shifting Systems

Both front and rear derailleurs are controlled by dual levers. However, the rear derailleur set of levers operates somewhat differently than the front set. I will describe each set individually, starting with the rear derailleur levers:

Rear Derailleur Dual-Shift Levers

The shift levers on the right side of the handlebars (mounted on the rear brake body) operate the rear derailleur.

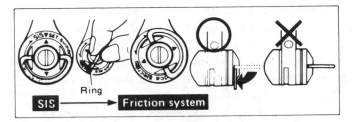

Fig. 2-3: *Older model single-lever index shifters give the option of changing from index to conventional friction-shifting in an emergency. To switch, just turn the ring.* Courtesy Shimano.

1. *To shift from a smaller rear cog up to the next largest cog:* Press lever "C" (Fig. 2-1) one click. You can start with the smallest rear cog and shift up one cog at a time. For example, if you have six freewheel cogs, you can start shifting from the small one, one cog at a time, all the way to the biggest (slow-speed) cog. You can shift the big lever to each cog, sequentially, or all the way to the biggest rear cog.

2. *To shift from the smallest rear cog all the way to the biggest rear cog:* Press lever "C" (Fig. 2-1) all the way. Or, press the big shift lever *all* the way to shift the chain to the biggest rear cog from any smaller cog. For example, if the chain is on the third cog and you want to shift to the biggest cog as you approach a hill, you press the big lever all the way.

3. *To shift from a bigger to a smaller rear cog,* use the small shift lever "D" (Fig. 2-1). Each time you press the small lever the chain moves from one large cog to the next smallest cog.

Both shift levers are spring-loaded and thus return to the original position as you remove finger pressure.

Front Derailleur Dual Index Shift Levers

The shift levers for the front derailleur, mounted on the front brake lever on the left of the handlebars, look like the levers for the rear derailleur, but they work differently. The big lever ("C" in Fig. 2-1) moves the chain from a small to a larger chainwheel. The small lever ("D" in Fig. 2-1) moves the chain from a larger to a smaller chainwheel.

1. *To shift from the smallest to the largest chainwheel:* Press the big lever ("C" in Fig. 2-1) a full stroke.

2. *To shift from the smallest chainwheel to the middle chainwheel, or from the middle chainwheel to the largest chainwheel:* Press the big

lever ("C" in Fig. 2-1) a half stroke. If you hear noise when shifting from the smallest to the middle chainwheel, gently press the small lever ("D" in Fig. 2-1). This corrects a slight overshift by moving the front derailleur cage slightly toward the small chainwheel.

3. *To shift from the largest to the smallest chainwheel:* press the small lever ("D" in Fig. 2-1) a full stroke.

4. *To shift from the largest chainwheel to the middle chainwheel, or from the middle to the smallest chainwheel:* Press the small lever ("D" in Fig. 2-1) a half stroke from the initial position.

Now, here's how to adjust your derailleurs.

DERAILLEUR ADJUSTMENTS

All shift systems have common adjustments. Index systems, including dual-lever shifters, require a few extra refinements. Let's start with common, garden-variety friction-shifted derailleurs, beginning with the rear derailleur. I'll give basic adjustments, then troubleshooting tips.

Tools You Will Need

1. Torque wrench (inch/pound model). Please review use of this wrench in Chapter 1.
2. Small Phillips head screwdriver.
3. 4-, 6-, and 8-mm Allen sockets for torque wrench.
4. Park fourth hand tool (optional).
5. Cable cutter.

Table 2-1 TORQUE TABLE FOR DERAILLEURS*

(Values in inch/pounds)	
Front and rear derailleur cable fixing bolts	35–50
Front derailleur clamp fixing bolt	53–65
Rear derailleur mounting bolt	70–85
Shift lever fixing (clamp) bolt	35–53
Jockey and idler wheel axle nuts	26–35

*See data on torque in Chapter 1 for use of torque wrench, and torque safety values.

NON-INDEXING FRICTION SHIFT SYSTEMS

Rear Derailleur Adjustment

All derailleurs have two adjusters to limit left and right movement (Fig. 2-4). These little bolts or adjusters keep the derailleur from overshifting to the right or to the left.

The low-gear adjuster ("L" in Fig. 2-4) limits movement to the left. If your derailleur does not have the letters "L" and "H" stamped on it, the "L" or low-limit adjuster is the one nearest the derailleur mounting bolt, at the top of the derailleur body. The "L" adjuster prevents the chain from being moved too far to the left, where it can fall off the big rear cog and jam between that cog and the spokes (Fig. 2-5). In such a jam, the chain can cut and sever one or more spokes and cause an accident. At the very least, a broken spoke will cause a misaligned wheel which in turn reduces braking capacity. You'll know when this happens from the loud grinding noise as the chain and spokes do battle, and pedaling becomes gritty and hard. Always inspect the spokes for cuts when this happens. A cut will weaken a spoke and cause later failure

Fig. 2-4: *Closeup of a rear derailleur showing limit bolts. "L" limits derailleur travel to the left, "H" to the right.*

Fig. 2-5: *Adjust the "L" bolt in Fig. 2-4 to prevent the chain from being shifted so far to the left that it moves off the big cog and jams between it and the chain, as shown here with arrows.*

Fig. 2-6: *Adjust the "H" bolt in Fig. 2-4 to prevent the chain from moving so far to the right that it jams between the small cog and the chain stay, arrows.*

miles from home. Always remove a severed spoke before cycling on. Then, with your spoke wrench, realign the wheel enough to get you home. Replace the spoke(s) as soon as possible. For wheel truing and spoke replacement instructions, see Chapter 11.

If the high gear adjuster on your derailleur ("H" in Fig. 2-4) moves the chain too far to the right, the chain can fall off the small cog and jam tightly between it and the chainstay (arrow in Fig. 2-6). Then you could experience pedal lockup, as though a strong arm had suddenly grabbed the pedal and kept it from moving. You may then lose control and balance, which could lead to an accident. Now let's learn how to adjust your rear derailleur so you can shift with ease, accuracy, and above all, with safety.

1. *Check for cable slack:* In Chapter 1 you learned that brake cables stretch with use and that such stretch must be removed to maintain safe

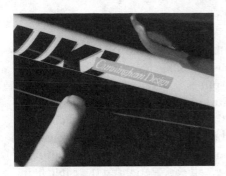

Fig. 2-7: Check for cable stretch by pulling cable about midway on the down tube.

braking. Derailleur cables also stretch, and that stretch must be removed to maintain accurate shifting. Here's how: With the rear wheel off the ground (ideally, the bike should be on a bike stand or suspended from the ceiling), shift the chain to the small rear cog. With your finger halfway down the down tube (Fig. 2-7), lift the rear derailleur cable. If there is any slack, the cable has stretched. The slack must be removed before making any other adjustments.

   2. *Remove minor cable slack:* Some derailleurs have a cable slack adjustment barrel (Fig. 2-8), which you can turn to remove cable slack. Turn the barrel counterclockwise to remove slack, clockwise to add slack. However, if you can't remove all the slack with the barrel adjuster, turn

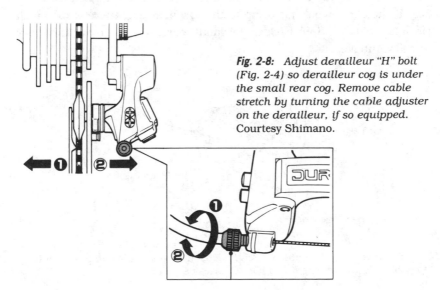

Fig. 2-8: Adjust derailleur "H" bolt (Fig. 2-4) so derailleur cog is under the small rear cog. Remove cable stretch by turning the cable adjuster on the derailleur, if so equipped. Courtesy Shimano.

it clockwise as far as it will go, then remove cable slack at the cable fixing bolt as noted below.

3. *Remove major cable slack:* Shift the chain to the small rear cog. To remove the slack, loosen the cable fixing bolt (Fig. 2-9). Pull the excess cable through with a pair of pliers.

Rotate the crank and use the shift lever to shift the derailleur all the way to the right, so the chain is on the small rear cog. If the chain won't shift to the small cog, you will need to let out a bit of cable through the cable fixing bolt. Try letting out about ⅛ of an inch at a time until you can get the chain to shift over to the small cog. Retighten the cable fixing bolt to 35 to 50 inch/pounds.

Leave the chain on the small rear cog. Now, look at the location of the top derailleur wheel. It should be directly under the small cog. Turn the high speed derailleur limit bolt ("H" in Fig. 2-4) one way or the other until the top derailleur wheel is under the small cog. For example:

a. If the top derailleur wheel sits to the *left* of the small cog, turn the high-speed adjuster counterclockwise until it is aligned.

b. If the top wheel sits too far to the *right,* turn the high-speed adjuster clockwise to make this alignment.

4. *Check low-speed adjuster:* While you turn the pedals, shift the rear derailleur to the big freewheel cog. If the derailleur top wheel is not aligned directly under the big cog, turn the low-speed adjuster ("L" in Fig. 2-4) one way or the other until the top wheel is aligned with that cog. If the chain won't move up to the low-gear cog, there is too much slack in the cable. Shift back to the small rear cog and remove this slack as shown above.

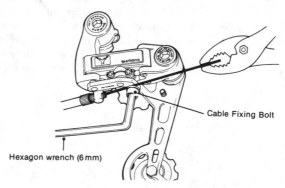

Fig. 2-9: *Remove major cable stretch by loosening the cable fixing bolt, pulling cable taut, tightening fixing bolt.* Courtesy Shimano.

5. *Check shifting on all rear gears:* While turning the pedals, shift up and down through all the gears to make sure the chain will seat accurately on all cogs, especially the low and high gears. Repeat this step several times. Make any fine-tuning adjustments necessary to keep the top wheel aligned directly under the high and low gear cogs. The chain should run smoothly and silently on both high and low gears. Any rubbing or grinding noises on either of these gears probably means that the derailleur top wheel is not directly aligned under each gear, causing the chain to seat inaccurately. This shortens the life of both the chain and the freewheel cog.

6. *Check derailleur mounting bolt:* The derailleur mounting bolt (arrow, Fig. 2-10) (a.k.a. fixing bolt) should be torqued to 70 to 85 inch/pounds. Use a 5-mm Allen wrench.

7. *Check and adjust chain wraparound:* The top wheel should be as close as possible to *all* freewheel cogs, without touching them. I like about a ⅛-inch clearance on all gears. The chain should fall on nearly half the teeth of each rear (freewheel) cog (Fig. 2-11). For example, on a 24-tooth cog, the chain should be wrapped around at least ten teeth; on a 34-tooth cog, around at least fifteen.

Fig. 2-10: Check derailleur mounting bolt, arrow. It should be tightened to 70 to 80 inch/pounds.

Fig. 2-11: Keep the rear derailleur adjusted for maximum chain wraparound. Good wraparound, "1," helps prevent chain skip. Poor wraparound is shown in gear "2" where the chain is on less than half the teeth.

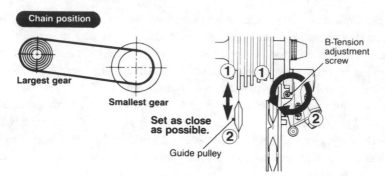

Fig. 2-12: *Adjust the derailleur limit bolts so the derailleur pulley is under the small cog and the big cog, as shown. Use the "B" tension bolt to bring the chain close to the big cog, with the chain on that cog and on the small chainwheel.* Courtesy Shimano.

Check chain wraparound on all gears by shifting through them and watching how close the top wheel is from each cog. Again, Fig. 2-11 gives an excellent illustration of good and bad chain wraparound. Chain "1" shows good wraparound with the chain on seven teeth of this 14-tooth cog. Chain "2" shows the chain on only four teeth, where it is more likely to skip. Again, when the chain skips or jumps, your foot will slip if you've been pedaling hard, and you could lose balance and control.

There are three simple ways to move the top wheel closer to the cogs:

a. Adjust the derailleur angle with its chain tensioner bolt, if your derailleur has one ("A" in Fig. 2-10 and in Fig. 2-12). Turn this bolt (also called "B-tension adjuster screw") counterclockwise to move the derailleur top wheel closer to the cog.

b. Move the wheel back farther in the dropouts, if your bike has horizontal dropouts. You won't be able to do this with vertical dropouts.

c. Remove a link or two from the chain for the same result. See the section on chains in this chapter for data on chain length change.

I would not quibble about a tooth more or less, though, just so the chain is hanging on half or a few teeth less than half. Anything less and you're risking chain skip and an accident. However, you can adjust the derailleur *too* close to the freewheel cogs. When the derailleur top wheel gets too close to the cog, the chain can jam between the top derailleur wheel and the right side of the derailleur cage plate. This condition can lock up the pedal motion unexpectedly, and contribute to loss of control and an accident.

8. *Lubricate rear derailleur pivot points* with light oil every month, more often if you ride a lot.

Changing the Front or Rear Derailleur Cable

Eventually a derailleur cable (as with all bike cables) will wear out. If you see a frayed strand before the cable clamp, it's time to change to a new cable. Cables come in two parts—the spaghettilike casing tubing and the stranded steel cable that runs inside the casing. The Shimano SIS cable with casing liner is flexible, without undue compression that tends to set up resistance to cable movement inside the casing. The SIS cable is the type Shimano recommends for their index shifting system, and any bike shop should have it in stock. One more point about cables and casings: avoid "flexible" steel casings. They are stiff and add back pressure to the cable.

Before you buy a replacement cable, check with your bicycle shop to *make sure it will be compatible with your shifting system. Here is how to change a cable:*

1. Release the cable fixing bolt at the derailleur (Fig. 2-9). Push on the casing near the shift lever until the leaded end of the cable comes out of the shift lever (Fig. 2-13).

2. Remove both casing and cable and replace with the new cable and casing. If you have cut the casing to trim off unneeded length, be sure to file off any burrs or rough edges on the cut end. I use a bench grinder for this purpose.

3. Put the free end of the cable into the shift lever, so the leaded end fits into a recessed opening in the lever.

Fig. 2-13: *Insert or remove a derailleur cable where shown, arrow, on single-lever index shifters.*

4. Remove cable slack as discussed above on rear derailleurs, and below, for front derailleurs. Recheck derailleur adjustments as noted above and below.

5. Leave about one or one-and-a-half-inch of cable beyond the cable fixing bolt. Snip off excess cable. Keep ends from unwinding after you cut off excess cable with a lead cap (available from bike shops) on the cut end. Melt the cap with a match or soldering iron. Or, solder about an inch of the cable *before* snipping it. The solder will keep the end from unwinding.

Check Derailleur Wheels

Remove, clean, and replace the derailleur wheels. Dust and dirt abrade and wear down top and idler wheels on a rear derailleur. I recommend that you replace these little wheels with sealed-bearing top and idler wheels (Fig. 2-14) for smoother shifting. They are made by SunTour and should be available from your bike shop. To clean and relubricate, just remove them, pry out the thin O-ring seals with a thin-blade knife, wash out old grease and dirt with kerosene and a small brush, and relube with a light grease. Then reinsert the seals and put the wheels back in the derailleur.

Fig. 2-14: *Install sealed bearing pulleys on the rear derailleur for smoothest shifting. These pulleys are made by SunTour.*

Rear Derailleur (Friction-Shift Type) Troubleshooting

1. PROBLEM: *Chain skip.* One or more of the freewheel cogs may be worn to the point where they get little lips or overhangs that catch the chain. A worn chainwheel also causes chain skip.

SOLUTION: *Install a new freewheel cog (Chapter 5) or a new chainwheel (Chapter 3).*

2. PROBLEM: *Chain skip.* Worn chain.

SOLUTION: Replace the chain (Chapter 4).

3. PROBLEM: *Chain noise from the freewheel.*

SOLUTION: If the chain seems to have trouble settling down on the cog you have selected and makes a grinding noise, it's telling you that you probably have not shifted accurately.

4. PROBLEM: *Can't shift to low rear gear.*

SOLUTION: If you have installed a new chain that's too short, the chain may not shift to the large cog (see Chapter 4).

5. PROBLEM: *Chain falls off gears.*

SOLUTION: If the chain is too long, it can flop around and fall off the rear cog of the chainwheel, especially when going downhill at high speed on a bumpy road when you have shifted to the high-speed gear. When riding an ATB down a rough downhill trail, keep the chain as taut as possible by shifting to the low-gear combination front and rear, or at least put the chain on the largest rear cog and the second largest chainwheel (most ATBs have triple chainwheels). You can always reshift after the downhill run is over.

6. PROBLEM: *Chain falls off or jams on the idler wheel (the bottom derailleur wheel).*

SOLUTION: Some rear derailleurs have a movable outer cage (Fig. 2-15) so that the derailleur can be removed without having to remove the chain. If the derailleur idler wheel axle nut ("C"in Fig. 2-15) is not tight, this movable outer plate ("B" in Fig. 2-15) may slip down and permit the chain to slip off the idler (bottom) wheel. Derailleur wheel axle nuts should be tightened to 50 to 60 inch/pounds.

7. PROBLEM: *The chain won't shift accurately to any gear.*

SOLUTION: Derailleurs do wear out, eventually. Wear causes excessive free play between these parts. Check the rear derailleur by shifting the chain to the small freewheel cog. Grasp the derailleur cage at the lower (idler) wheel. Move the cage briskly from side to side. If you feel looseness, you need a new derailleur.

8. PROBLEM: *Index shifters do not shift accurately.*

SOLUTION: See section on index shifters in this chapter.

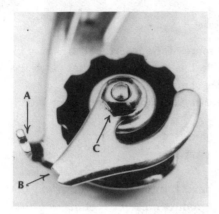

Fig. 2-15: To remove chain from this SunTour derailleur without taking the chain apart, loosen the pulley axle bolt "C" and move the cage section "B." Be sure to close the cage section to point "A" and tighten the axle bolt.

9. PROBLEM: *Cannot replace chain back onto derailleur.*

SOLUTION: Fig. 2-16 shows you how the chain should fit on the derailleur wheels. If you have changed the derailleur or removed the chain for cleaning, you may puzzle for awhile about which wheel and in which direction on each wheel the chain should fit. As Fig. 2-16 shows, the chain should be:

a. On *top* of the freewheel cog.

b. In *front* of the derailleur upper (jockey wheel).

c. *Behind* the derailleur bottom (idler) wheel.

10. PROBLEM: Derailleur and chain interfere with rear wheel removal.

SOLUTION: To remove the rear wheel:

a. Shift the chain to the small rear cog and the small chainwheel.

b. On a road bike, open the brake release. On an ATB, remove the crossover wire. See Chapter 1 for this procedure.

c. Open the quick-release lever or loosen the axle mounting bolts (Chapter 7).

d. Grasp and pull the derailleur body backward so its jockey wheel clears the freewheel cogs. If you need more chain slack, slip the chain off the small chainwheel, down onto the bottom bracket shell.

Modern top-of-the-line rear derailleur design has solved most of the shifting problems that have plagued cyclists for years. The better derailleurs, the more expensive ones, for example, have sealed mechanisms, sturdy single- and double-spring mechanisms, plus a movement which keeps the top wheel a uniform distance from the freewheel cogs.

Fig. 2-16: *When replacing a chain, note that it goes over the freewheel cog, in front of the top derailleur pulley, and behind the bottom derailleur pulley.*

Front Derailleur Adjustment (Friction Systems)

As with the rear derailleur, it is very important that the front derailleur be correctly adjusted for safety and for ease of shifting. Here's how:

1. *Shift the chain to the low-gear position* (small chainwheel).
2. *Check parallel position:* The derailleur cage should be positioned parallel to the large chainwheel (as shown in Fig. 2-17).

3. *Check derailleur clearance:* If you have an elliptical chainwheel, the cage should be $1/_{32}$ inch to $1/_8$ inch above the highest point of the chainwheel ellipse. If you have a round chainwheel with longer teeth at one section, the cage should be $1/_{32}$ inch to $1/_8$ inch above that section (as shown in Fig. 2-17).

4. *To reposition the derailleur for positions 2 and 3 above:* Loosen the derailleur clamp fixing bolt (Fig. 2-18 and "5" in Fig. 2-19) and move the derailleur up or down and to the right or left as necessary. Tighten the clamp fixing bolt to 53 to 65 inch/pounds.

5. *Remove cable slack.* Shift the chain to the small chainwheel. Using your finger, lift the cable about halfway down the down tube (Fig. 2-7). If there is any slack, remove it by loosening the cable fixing bolt. Pull excess cable through the fixing bolt and tighten this bolt to 35 to 53 inch/ pounds. Leave about one or one-and-a-half inch of cable beyond the cable fixing bolt.

6. *Adjust left and right derailleur travel.* Like a rear derailleur, the front derailleur has two adjusters—a high-speed adjuster, which limits its travel to the right, and a low-speed adjuster, which limits its travel to the left. Fig. 2-20 shows them in closeup. As you can see, these little bolts limit derailleur travel to the left and to the right. The LO adjuster (closest to the mounting clamp) controls or limits derailleur movment over the small chainwheel. The HI adjuster limits derailleur movement to the right, over the large chainwheel.

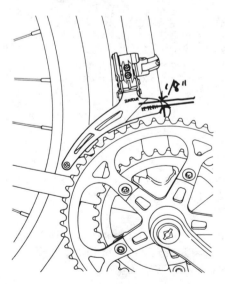

Fig. 2-17: *Move the front derailleur up or down to keep about ⅛ inch clearance between the derailleur cage and the chainwheel teeth. Derailleur cage should also be parallel to the chainwheels.*

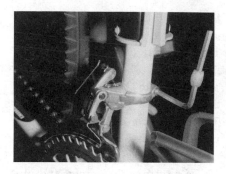

Fig. 2-18: *The Allen wrench shows the location of this front derailleur clamp fixing bolt holding the derailleur onto the seat tube.*

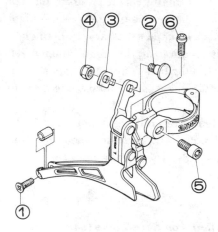

Fig. 2-19: *Exploded view of a front derailleur.* Courtesy SunTour.

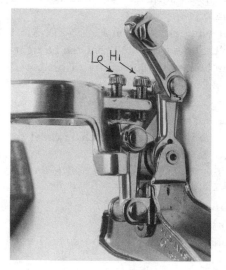

Fig. 2-20: *Super close-up of a front derailleur, showing left,* LO, *and right,* HI, *limit bolts.*

7. *Adjust low-gear (left) travel.* With the shift lever, move the front derailleur so its cage is over the small chainwheel (as shown in Fig. 2-18). If you can't shift the derailleur far enough to the left, turn the low-speed adjuster counterclockwise until the cage is centered over the small chainwheel. If the derailleur cage travels so far to the left that it throws the chain off the chainwheel, turn the low-speed adjuster clockwise to limit derailleur movement to the left. Shift the derailleur several times to make sure the chain moves accurately onto the smaller chainwheel, and fine-tune the low-gear limit adjuster as necessary.

8. *Adjust high-gear (right) travel.* While turning the cranks, shift the front derailleur so the large chainwheel (high gear) is close to, but not touching, the right inner surface of the chainguide plate. Turn the high-gear adjuster clockwise or counterclockwise, as necessary, to limit right movement of the derailleur to this location of the large chainwheel. Check both high- and low-gear adjustments by shifting the chain several times from the small to the large chainwheel and readjust one or both limit adjusters as necessary.

Use #242 Loctite to keep the cable clamp nut, derailleur limit bolts, front and rear derailleur mounting bolts, and rear derailleur top and idler wheel bolts from working loose under road vibration.

Front Derailleur Troubleshooting

1. PROBLEM: *Front or rear derailleurs on a road bike (shift levers on the down tube) seem to shift by themselves* so that you find the chain on a gear combination you don't want.

SOLUTION: Check the shift lever wing nut ("A" in Fig. 2-21). Most friction-type levers have a wing bolt. Some use a bolt that can be tightened with a dime. In any case, the bolt works loose after a time, and needs to be retightened periodically.

2. PROBLEM: *The chain moves too far to the left,* falls off the small chainwheel and onto the bottom-bracket shell where it may jam between the fixed cup of the bottom bracket and the base of the chainwheel.

SOLUTION: Readjust left travel as described above.

3. PROBLEM: *The chain moves too far to the right* so it falls off the large chainwheel and down onto the crank.

SOLUTION: Readjust the travel as described above.

4. PROBLEM: *The chain rubs on the derailleur cage.*

SOLUTION: The derailleur cage may not be parallel to the chainwheels. Check and readjust as shown above.

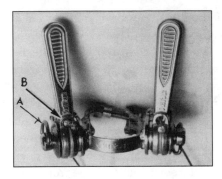

Fig. 2-21: Keep wing nut "A" tight to prevent shift lever(s) from working loose and shifting the chain. "B" points to leaded end of derailleur cable.

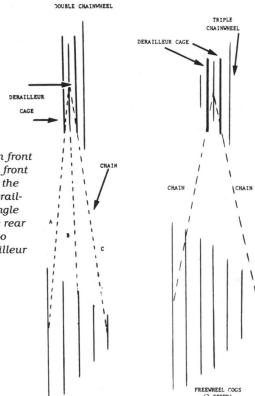

Fig. 2-22: Correct chain rub on front derailleur cage by moving the front shift lever slightly one way or the other after shifting the rear derailleur. As you can see, chain angle changes as you shift from one rear cog to another. If angle gets too acute, chain rubs on the derailleur cage.

5. PROBLEM: *Grinding noise or chain-rubbing sound from front de-railleur.*

SOLUTION: If you hear a grinding noise coming from the front de-railleur cage after shifting to a higher or lower rear cog *without shifting the front derailleur,* it's because the chain assumes an increasing angle as you shift, as shown in Fig. 2-22. As you can see, chain angle becomes greater inside the derailleur cage as you shift from the biggest to the smallest *rear* cog. This problem is especially acute with a 7-speed freewheel. Keep the chain from rubbing on the front derailleur cage by moving the cage slightly one way or the other until the grinding noise stops, and the chain and chainwheel are centered inside the derailleur cage. Check this for yourself. With the bike on a stand or suspended from the ceiling, shift the chain to the third gear of a 5- or 6-speed freewheel, or the fourth gear of a 7-speed freewheel. With the front shift lever, adjust the front derailleur until the chain is centered in the derailleur cage. Now shift the chain to the smallest rear cog. You will see that the chain moves closer to the right front derailleur cage plate as you do so. Shift the chain to the largest rear cog. You will note that the chain moves closer to the left front derailleur cage plate. This causes an increase in chain angle in the front derailleur cage as you shift the chain from one rear cog to another. The chain then rubs on the derailleur cage, even though derailleurs are correctly adjusted. Index shifting minimizes but does not eliminate this problem. You still have to move the front derailleur right or left to prevent chain rub on the derailleur cage.

6. PROBLEM: *Chain jumps off chainwheel.*

SOLUTION: Another cause of chain jump is a bent chainwheel. Most chainwheels are made of aluminum. They can be bent if the bike is dropped on them, or if another bike runs into them, or by other impacts. If you suspect a chainwheel is bent, remove the chain from it, spin the cranks, and eyeball the chainwheel from the rear. Mark any bent place with chalk. With a crescent wrench, *gently* force the chainwheel back to true. When you do this, remember that aluminum is a lot more brittle than steel. It takes little bending back and forth to break it. Try to make only one bend back to true.

7. PROBLEM: *You can shift the chain to the large chainwheel but have trouble shifting back down to the small chainwheel.*

SOLUTION: The derailleur is too high above the chainwheel. Readjust as shown above.

8. PROBLEM: *You cannot shift up to the large chainwheel.*

SOLUTION: The derailleur is positioned too low above the large chainwheel, where it rubs on the large chainwheel. Readjust as shown above.

INDEX SHIFTING SYSTEMS

Index shifting systems take the guesswork out of accurate shifting from one gear to another. Originally developed so racing cyclists could shift quickly and accurately during a race, these systems are now on the market as original equipment on most makes of bicycles.

Properly adjusted, index shift systems are a safety device as well as a convenience for fast and precise shifting. It takes practice to shift with a conventional derailleur system as you try to move the chain to the correct gear. Inaccurate manual shifting may leave the chain partly on a cog. Such shifting not only wears out the cog and the chain faster, it can contribute to chain skip, loss of control, and an accident. This type of accident can be avoided, of course, by learning how to shift smoothly and accurately. Index shifting automatically gives you smooth, accurate, and safe shifting to the gear you want. It moves the chain precisely onto the cogs of the freewheel and chainwheel without guessing or fiddling with shift levers. You always know which gear you're in. You won't ever have to look down and back at the rear cogs to see which gear the chain is in, or down at the chainwheel for the same reason. All of which means *safety* because you can concentrate on traffic, road, or trail conditions.

Even uphill shifting is easier, because you can get the chain to a lower gear quicker than with a conventional system. With index shifting, the chain moves fast, precisely, and usually without need to fine-tune where you have placed the chain. The system is self-tuning, if it's adjusted correctly in the first place.

How to Adjust Single-Lever Index Shifting Systems

The first commercially available index shifting system was the single lever design (Fig. 2-13) introduced to the U.S. market in 1984. Since that time index systems have been refined to the point where they are fairly foolproof. Latest versions use two levers each for front and rear shifters. I'll review adjustments for the single-lever index system first, then cover the newer double-lever systems.

First, if the index feature won't work, you can quickly and easily shift to old-fashioned friction shifting. Do this by turning the dial on the shift lever from INDEX to FRICTION (Fig. 2-3). For example, if the cable stretches while you're out on a ride so the index shift goes on strike on some gears, just switch to friction and pedal on. Earlier single-lever index shifting systems operate with a definite click which you hear each time you shift the chain on the freewheel cogs or on the chainwheels.

These are the steps in adjusting single-lever index shifting systems:

1. *High speed adjustment.* Shift to the small freewheel cog. Eyeball the derailleur top wheel and this cog. The top derailleur wheel should be parallel to and aligned under the left edge of the small freewheel cog (as shown in Fig. 2-23). If not, turn the high-speed adjuster clockwise or counterclockwise until the derailleur wheel is lined up as above.

2. *Low speed adjustment.* Shift the chain to the big freewheel cog (low gear). The derailleur top wheel should be parallel to and a tad to the right of that cog (as shown in Fig. 2-24). If not, adjust the low speed adjuster clockwise or counterclockwise until the top wheel is lined up with that cog.

Remove excess cable slack. Maintaining correct cable tension is critical for all index systems. If the cable is too slack, the chain won't shift from high (small cog) to the next cog. If it's too tight (too much cable

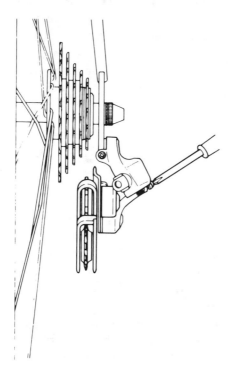

Fig. 2-23: *On dual-lever index shifters, align the top derailleur wheel a bit to the left of the small freewheel cog.* Courtesy Shimano.

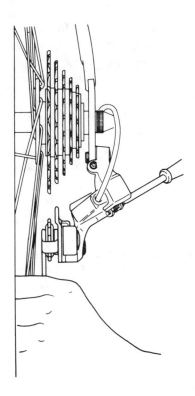

Fig. 2-24: *Align the top derailleur wheel a bit to the right of the large rear cog, on dual-lever index shifters.* Courtesy Shimano.

tension) the chain may skip a gear as you shift to a lower gear. Move the rear derailleur shift lever wing bolt to the friction mode (as shown in Fig. 2-3). Be sure to turn the little ring back down flat again after you switch from one mode to the other. If the ring is not flat, the derailleur system can switch from one mode to the other, which may be a bit disconcerting.

Shift to the high (small rear cog) gear. Pull excess cable through the derailleur cable fixing bolt and tighten it to 35 to 53 inch/pounds. Fine-tune cable tension with the derailleur's *inner cable tension barrel,* as you make the following adjustments.

Adjust Cable Tension

1. Turn the shift lever wing bolt so the system is in the index mode (as shown in Fig. 2-3).

2. Now shift from the small freewheel cog to the next biggest cog. If the chain won't move to this gear, turn the cable slack adjuster on the

derailleur ("A" in Fig. 2-25) or on the shift lever body ("D" in Fig. 2-26) counterclockwise one or two turns. Try shifting again. If the chain overshifts and moves to the third gear, turn the cable slack adjuster clockwise a half a turn to one turn and continue this fine-tuning until the chain falls exactly on the second gear.

3. With the chain resting on the second gear, turn the inner cable tension adjuster (Fig. 2-25 or Fig. 2-26) counterclockwise while you turn the pedal forward, as if you were cycling. As you turn the adjuster, watch the rear third cog and the chain. As the chain just begins to approach the third cog, stop twisting the adjuster.

4. Shift back to the small rear cog. Repeat Step 6 below on each of the freewheel cogs, fine-tuning with the cable tension adjuster on the derailleur as necessary.

5. Put the chain on the smallest chainwheel and the largest freewheel. Turn the rear derailleur angle adjustment screw ("B" in Fig. 2-25) to bring the derailleur top wheel as close to the big rear cog as possible, without touching it.

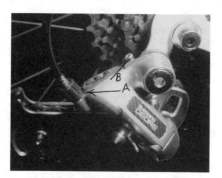

Fig. 2-25: Remove minor *cable stretch with the cable adjuster at the derailleur, "A."*

Fig. 2-26: Remove minor *cable stretch with the adjuster on the shift lever, "D." "A" shows the screw holding the cable plate; "B," the small shift lever; "C," the large shift lever.*

6. For the final adjustment step, crank in reverse (backpedal). If the chain rubs as you're backpedaling, the top wheel is too close to the large rear cog. Turn the angle tension adjustment screw clockwise ("B" in Fig. 2-25) until you can backpedal without having the derailleur top wheel rub on the big (low-gear) rear cog.

7. Adjust the front derailleur as noted in the section above, "Front Derailleur Adjustment." Front derailleur adjustments for single-lever index shifters are the same as for conventional shift systems.

How to Adjust Dual-Lever Index Shifting Systems

Adjustments for front and rear dual-lever indexing shift systems may seem the same as for conventional friction shift systems. However, there are important differences. So please review the data that follows if you have a dual-lever index system on your bicycle. The same bolt-and-nut torque specs apply to both friction and index systems, however. Instructions for adjustments and troubleshooting are combined below.

Troubleshooting the Rear Dual-Lever Index Shift System

1. PROBLEM: *Chain won't shift smoothly to the largest freewheel cog.*

SOLUTION: Check and adjust for cable stretch as shown earlier in this chapter on friction shift systems. Note: You can remove minor cable stretch at the cable tension barrel on the shift lever (Fig. 2-26) and/or at the derailleur (Fig. 2-25), if these adjusters are on your components.

2. PROBLEM: *Chain won't move up from the smaller to the next-larger rear cog.*

SOLUTION: Adjust the cable tension barrel on the derailleur or shift lever (Fig. 2-25 or Fig. 2-26) counterclockwise a quarter turn; repeat as necessary.

3. PROBLEM: *Chain moves past the second gear as you attempt to shift to it.*

SOLUTION: Turn the cable tension barrel (Fig. 2-25 or Fig. 2-26) clockwise a quarter turn; repeat as necessary. Then shift the chain to the next-smallest rear cog. Turn the crank so the chain moves the rear wheel. Turn the tension barrel counterclockwise until you hear the chain make noise against the third cog (up from the smallest cog).

4. PROBLEM: *Chain moves past the small cog and jams between it and the chain stay.*

SOLUTION: Align the derailleur top wheel under the small cog, or slightly to its right. See above on friction and single-lever index shifters.

5. PROBLEM: *Chain skips while you pedal or as you shift.*

SOLUTION: Shift the chain so it is on the smallest chainwheel and the largest rear cog. While turning the crank backward (backpedal) turn the cage tension bolt ("B" in Fig. 2-25) counterclockwise to bring the rear derailleur upper pulley almost but not quite to where it touches the big rear cog. Now shift to the next smallest rear cog, then back to the big cog. Should the top derailleur pulley touch the big cog, turn the cage tension adjuster clockwise to bring this pulley to just below the big cog.

6. PROBLEM: *Chain skips or is noisy as you pedal.*

SOLUTION: Chain or cog teeth, or both, may be worn. See section on friction shifting above, and on chain wear later in this chapter. Replace worn cogs and chains.

Troubleshooting Chainwheel Dual-Lever Index Systems

1. PROBLEM: *Can't shift from a smaller to the largest chainwheel.*

SOLUTION: The cable has stretched. Shift to the smallest chainwheel. Remove minor cable stretch with the cable adjuster barrel at the shift lever ("E" in Fig. 2-1), if your shifters are so equipped. Remove major cable stretch as described in the section above on friction front shifters.

2. PROBLEM: *Chain overshifts off the small chainwheel. Chain falls off the left.*

SOLUTION: Shift the chain to the smallest chainwheel and to the largest freewheel cog. Adjust the low gear limit bolt (Fig. 2-27) until the clearance between the chain and the front derailleur chain guard inner plate is around $1/64$ to $1/32$ inch. Check shifting and readjust the low-gear limit bolt as necessary.

3. PROBLEM: *Chain overshifts and falls to the right off the large chainwheel.*

SOLUTION: With the chain on the big chainwheel and smallest freewheel cog, turn the high-gear limit bolt (Fig. 2-27) on the front derailleur so there is a bare minimum clearance between the chain and the inside of the outer front derailleur cage plate. Check to make sure the chain does not rub on the cage plate.

4. PROBLEM: *Can't shift accurately to the center chainwheel. Chain seems to jump or skip off this gear.*

SOLUTION: Turn the high gear limit bolt (Fig. 2-27) one or two turns counterclockwise. Check shifting and readjust this bolt as necessary.

5. PROBLEM: *Difficulty shifting from the center to the big chainwheel.*

SOLUTION: Adjust the high-gear limit bolt (Fig. 2-27) counterclockwise a quarter turn or so.

Fig. 2-27: *Low- and high-gear limit bolts on Shimano front derailleur, left, and SunTour front derailleur, right.*

6. PROBLEM: *Difficulty in shifting from the center to the small chain-wheel.*

SOLUTION: Turn the low-gear adjuster bolt (Fig. 2-27) a quarter turn counterclockwise. Check shifting, readjust this bolt as necessary.

7. PROBLEM: *When chain is on big chainwheel it rubs on the outer (right side) of the derailleur cage plate.*

SOLUTION: Turn the front derailleur clamp bolt ("2" in Fig. 2-28) two or three turns to loosen it. Move the front derailleur up or down until the outer cage plate clears the chain $1/_{32}$ to $1/_8$ inch. Tighten the clamp bolt to 35 to 52 inch/pounds.

8. PROBLEM: *After solution above, chain now rubs on inner or outer cage plate.*

SOLUTION: Shift the chain up to the big chainwheel. Loosen the front derailleur clamp bolt as in the solution above. Pivot the derailleur until its outer cage plate is above and parallel to the large chainwheel.

On all dual-lever shifters:

PROBLEM: *None of the above problems can be solved on either front or rear shifters.*

SOLUTION: The ratchet mechanism may be defective. The rear shift lever has some 36 parts in it, a watchmaker's dream. Have your dealer replace it. This is a shop job.

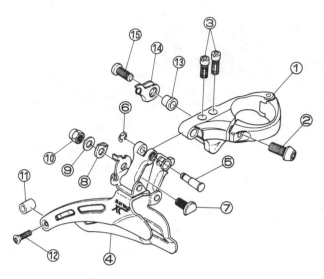

Fig. 2-28: *Exploded view of a front derailleur: "10" is the cable fixing bolt, "2" is the derailleur clamp bolt.* Courtesy SunTour.

Retrofitting Dual-Lever Index Shifters

Note: You can adjust the reach of dual-index shift levers to suit your finger length. Turn the reach adjuster ("B" in Fig. 2-30).

Retrofitting dual-lever index shifters on your old bike can be a real can of worms, as far as I am concerned. First, you have to be absolutely sure that the chain, freewheel, and front and rear derailleurs are matched components. Using components of different makes, let alone unmatched

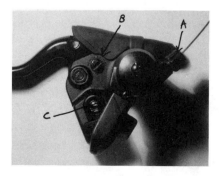

Fig. 2-30: *View from the underside of a dual-lever index shifter/brake lever combination. "A," cable stretch adjuster; "B," reach adjuster; "C," clamp bolt holding unit onto handlebars.*

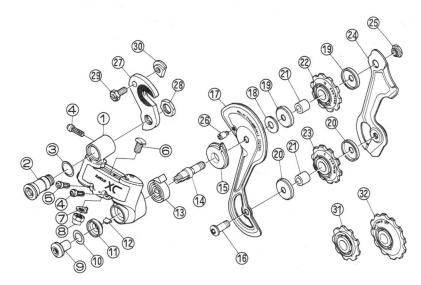

Fig. 2-29: *Exploded view of a rear derailleur: "2" is the bolt that holds the derailleur on the rear wheel dropout; "8" is the cable fixing bolt.*

parts of the same make, is an invitation to disaster. Some makes of shifters, for example, are designed for a specific number of freewheel gears. This is because the shifter ratchet mechanism has to be designed with exactly the number of freewheel cogs you use. A 6-speed ratchet shifter will not work with a 7-speed freewheel, for example.

The hanger, where the rear derailleur is mounted, has to be exactly aligned with the frame, or the dual shifters will not shift accurately. Shimano makes an excellent hanger alignment tool to check this, but it's expensive. By the time this book reaches you, I would imagine a good bike shop would have this tool, though.

For all the above reasons I am not going to cover retrofitting dual lever systems, or even single-lever shift systems, in this book. This is properly a shop job. You will likely need a new freehub and freehub cassette, a new rim and spokes, a wheel building job, new chain, new rear derailleur, new cable, and of course the dual-index shifter/brake combination plus labor. The total comes to around $230. If your frame was designed for a 5-speed freewheel and you go to a 6- or 7-speed freewheel, the frame reworking would add another $30. If the dropout or chain stay or frame is out of alignment, add another $30 or more for frame realignment. It makes a lot more sense to me to spend another

$200 or $300 and get a new bike with the dual index shifters, if you want to go that route. Excellent bikes for $500 or $600 with these shifters are now on the market.

CABLE REPLACEMENT

How to Replace a Cable on Dual-Lever Index Shifters

Replacement of the cable on the front or rear of these shifters is similar to cable replacement of single-lever index shifters and friction shifters, with one small difference. The difference lies in how you snake the cable end through the shift lever body.

To change a derailleur cable:

1. Shift the chain to the small rear cog if you are changing a rear derailleur, or to the small chainwheel if you are changing a front derailleur cable.

2. Remove the small screw ("A" in Fig. 2-26) and the plastic plate it holds (under the short shift lever) using a small Phillips screwdriver. (If your shifters do not have this piece, as on some models, continue with the steps below.)

3. Loosen the cable binder bolt ("10" in Fig. 2-28) on a front derailleur, or the same bolt ("8" in Fig. 2-29) on a rear derailleur, that holds the cable in the unit. Pull out the old cable.

4. Remove the old cable from the spaghetti tubing and push the leaded end out of the shift lever ("B" in Fig. 2-1 or Fig. 2-21).

5. Push the end of the new cable (be sure to use the same make cable; check with your bicycle shop) through the shift lever. This is a bit tricky, as you may have discovered at this point. It's almost impossible to see the tiny orifice the cable has to go through. Start the cable insertion just under the small shift lever (Fig. 2-1) and poke and prod until it comes out the other side, through the cable slack adjuster. This can be a stinker of a procedure, I know. Stick with it, you'll get there. It helps if you remove the cable slack adjuster ("D" in Fig. 2-26) from the shift lever. Be sure to replace it later.

6. Pass the new cable through the spaghetti tubing, through the frame-mounted cable stops, the rear derailleur cable slack adjuster, and into the cable binder bolt.

7. Pull up hard on the new cable, about halfway down the down tube, to prestretch the cable.

8. Hold the cable taut with a fourth hand tool or needle-nose pliers and tighten the cable binder bolt to 35 to 52 inch/pounds.

9. Recheck all shift adjustments. Review the troubleshooting procedures above for rear and front derailleurs and readjust as necessary.

10. Replace the plastic piece you removed in Step "1" above.

How to Replace a Cable on Friction Shifters

Replacing a cable on friction shifters is simple. Just loosen the cable fixing bolt on the derailleur, pull the old cable out of the shift lever (Fig. 2-21), and install a new one, as described above for dual shifters. Readjust the derailleurs as described in the friction shift section at the beginning of this chapter.

Road-bike shift levers are usually mounted on the down tube (Fig. 2-21). Shifting is snappier, more responsive from this position, but the rider has to bend over slightly to reach the levers. This momentary distraction could cause an accident. Shift levers on cheaper road bikes are often mounted on the stem. In this location shift levers can be reached without bending down. However, cables are longer so shifting is sluggish, compared to down tube–mounted levers. On the stem, these levers are a hazard, especially for men, should an accident propel the rider over the handlebars.

Bar-end shifters (Fig. 2-31) are an excellent solution to the disadvantags of down-tube stem-mounted shifters. They are located at the ends of road bike downturned handlebars. Here the rider can reach them without bending down. The cable length is shorter than stem shifters. Shifting is snappy. Follow these steps to install bar-end shifters:

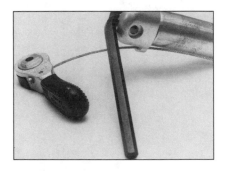

Fig. 2-31: *Bar-end shifters on a road bike are easy to reach, provide snappy shifting.*

1. Remove the plug from each end of the handlebar. Remove the handlebar tape.

2. Insert the shift cable into the shift lever and through the guide hole in the shifter body (Fig. 2-31).

3. Insert the shift lever body into the handlebar end and tighten it with an Allen wrench (Fig. 2-31).

4. Replace the shift lever in the handlebar body, and tighten the mounting bolt with a screwdriver (Fig. 2-32).

5. Replace the shift lever bolt cap (arrow, Fig. 2-33) on the shift lever mounting bolt.

6. If you are replacing down tube–mounted shifters, you will need longer derailleur cables. Install these cables. Readjust derailleurs as above, if necessary.

7. Tape about six inches of the cable along the bottom edge of the handlebars. Continue the tape behind the cables and finish taping. The cables should curve outward from the handlebars so as not to bind cable movement.

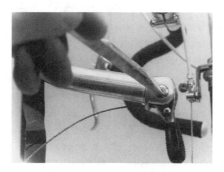

Fig. 2-32: *Tighten bar-end shift-lever mounting bolt with a screwdriver.*

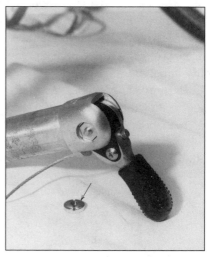

Fig. 2-33: *Install shift-lever mounting bolt cap, arrow.*

3

Chainwheels, Cranks, and Bottom Brackets

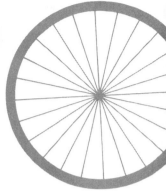

I n this chapter you will learn how to care for your chainwheels, cranks, and bottom bracket. I will start with chainwheels. First, here are tools you will need. Please note that chainwheel bolts and nuts vary in size from bike to bike, as do bottom-bracket bolts, adjustable cups, and lockrings. The following list is generic only. Check with your bike shop for the sizes you need.

Tools You Will Need

1. Chainwheel nut wrench ("A," Fig. 3-1).
2. Crank puller ("B," Fig. 3-1).
3. Allen wrench for chainwheel bolt ("C," Fig. 3-1).
4. Wrench for bottom-bracket axle (a.k.a. spindle) bolt, usually 14 or 15 mm ("D," Fig. 3-1 and "2," Fig. 3-2). Or a thin–wall socket wrench in these sizes. If you have a Shimano bottom bracket with an Allen bolt, you need a 5-mm Allen wrench and won't need the crank puller.
5. Bottom bracket lockring and fixed-cup wrench ("1," Fig. 3-2).
6. Pin wrench ("3," Fig. 3-2) for bottom bracket adjustable cup.
7. Torque wrench (Fig. 1-2). Please review the data on torque and use of the torque wrench in Chapter 1.
8. If your bike has a Phil Wood sealed-bearing bottom bracket, a special wrench for the adjustable rings (Fig. 3-3).

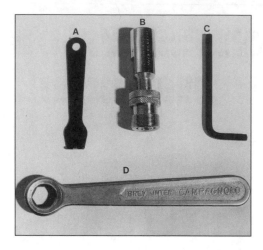

Fig. 3-1: *Chainwheel and bottom-bracket tools. "A," chainwheel nut wrench; "B," bottom-bracket crank puller; "C," Allen wrench for chainwheel bolt; "D," bottom-bracket crank binder bolt wrench.*

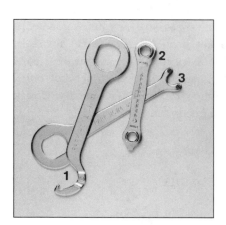

Fig. 3-2: *Bottom-bracket tools. "1," lockring and fixed-cup wrench; "2," bottom-bracket axle bolt wrench in 14-, 15- and 16-mm sizes; "3," adjustable-cup pin wrench on one end, fixed-cup wrench on the other end.* Courtesy Park Tools.

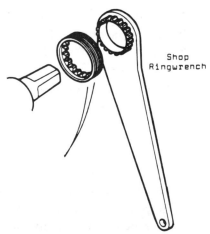

Fig. 3-3: *Shop-type wrench for Phil Wood cartridge-type bottom-bracket left and right cups.*

9. A 15-mm open-end wrench to remove the pedals from a one-piece crankset on inexpensive bicycles. Pedals must be removed to remove the one-piece cranks and axle so you can remove the bearings for cleaning and relubrication.

10. Supply of lubricant for the bottom bracket bearings. I recommend boat-trailer wheel-bearing grease, available from any marine supply outlet and some hardware stores.

Table 3-1 BOLT-AND-NUT TIGHTENING TORQUE SPECIFICATIONS

	(Inch/pounds)
Crank-to-bottom-bracket axle bolt	200–300
Chainwheel binder bolts (holds chainwheels together)	70–90
Bottom-bracket lockring	600–900
Bottom bracket fixed cup (right hand chainwheel side)	600–900

CHAINWHEEL MAINTENANCE

Follow These Maintenance Tips for Long-Lived Chainwheels

1. *Abrasives such as sand and road dirt can wear out the aluminum-alloy teeth of a chainwheel.* It's not easy to reach behind the chainwheels, especially in the middle of a triple chainset (Fig. 3-4), but it's important you get both sides of all the teeth on all the chainwheels clean, to prevent

Fig. 3-4: Be sure to clean all teeth of your chainwheel. The center and small rings are hard to reach, but important to keep clean. Note gunk on the small chainring. Allen wrench is used to tighten chainwheel binder bolts.

their premature wear and costly replacement. The middle chainwheel and the inner (right) side of the small chainwheel are tough to get at. Use a small brush dipped in kerosene, or a kerosene-soaked rag, to remove the kind of gritty buildup you can see on the small chainring in Fig. 3-4.

2. *If chainwheel teeth are worn* it's time to replace the chainwheel. Most ATB cyclists used the smaller of a double chainwheel or the middle of a triple chainwheel on slow-speed off-road rides. Inspect those chainwheels closely for wear after every 200 miles of cycling.

3. *Look for a bent chainwheel.* A bent chainwheel can cause chain skip. If you have an expensive bike I recommend that the straightening be done at a bike shop. The chainrings are also costly and if they break while being straightened, a replacement could cost at least $15, plus labor. You could gently force a bent chainwheel back to true with a 6-inch adjustable crescent wrench. If you go this route, remember that aluminum is a lot less elastic and more brittle than steel. So go easy, and try to true it up in one direction only.

4. *Check for loose chainwheel binder bolts.* I was ride-testing a new bike for a magazine article a few years ago. When I shifted the chain from the small to the large chainwheel, the pedals suddenly locked and I almost lost control. I found that the chainwheel binder bolts (Fig. 3-5) either had not been sufficiently tightened, or had worked loose, which

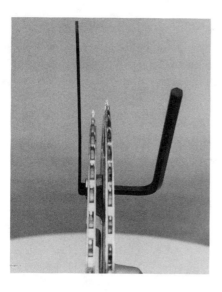

Fig. 3-5: Check tightness of chainwheel binder bolts and nuts at least every six months. Tighten them to 70 to 95 inch/pounds.

allowed the two chainwheels to spread apart. When I shifted, the chain fell down between them. These bolts *can* work loose, so check them after every long trip, or every few months. You'll need a 5-mm Allen wrench and a slot wrench (Fig. 3-1). A double chainwheel set has five binder bolts, and a triple chainwheel set has ten binder bolts. To tighten these bolts, use the slot wrench to hold the binder bolt nut and the 5-mm Allen wrench to tighten the binder bolt. Tighten each bolt to a torque of 70 to 95 inch/pounds.

If you have a worn chainwheel, or wish to change to a different size chainwheel for improved gearing, here is how to do it. First, however, I recommend you review Chapter 6 on gears and gearing for an overview on gear selections.

Here's How to Remove the Chainwheels and Replace a Chainwheel

1. Remove the dust cap (Fig. 3-6 and Fig. 3-7), depending on design, use an Allen wrench, screwdriver, or pin wrench.

2. With a 14- or 15-mm wrench (see Figs. 3-1 and 3-2), turn the crank binder bolt counterclockwise (Fig. 3-8). Remove it and its washer (Fig. 3-9). If your bike has a Shimano one-key release (Fig. 3-10), use a 6-mm Allen wrench (Fig. 3-11) and skip Step 3 below, because this setup combines a crank axle binder bolt and a crank puller. Be careful when using the Allen wrench to loosen this bolt. It's easy to slip and skin your knuckles. The Allen bolt is integral to the crank and remains in it when the crank is removed from the spindle. The Allen bolt crank was

Fig. 3-6: *Remove this dust cap with an Allen wrench.*

Fig. 3-7: Use a screwdriver to remove this dust cap.

Fig. 3-8: Remove the crank binder bolt (holds crank on bottom-bracket axle).

Fig. 3-9: Remove axle binder bolt and washer.

Fig. 3-10: *Close-up of a Shimano one-key axle binder bolt. This unit also doubles as a crank puller.*

Fig. 3-11: *Loosen the one-key axle binder bolt with a 5-mm Allen wrench. Keep turning until the crank is loose and can be removed from the axle.*

a great idea because it was so easy to remove. Thieves agreed; soon after they were introduced, a lot of $130 chainwheels and cranks, along with attached $85 pedals, disappeared.

3. Thread in a crank puller tool (Fig. 3-12). Be sure to retract this tool before installing it in the dust cap threads. Hold section "A" while you turn section "B" until that part is retracted all the way, flush with the end section "A" as shown in Fig. 3-12. Thread section "A" into the dust cap threads (Fig. 3-13), turning it by the knurled section. Be very careful to start this tool so as not to strip or cross-thread the dust cap threads. Remember—the tool is steel, the dust cap threads are aluminum. It is *very* important, too, that the tool be threaded *all* the way into the dust cap opening, so it uses *all* the dust cap threads. The crank puller puts an awful lot of pressure on dust cap threads. If this tool is not all the way in, the tool will pull right off the dust cap threads, stripping them as it goes. You will have a costly shop job to rethread the crank dust cap threads.

4. Turn the crank puller clockwise with a wrench on the flats ("C" in Fig. 3-12) until the crank is loose on the bottom-bracket axle (Fig. 3-14). If you meet a lot of resistance and can't get the crank to break loose, tap the end of the crank puller briskly with a ball peen hammer a few

Fig. 3-12: Bottom-bracket crank-puller tool. Be sure the tool is adjusted so it looks just like this photo, before inserting it in the dust cap threads.

Fig. 3-13: Crank puller in dust cap threads. Make sure it is in straight (not cross-threaded) and in as far as possible.

Fig. 3-14: When the crank puller has loosened the crank, remove the crank from the axle and the tool from the crank.

times, then keep turning. Repeat as necessary. When the cranks and chainwheels are off the axle, remove the crank puller tool.

5. Dunk the chainwheels in kerosene and clean them thoroughly. (Note: You do not *have* to remove the chainwheels to clean them.) Check the tightness of all chainwheel binder bolts (Fig. 3-5), as noted above, to a torque of 70 to 95 inch/pounds.

6. If you wish to change chainwheels, now is the time to do it. Please see Chapter 6 for information on gearing to help you select the right size replacement chainwheel. Or, if your chainwheel is bent or worn, you should also replace it. Here is how:

a. First, look at Fig. 3-15. Note the little bolts, "E," and washers, "D." If you change from a double to a triple chainwheel setup (see instructions on changing the bottom bracket-axle to a longer one, below), you will need to buy a new, longer set of these bolts, and, possibly, washers of a different thickness. Since the first edition of this book in 1981, dozens and dozens of makes and sizes of chainwheels have appeared on the market. There simply is not space enough in this book to even attempt to tell you which size bolts and washers should be used on the many, many chainring combinations you could use. In addition, not all chainrings are compatible and will fit on your particular crank ("A" in Fig. 3-15). My advice is for you to take your old crank, together with chainrings, to your bike shop and let the mechanic help you select new rings to fit your old crank.

b. Fit the new chainring(s) on the crank, using the bolts, washers, and nuts (yes, there is a bolt for each nut, though only one is shown, "C" in Fig. 3-15). Tighten them (as in Fig. 3-5) to 70 to 95 inch/pounds.

7. *A word of warning about elliptical chainwheels.* When reinstalling chainwheels on the crank, make sure the topmost part of the chainwheel (the apex of the ellipse) is in line with the crank (as shown in Fig. 3-16). As you replace the crank/chainwheel combination on the axle, make sure the top of the ellipse of all the chainwheels is about $\frac{1}{32}$ inch from the outer front derailleur cage plate, vertical to the ground and parallel to each other. Otherwise you negate any benefit the oval ring imparts. This warning also goes for some makes and models of 1990 round chainwheels where the teeth are slightly higher in one area than in others. Rotate the new round chainwheels to find where the longer teeth are located.

Fig. 3-15: *Triple chainwheel setup: "A," crank; "B," chainwheels; "C," dustcap; "D," spacers; "E," bolts.*

Fig. 3-16: *Elliptical chainwheels. Note that the highest point of each chainwheel's ellipse is parallel to the crank.* Courtesy Shimano.

Table 3-2 BOTTOM-BRACKET SPECIFICATIONS

	Model No.	Spindle Mark	Sell Width	A	B	C	D
DEORE XT	BB-M730	D-3A	68	117.5	52	33.5	32
	BB-M730	D-3NL	68	122.5	52	36	34.5
	BB-M730	D-5A	70	117.5	54	32.5	31
	BB-M730	D-5NL	70	122.5	54	35	33.5
DEORE	BB-MT60	D-3A	68	117.5	52	33.5	32
	BB-MT60	D-3NL	68	122.5	52	36	34.5
	BB-MT60	D-5A	70	117.5	54	32.5	31
	BB-MT60	D-5NL	70	122.5	54	35	33.5
	(FC-B124)	3SS	68	121.5	52	37.5	32
	(FC-B124)	5S	70	124.5	55	37.5	32
EXAGE mountain	BB-M450	3A	68	117.5	52	33.5	32
trail	BB-M450	5A	70	117.5	54	32.5	31

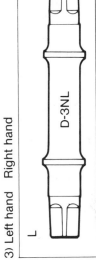

Shell width

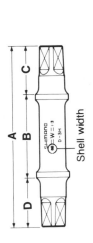

L   R

D-3NL

3) Left hand   Right hand

4) Explanation of spindle mark

① ② ③ ④

Going from a Double to a Triple Chainwheel

As I noted earlier in this chapter, if you wish a lower gear for hill climbing, plus a much wider selection of gears, you can install a third chainwheel on your crank. See the chainwheel data above for instructions.

You will also need a bottom-bracket axle with a longer section on the right side for the now wider triple chainwheel. The longer axle is required to provide clearance between the small chainwheel and the chain stay. Without such clearance the chainwheel will rub on the chain stay.

There are too many makes and types of bottom-bracket axles available to be able to show you a full range of which axle is compatible with which crank. Table 3-2, for example, gives all the variations of spindle dimensions for just one make of chainwheels, Shimano. You must have an exact match if you buy a spindle. See your bike shop for the right match.

Now that you have the chainwheels and crank removed from the bottom bracket, proceed with maintenance of the bottom bracket assembly.

BOTTOM BRACKET MAINTENANCE

The bottom bracket (Fig. 3-17) consists of the axle "A"; axle bolts, "B"; adjustable cup, "C"; lockring, "D"; axle bolt washers, "E"; ball bearings in a retainer, "F"; and fixed cup, "G," that goes on the right side of the bottom-bracket shell. Some bottom brackets use sealed cartridge bearings which are *not* removable except with an arbor press. However, some types of sealed-bearing bottom brackets can replace conventional units. I'll discuss these sealed units later on in this section. Let's start with the ball bearing–type bottom bracket, which are on most of the bicycles on the market today.

Disassembly

1. Remove both cranks. See instructions above under "Here's how to remove the chainwheels and replace a chainwheel."

2. Remove the lockring counterclockwise with the special wrench, as shown in Fig. 3-18.

Fig. 3-17: *Bottom-bracket assembly: "A," axle; "B," bolts to hold cranks onto axle; "C," adjustable cup; "D," lockring; "E," washers for bolts "B"; "F," ball bearings in retainers; "G," fixed cup.*

Fig. 3-18: *Remove lockring with special wrench.*

3. Remove the adjustable cup counterclockwise (Fig. 3-19). Use the pin wrench.

4. Remove the outer set of bearings, the axle, the inner set of bearings, and any plastic seal (Fig. 3-20). The bearings in older bikes may be loose instead of in a retainer, so be ready to catch them.

5. Clean dirt and old grease from cups and bearings with kerosene.

6. Inspect the bearings for wear. If your bike is relatively new and hasn't had much use, chances are that all you will need to do, after cleaning the bearings, cups, and spindle, is to repack the bearings with grease and replace them. If the balls are in a retainer, I recommend

Fig. 3-19: Remove adjustable cup with pin wrench.

Fig. 3-20: Remove plastic seal from inside bottom bracket.

scrapping the old balls along with their retainer and replacing them with loose balls. Use new ones; they aren't that expensive. This will give you eleven instead of nine balls per bearing set, so the bottom-bracket spindle will run more smoothly. The additional balls will add to both bearing and cup life. Most modern bottom brackets use ¼-inch balls, but take your old ones to the bike shop to make sure you get the same size replacements.

7. Inspect the cups for signs of galling or brinelling, indicated by pitting or grooves worn in the racetrack, and replace them if necessary.

Reassembly

Now that you have cleaned your ball-and-cup–type bottom bracket and replaced any worn parts, you are ready to grease and put it back together. I recommend boat-trailer wheel-bearing grease. It adds a bit more pedaling drag but won't wash out as fast as ordinary grease when you run through water or mud. Here are the steps for reassembly:

1. Roll the loose balls in grease until they are thoroughly covered.
2. Put a layer of grease on both cups.
3. Put the loose balls in the cups. The grease will hold them in place.
4. Insert the spindle (a.k.a. axle) into the bottom bracket. Make sure the longer spindle end goes in first, because that's the spindle side for the chainwheels. If your bottom bracket did not come with a plastic protective cover, it's a good idea to install one (Fig. 3-20) to keep away abrasives and water that can get into frame tubes and work down into the bottom-bracket shell.
5. Thread the adjustable cup clockwise into the bottom-bracket shell and turn it by hand as far as possible. Use the pin wrench to continue turning it until it's snug. Back the cup off a half-turn.
6. Thread the lockring onto the adjustable cup by hand. Hold the adjustable cup with the pin wrench so it can't turn, and tighten the lockring firmly with the lockring wrench.
7. Check bearing adjustment for tightness. Twirl the spindle with your thumb and a finger. It should rotate smoothly. If it feels rough or is hard to turn, loosen the lockring and turn the adjustable cup counterclockwise about a quarter turn, and tighten the lockring. Check the adjustment and repeat this step as necessary. Hold the spindle with your fingers and push it up and down. If it feels loose, loosen the lockring, turn the adjustable cup clockwise a quarter turn, and retighten the lockring. Repeat these adjustments as necessary. See Step 9 below for additional check.
8. Install both cranks. *Do not lubricate the spindle flats, where the cranks fit!* The crank-to-spindle is a *drive* fit. Tighten the crank binder bolt to 220 to 300 inch/pounds. Replace the dust caps.
9. Again check the bearing adjustment for looseness. Place one crank at the twelve o'clock position. Move both cranks sharply from side to

side, toward and away from you. If you feel looseness, turn the lockring counterclockwise until it's loose and turn the adjustable cap clockwise about a quarter turn. Hold the adjustable cup with the pin wrench and tighten the lockring. Check this adjustment and repeat this step as necessary. The cranks should rotate smoothly and stop gradually.

10. Retighten the bottom-bracket crank-fixing bolts every 50 miles for the first 200 miles. This is important. As I said, the crank-to-spindle attachment is a drive fit. The fixing bolt forces the crank onto the spindle flats. The crank is aluminum (except for bargain-basement cranksets which are steel), the spindle is steel. Just a few miles of pedaling will destroy a crank if the fit is loose. Then you will be faced with spending upwards of $125 for a crankset of equal quality (plus labor).

Replacing the Bottom-Bracket Unit

If the adjustable cup bearing surface is worn, pitted, or grooved, it should, of course, be replaced. Replace the fixed cup also because it too will be shot. Be sure you buy an exact replacement bottom-bracket set that matches the dimensions of your cranks (use your old cranks). Here's how to install a new ball-bearing bottom bracket:

1. Remove cranks and adjustable cup and its lockring as described above, in the sections of this chapter on crank removal and on bottom bracket disassembly.

2. Remove the fixed cup. The fixed cup has flats for a special wrench (Fig. 3-21), so you must use the one that fits your fixed cup. However, I recommend that you not invest in this tool for only this one-shot purpose. It's a tough job and you could damage the frame if you are not careful. Most fixed cups, particularly on older bikes, are on so tight it

Fig. 3-21: *Fixed cup is removed clockwise on most bikes with this special wrench. See text.*

takes a lot more torque (turning energy) than you can supply with this tool. Have the fixed cup removed by a bike shop which has special tools for this operation. As I noted, the only reason to remove the fixed cup is to change to another make or model bottom-bracket assembly. You could remove the fixed cup by holding the cup flats in a machinist's vise and turning the entire bike. Your vise should have undamaged jaws for this operation, otherwise the fixed cup flats will slip out of the vise. If the bike was made in the U.S.A., France, or Italy, turn the bike clockwise. If it was made anyplace else, chances are that the cup is right-hand threaded, so turn the bike counterclockwise.

3. Replace the new bottom-bracket assembly. See instructions above in the section in this chapter on bottom bracket disassembly.

Sealed Bearing Bottom-Bracket Maintenance

There are two types of sealed-bearing bottom brackets. Both types use electric motor–type cartridge bearings. In one type the bearings are not removable. If they wear out, it takes special tools, such as a machine shop arbor press, to remove and replace them. Fisher, Klein, and some European makes such as the Alex Singer come with these bearings. Lubricating these at least yearly, more often if you ride a lot, especially over sand or through water, they will last many years.

To lubricate these bearings:

1. Remove the cranks. See crank removal instructions in the section on crank removal earlier in this chapter.

2. Remove the circlip (split washer) if there is one.

3. Pry out the neoprene seal with a thin-bladed knife (Fig. 3-22), being careful not to damage the seal. Stuff in grease with your fingers, and replace the seal, circlip, and cranks.

Replacing Ball-Bearing Bottom Brackets with Cartridge Sealed Units

For increased reliability, I recommend that you replace your conventional ball-bearing bottom-bracket set. If I were to safari cross-country anywhere, I would install one of these units. Maintenance is nil except for lubrication, as noted above.

Phil Wood (Fig. 3-23) and Bullseye (Figs. 3-24 and 3-25) make excellent replacement sealed-bearing, cartridge-type bottom brackets. Just be sure, as noted above, that the angles of the flats on the axle match

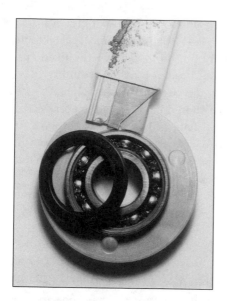

Fig. 3-22: Pry out a sealed bearing seal with a thin blade so you can stuff grease into the bearing.

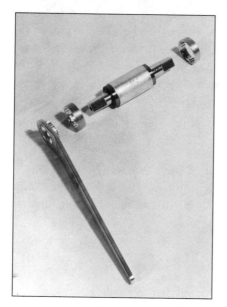

Fig. 3-23: Phil Wood cartridge-type sealed-bearing bottom bracket.

Fig. 3-24: Bullseye cartridge-type sealed-bearing bottom bracket. Bearings are moved to the right for chainline.

Fig. 3-25: Bullseye cartridge-type bottom bracket. Bearings are moved to the left for chainline.

your existing crank flats. Check this with the bike shop before you buy. If you can't find either of these sealed cartridge units, write to the manufacturer: Phil Wood & Co., 580 N. 6th St., San Jose, CA 95112, or phone: 408-298-1540. Contact Bullseye Cycle Corp. at 418 Varney St., Burbank, CA 91502, or phone: 1-800-874-0600 or 818-846-9163. The Phil Wood model is strong as a tank, without the tank's weight. Bearings are not owner-replaceable in this unit; that's a shop job best done by Phil Wood. But that's nothing to worry about so long as you are faithful about lubrication. Bullseye bearings (Fig. 3-22) are owner-replaceable. These are both excellent units. They use electric motor-type high-quality sealed bearings, are very strong, and should last for many years.

A WORD ABOUT CHAINLINE

I am going to discuss chainline adjustments in the paragraphs that follow. If you change the number of cogs in the freewheel or the number of chainwheels up front, you must adjust chainline, as I will explain below. However, a word of caution: *do not change your gearing setup if you have any type or make of index shifting. The total complement of index shift levers, front and rear derailleurs, frame design, chainwheels, freewheel and rear wheel alignment are all designed together*. If you change any of these components your precisely aligned index shift system will probably go crazy and refuse to work.

If you do not have index shifting, you can change freewheel cogs and/ or chainwheels to a gear configuration better suited to your needs than the one that came with the bike (spell that "granny gears" for most of

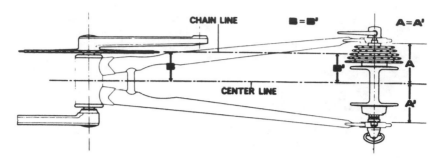

Fig. 3-26: Chain alignment for single chainwheel and 5-cog freewheel.

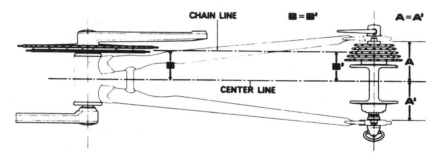

Fig. 3-27: Chain alignment for double chainwheel and 5-cog freewheel.

us, including me). Again, please see Chapter 6 for a discussion of gears and gearing. If you make these changes you will need to realign the chainline. For example, if you decide you want more gears and wish to change from a 5- to a 6- or 7-speed freewheel, and/or go from a double to a triple chainwheel, you must also readjust the chainline. Fig. 3-26 shows chain alignment for a 5-speed freewheel and a single chainwheel. Here the chainwheel is aligned on the third freewheel cog. Fig. 3-27 shows the midpoint between a double chainwheel aligned on the third of a 5-cog freewheel. Fig. 3-28 shows the third cog of a 5-cog freewheel aligned on the center of a triple chainwheel. Fig. 3-29 shows the correct alignment of a 6-speed freewheel and a double chainwheel, with the chain midway between the third and fourth freewheel cogs and midway

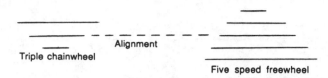

Fig. 3-28: Chain alignment for triple chainwheel and 5-cog freewheel.

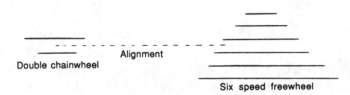

Fig. 3-29: Chain alignment for double chainwheel and 6-cog freewheel.

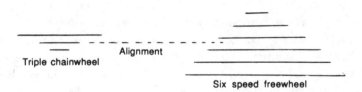

Fig. 3-30: Chain alignment for triple chainwheel and 6-cog freewheel.

between the double chainwheels. Fig. 3-30 shows the correct chain alignment for a triple chainwheel and a 6-cog freewheel, with the chain on the center chainwheel and midway between the third and fourth freewheel cog. Fig. 3-31 shows chain alignment for a triple chainwheel and a 7-cog freewheel; the center chainwheel should align with the fourth freewheel cog. Now, don't get me wrong—if I show a chain alignment where the chain falls *midway* between chainwheels or freewheel cogs, that *does not* mean that that is where the chain should ride as you pedal. Where the chain rides is a function of the manual shift lever adjustment, and rear and front derailleur adjustments (see Chapter 2). Chain alignment assures optimal chain placement on gears, without chain rub on adjacent cogs or freewheels. It also helps reduce the need to make minor

TRIPLE CHAINWHEEL   ALIGNMENT   SEVEN SPEED FREEWHEEL

Fig. 3-31: *Chain alignment for triple chainwheel and 7-cog freewheel.*

readjustments of the shift lever(s) to avoid chain rub every time you shift.

If you do not have a Phil Wood or Bullseye cartridge-type bottom bracket, there is only one other way you can adjust the chainline. You can add one or more washers of various thicknesses to one side or the other of the hub, as necessary. For example, add washers to the freewheel side of the hub to move rear cogs to the left, and vice versa to the right. You can't move the chainwheels left or right on a conventional ball-bearing bottom bracket set (Fig. 3-32). If you add washers to the rear hub, you will have to realign the rear wheel dish (see Chapter 11 for an explanation of rear wheel dishing). The amount of rear hub movment left or right is also strictly limited by the clearance between the small freewheel cog and the chain stay. When the chain is on the small rear cog it must not rub on the chain stay.

An advantage of a cartridge-type sealed-bearing unit is that it can be adjusted to meet your chainline needs. You won't have to add or remove washers on the rear hub, and then have to redish it (see Chapter 12 on dishing a wheel). The sealed bottom bracket can also be moved much farther to the right or left, so you have much greater flexibility in chain-line adjustment than doing it on the rear wheel. Take a look at the Phil Wood and Bullseye bottom brackets in Figs. 3-23 to 3-25. You can see that both left- and right-side cups are movable to the left or right. In Fig. 3-24, for example, the entire cartridge has been slid far to the left; in Fig. 3-25, it is slid to the right. This is an extreme position, to be sure, but I did it so you get the point. On the Phil Wood sealed unit, as on the Bullseye, the rings really aren't cups, of course, but they serve the same purpose as cups in holding the sealed bearings securely in the bottom bracket, in their cups, so to speak.

To install the Phil Wood unit, you will need the special tool for the adjustable cups shown at the left in Fig. 3-23. To install the Bullseye

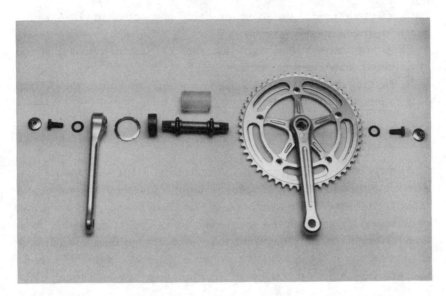

Fig. 3-32: Conventional ball-bearing bottom bracket cannot be moved left or right to adjust chainline.

unit you will need 2-mm Allen wrenches. For both makes, you will of course need the tools mentioned at the beginning of this chapter to remove and reinstall the cranks on the bottom-bracket axle.

To Install a Cartridge-Type Bottom Bracket

1. Remove both cranks (see section in this chapter, above, on crank removal).

2. Remove the left-side lockring and adjustable cup.

3. Remove axle and ball bearings.

4. Remove the fixed cup clockwise (on the right side).

5. Thread in the fixed cup replacement (right side) about halfway. Remember, this side is a reverse thread, so it threads *on* counterclockwise.

6. Insert the bottom-bracket cartridge with the longest side of the axle first, into the empty bottom-bracket shell.

7. Thread the left side adjustable "cup" (Fig. 3-22) on clockwise and snug it up tightly. Spin the axle between your fingers. If you feel binding,

back off the left side cup about an eighth of a turn and check again; repeat as necessary.

8. Adjust the left- and right-side cups as necessary to adjust the chainline as shown in Figs. 3-26 to 3-31.

9. Note: Bullseye bottom brackets come with refreshingly lucid and easy-to-follow instructions, so I won't repeat them here.

About Elliptical Chainwheels

A few years ago, elliptical chainwheels (Fig. 3-16) were touted as a sure route to more efficient, easier pedaling. Now they are passé, and today hardly a new bike has them. We are back to the good old round chainrings. The elliptical rings created an uneven pedal stroke that bothered a lot of cyclists, so they fell out of favor. If your bike has elliptical chainrings, I'd leave them on. In my opinion, the cost and time to convert to round from elliptical is not justified from a performance standpoint.

Cottered Crankset Maintenance

Cottered cranks (Fig. 3-33) were very popular ten or fifteen years ago. They were even on some fairly expensive touring bikes, even though

Fig. 3-33: Remove cottered cranks over a notched 2 × 4 to avoid damage to bearings: "A," cotter; "B," 2 × 4; "C," 2 × 4 notch.

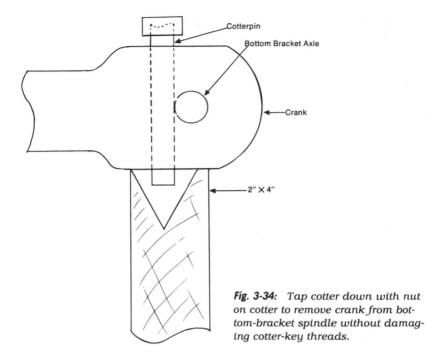

Fig. 3-34: *Tap cotter down with nut on cotter to remove crank from bottom-bracket spindle without damaging cotter-key threads.*

they were made of steel and quite heavy. Today you'll only find them on inexpensive bicycles. Cottered cranks are held on the bottom-bracket spindle by a tapered cotter key that matches the taper of the spindle. To remove them, cut a V-notch in a two-by-four and brace the crank against it (Figs. 3-33 and 3-34). Turn the cotter key nut (Fig. 3-34) counterclockwise two or three turns, but not all the way off. With the cranks braced as shown in Figures 3-33 and 3-34, hammer the cotter key down until it pops out. The two-by-four absorbs hammer shock that would otherwise damage the bottom-bracket bearings. With cranks removed, you can remove and relube the bottom-bracket bearings as described earlier in this chapter. To reinstall these cranks, reverse the above steps.

One-Piece "Ashtabula" Crank Maintenance

One-piece heavy steel cranks (Figs. 3-35 and 3-36) are today found only on inexpensive bikes. But back in the 1970s some fairly decent bikes came with these cumbersome assemblies. Schwinn's SuperSport

Fig. 3-35: *One-piece steel "Ashta-bula" bottom bracket and crankset.*

Fig. 3-36: *Another make of "Ashta-bula" bottom bracket.*

was one such. This was a beautiful machine with a frame of light, excellent tubing. It came with high-quality components, except for the bottom bracket. It was like putting a cast-iron saddle on a spirited race horse. If you have such a bike, or one similarly afflicted, Bullseye has a cure for you. All you need to do is remove the one-piece assembly and bolt in the Bullseye sealed-bearing cartridge bottom bracket (Fig. 3-37).

Fig. 3-37: This Bullseye bottom bracket is designed to replace the much heavier one-piece "Ashtabula"-type bottom-bracket sets.

The unit's spindle has flats which fit the cranks that come with modern bicycles. You will, of course, have to buy new cranks and chainwheels. But, if you have a SuperSport or similar high-quality oldie-but-goodie bike, the cost of about $150 will be well worth the weight savings of a couple of pounds. Besides, aluminum-alloy cranks and chainwheels *look* so much better than clunky one-piece cranksets.

Back to the Ashtabula heavies. Please note that in Fig. 3-35, the lockring is removed by a 12-inch adjustable crescent wrench, and in Fig. 3-36, the lockring is removed by a standard wrench (Fig. 3-2). To maintain and/or remove these cranks:

1. Remove the pedal from the left crank.

2. Remove the bottom-bracket locknut and adjustable cap (see instructions on bottom-bracket maintenance in this chapter).

3. Pull the crank and chainwheel assembly out through the right (chainwheel) side of the bracket shell, along with the bearings.

4. Remove, clean, and relube the bearings as described earlier in this chapter.

5. Reinstall the crankset, bearings, and adjustable cone.

6. Adjust bearing clearance with the adjustable cone as described earlier in this chapter.

The Long Crank Controversy

Longer ago than I care to think about, a cyclist built long cranks and claimed a new record for climbing a mountain in, I think, New Hampshire. He published his results, which set off a controversy in the bicycle racing community. Racing cyclists are no different than athletes in other sports. They are win, win, win-oriented. Well, oriented isn't the right word; obsessed is more like it. If it takes long cranks to do it, then long cranks they *must* have.

It seems reasonable that long cranks make for more powerful strokes. Archimedes said it first. But bikes today do not come with long cranks. The average bike has 170-mm cranks. (If you want your millimeters by the inch, just multiply inches by 228.6. To go the other way, multiply by .03937.) Standard cranks also come in 172.5- and 175-mm lengths. The five millimeter difference between the shortest (170 mm) and the longest (175 mm) cranks is not much of a lever advantage, in my opinion. The reason for the 172.5-mm and 175-mm crank lengths is to give tall people with long legs a small fulcrum advantage over the rest of us. Or to fit them better on bigger frames. Or both.

Now if you want *really* long cranks, you could try Bullseye combined sealed-bearing bottom-bracket and 190-mm cranks (Fig. 3-38). As usual with Bullseye products, the unit comes with excellent installation instructions. Fig. 3-39 shows the 190-mm crank alongside a 170-mm crank. If you go this route, observe these precautions. First, make sure the inboard crank and pedal won't scrape the ground on a sharp turn. If you have an ATB, with higher ground clearance, such contact will be less likely, but check it out with a ruler before switching to longer cranks. If you are, say, 5'9" tall or less, your legs may be too short for effective, full-stroke use of the longer cranks (I'm thinking 190 mm here). We have all seen kids riding their dad's old bike, with their little fannies bobbing up and down on a frame way too big for them. On the other hand, if you are six feet or taller, and have a 24-inch or bigger ATB, the long cranks will give you better leverage on slow, steep hill climbs.

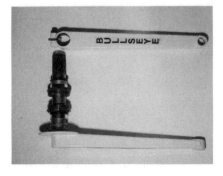

Fig. 3-38: *For long crank afficiona-dos, this Bullseye bottom-bracket set features 190-mm cranks and sealed bearings.*

Fig. 3-39: *190-mm crank, at bottom, compared with 170-mm crank, at top.*

You could also get the same effect on any size bike by changing gear ratios (bigger freewheel cogs and/or smaller chainwheel; see Chapter 6). On the flats, I can't see any improvement with longer cranks. Unless you are wearing stilts, which could just be a mite awkward.

TANDEM CHAINWHEELS

Follow maintenance instructions for ball-bearing or sealed-cartridge–type bottom brackets and for chainwheels as noted above.

In reinstalling the chainwheels with their cranks, you have two choices. You can install the cranks so they rotate in phase, synchronously. In this mode both pedals on the same side are always in the same position, as shown in Figs. 3-40 and 3-41, and on the tandem in Figure 3-44. Or, you could install the cranks out-of-phase, so that when one set of pedals is at the two o'clock and seven o'clock positions, the other set is at the twelve o'clock and six o'clock positions (Fig. 3-42). Or, in out-of-phase positions with the front pedals at the nine o'clock and three o'clock positions (Fig. 3-43).

Advantages of Tandem Pedals in Phase

1. Tandem is easier for both riders to mount and take off. The riders straddle the top tube, put one pedal at the two o'clock position, push that pedal down while hoisting themselves into the saddle, snap the other foot into the pedal and shoot smoothly off down the road.

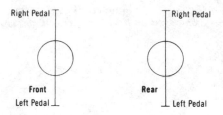

Fig. 3-40: Cranks are in phase. Both sets of pedals are in the position of least power application, at twelve o'clock and six o'clock positions.

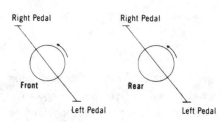

Fig. 3-41: In-phase cranks make take-off from a standing start easier and smoother.

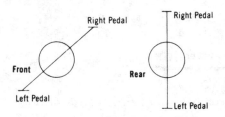

Fig. 3-42: Out-of-phase cranks permit one rider to apply power when the other rider cannot. Here the captain's pedals are at the null power position, while the stoker's right pedal is in a power downstroke.

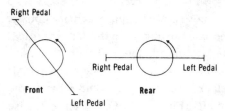

Fig. 3-43: Here cranks are out of phase. Now the stoker cannot apply power, while the captain can.

2. You can also feel how much work the other rider is doing. If one of you is goofing off, the other will know it.

3. Both riders can get their butts up off the saddle, stand up on the pedals and thus make steeper hills, or leave a single rider in the dust, if the mood so strikes.

Advantages of Tandem Pedals Out-of-Phase

1. One pedal will always be in a power stroke, with the pedal at just past the twelve o'clock position. The other rider's pedals will be parallel to the ground, with little power applied, as you can see in Figs. 3-42 and 3-43. With in-phase pedals, on the other hand, both riders' pedals will be at the no-power positions of six o'clock and twelve o'clock at the same time (Fig. 3-40 and Fig. 3-41), so power application will be jerky. Thus out-of-phase pedals permit smoother power to the rear wheel, an important advantage particularly on uphill climbs.

2. Because power is more efficiently applied with out-of-phase pedals, cadence (rate of pedal spin) can be faster and smoother. A higher cadence without extra effort means higher speeds in a lower gear, and the ability to pedal on downhill runs when in-phase tandems have to coast.

3. More efficient human effort applied to go-power cuts stress on moving parts. Chainwheels and freewheel wear is less. Chain breakage, more common to in-phase tandems, becomes a rarity on out-of-phase tandems.

4. Increased pedaling smoothness makes the tandem much easier for the captain (the person up front) to control. The captain, at least, will be less fatigued because he won't have to fight the wobble which is characteristic of in-phase tandems. In-phase tandems have both riders' power stroke on the same side of the bike at the same time, with accompanying simultaneous body-weight shift on that side. On the other hand, in-phase pedals, with both sets of pedals on a simultaneous power stroke, make slow speed climbs up steep hills easier for both stoker and captain.

Fig. 3-44: *This bottom bracket axle broke because of metal fatigue.*

Fig. 3-45: *Cranks are in phase on this tandem; i.e. cranks on both sides are in line with the seat tube.*

THINGS FALL APART

Nothing lasts forever. Even bottom-bracket axles can break off under the stomping stress of a strong cyclist or, rather, after many, many such stomps. It's called "metal fatigue." Steel gets tired after long years of hard work, and eventually breaks down, just like people do. Rest will cure us, but when steel breaks, like the bottom-bracket axle in Fig. 3-44, well, we can just hope and pray that the rider can control the bike and come to a safe stop when it happens, and that it occurs right outside a bike shop. *If* it happens. I offer this photo as a suggestion and reminder to you to closely inspect all working parts of your bike—those that can be seen, at least—for signs of metal fatigue which foretell imminent failure. Look for cracks, crazed lines, and cracked paint on tubing, especially after you have had an encounter with an unyielding object, such as a rock or tree.

In Chapter 4 we discuss chains, the one part that needs lots of love and care to stay healthy longer, and to keep from breaking when you least expect it, far from the madding crowd.

4

All About Chains

More than any other part of your bike, the chain is not only exposed to abrasives such as dirt, sand, and mud, but to water as well, which washes away protective lubricants. It's the one part of your bike that wears out fastest and needs the most maintenance. All-terrain bicycle chains, especially, need more frequent maintenance if the bike is ridden on sandy trails or though water. A new chain should last 2,000 to 3,000 miles; if exposed to abrasives, without being properly maintained, it can wear out in only 500 miles. A worn chain can jump or skip off gear teeth and cause an accident.

WHY CHAINS WEAR

Normal contact between the moving parts of a chain cause them to wear. Exposure to abrasives such as dirt and sand, coupled with a lack of lubrication, causes these parts to wear even faster. For example, look at Fig. 4-1, showing chain parts: "A," roller; "B," outer side plate; "C," inner side plate; "D," rivet; "E," bushing.

Wear points on a chain include the inside surfaces of plates, the roller, and the roller journal. Stretch is due to internal rearrangement of molecules in chain plates, and wear on rollers, bushings, inside chain plates, and rivets.

Fig 4-1: *Anatomy of a chain: "A," roller; "B," outer side plate; "C," inner side plate; "D," rivet; "E," bushing.*

Wear causes the chain to stretch. When the chain stretches, the pitch of the chain becomes greater than the pitch of the teeth of the freewheel cog and the teeth of the chainwheel. The pitch of the chain and the pitch of the cogs are thus mismatched. The load is carried by only one tooth at a time, instead of by however many cog teeth the chain is on (a function of chain wraparound discussed in Chapter 2). This concentrated wear puts additional stress on the chain and further accelerates chain wear. In addition, if the cogs carrying the chain are worn, the chain is prone to hang up on that cog, which causes the chain to slip and jump to the next cog. Such chain skip and jump can cause erratic pedaling, a distraction the rider does not need, especially in traffic. Chain slippage while the rider is straining uphill, off the saddle, may also cause the rider to come down suddenly on the top tube, a painful condition for either gender. It may also cause loss of control and an accident.

Here's How to Care for Your Chain and How to Tell When It Should Be Replaced

Clean your chain any time it looks dirty and before every long trip. A dirty chain not only wears out faster, it also wears down the teeth of

Fig. 4-2: Park chain cleaner fits over the chain.

Fig. 4-3: Vetta chain cleaner fits over the chain.

your freewheel and chainwheels, and *their* replacement costs a bundle. Clean your chain while it's on the bike or remove it for a more thorough cleaning.

On the bike, clean it with a chain cleaner (Figs. 4-2 and 4-3). With these cleaners, the chain passes through kerosene and over brushes as you turn the crank counterclockwise. The cleaners are small and light enough to carry along on a trip. If your cookstove uses kerosene you can use the same fluid in the cleaner. Or you could spray the chain with a degreaser, which flushes out dirt and cleans the chain. Be careful not to get any of this spray, or any spray-type lubricant, on the tires or brake pads!

Follow These Steps to Remove the Chain from the Bike for a More Thorough Cleaning Job

1. Buy a chain breaker tool (a.k.a. rivet remover) (Fig. 4-4). Always carry this tool with you on a trip. If the chain breaks on the road, you will need the tool to remove the broken link and put the chain back together. The day I left my chain tool home was, of course, the day the chain broke on a rural road in Wisconsin. I pounded the broken link pin out with an old nail and rock I found nearby. I removed the broken link and pounded the pin back into the now shorter chain, using the nail and the rock. You should also carry a couple of spare links. You can't buy individual links or sections of chains, so buy an extra chain and remove a couple of links as take-along spares. If you are on a safari, take the entire extra chain. If you carry a few links, they *must* be the same make and model as the chain on your bike. Just being the same make won't do; busy R&D types are always developing new chain configurations

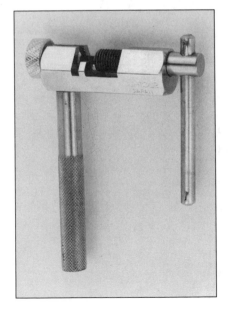

Fig. 4-4: SunTour chain-breaker tool.

such as bowed-out sideplates, narrower chains, etc. Links from the same makes but different model years of chains are not necessarily compatible.

3. The SunTour tool shown in Fig. 4-4 is excellent. The knurled knob at the top (Fig. 4-5) can be adjusted for different-length rivets. The idea is to push the rivet out of the chain link until about $\frac{1}{64}$ inch of the rivet remains inside the chainplate (arrow, Fig. 4-6). The protruding rivet (Fig. 4-7) will hold the chain together as you snap the links back, long enough to push the rivet back in.

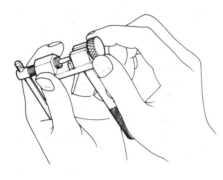

Fig. 4-5: *Adjust the knurled knob on this SunTour chain breaker to limit how far the pin is pushed.*

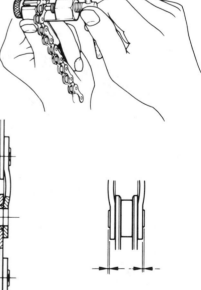

Fig. 4-6: *Keep about $\frac{1}{64}$ inch of the chain pin inside the chain plate, as shown, so chain can be snapped back and held while you push the pin the rest of the way back.*

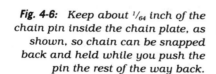

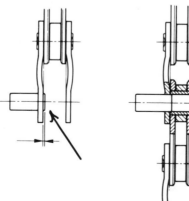

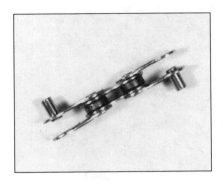

Fig. 4-7: *Another view of a chain link, showing the chain pin nearly flush with the inside of the chain plate, the correct distance to stop the pin.*

4. Shift the chain to the small rear and front cogs. Better yet, lift the chain off the small chainwheel and drop it down onto the bottom-bracket shell, to the left of the small chainwheel.

5. Put the chain breaker on a rivet (Figs. 4-8 and 4-9). Hold the chain breaker by the handle while you turn the lever until the rivet is nearly out. Six complete turns of the handle should work for $^3/_{32}$-inch derailleur chains. Use seven and a half turns for single- and 3-speed coaster-brake hub chains. The SunTour tool, as I said, takes the guesswork out of how far to push the rivet out.

Fig. 4-8: *Chain tool in place, with chain pin pushed out.*

Fig. 4-9: *This chain definitely needs to be removed and cleaned.*

6. Remove the chain. Before wasting time cleaning it, check it for wear by one of the two methods listed here:

a. Lay the chain flat. Count off 24 links. Since link pins (rivets) are a half-inch apart (Fig. 4-10), 24 links should measure 12 inches. If they measure much more, say 12¹⁄₁₆ inches, replace the chain.

b. Or, bend the chain and compare it to a new chain (as shown in Fig. 4-11). The chain at the bottom is worn and should be replaced. Replace a worn chain with an exact duplicate, especially if you have index shifting. If the chain is not worn, follow the steps below to clean and relube it.

7. Immerse the chain in kerosene (danger! do not use gasoline or any other highly flammable solvent). Move the chain around in the kerosene (Fig. 4-12) until it is clean.

8. Remove the chain and dry off the kerosene with a rag or paper towel.

9. *Relube a clean chain* by laying it on newspapers, on the garage floor, side plates vertical. Spray the chain with a good lubricant in a spray can, one containing molybdenum or Teflon in a petroleum base. This type of lubricant is thin enough to minimize abrasives pick-up from the road, yet provide excellent lubrication. After spraying one side, turn

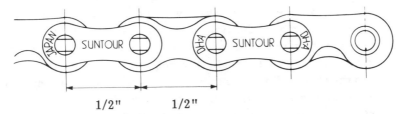

Fig. 4-10: *Chain pins are a half-inch apart, so 24 links should measure 12 inches. If links are much farther apart, chain is worn and should be replaced.*

Fig. 4-11: *Another way to check chain wear. Chain at the top is new. Chain at the bottom is worn.*

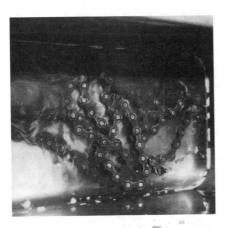

Fig. 4-12: *Dunk the chain in kerosene (not gasoline or other highly flammable solvent!) and swirl it around to clean it.*

the chain to the other side and spray it. If possible, let the lubricant penetrate for a couple of hours, or overnight, before reinstalling the chain.

10. Wipe off excess lubricant to prevent drip. Replace it this way on the freewheel cogs, near derailleur wheels, and chainwheel:

a. Start with the end of the chain without the protruding rivet.

b. Thread it through the front derailleur cage, then on *top* of the freewheel cog, then in front of the derailleur upper (jockey) wheel, then behind the derailleur bottom (idler) wheel.

c. So the chain will run the same way it was before you removed it, face it the way you pushed it out. If you pushed the rivet out toward the left side of the bike, push it back with the chain tool from the right side. It's a bit more trouble to do it this way, but it's better for the chain because it will keep the same wear pattern.

11. Chain reriveting is easier if you hold the chain together with a tool such as the Quick Link (Fig. 4-13).

12. Snap the two ends of the chain together. If you have about $1/_{64}$ inch of the rivet left inside the side plate, you should be able to force (snap) that much of it back into the chain.

13. Push the rivet the rest of the way in with the chain tool, until the same amount of the rivet shows on both sides.

14. The chain will most likely be stiff at this joint. Grasp the chain links on both sides of the section you reriveted, and twist the chain from side to side until it feels loose. If you don't free up this stiff link now you will have chain jump.

15. Replace the chain on the small chainwheel.

INSTALLING A NEW CHAIN

1. *The new chain should be the same length and make as the old one.*

2. Lay old and new chains side by side on the floor. Remove unneeded links with the chain tool. Install the new chain as described above, except here it makes no difference which side the rivet is on.

3. *Check to be sure the chain is the correct length.* Chains come in 112-, 116-, or 120-link sizes. The chain should be long enough so you can shift to the large freewheel cog; short enough so the chain won't skip or jump off a gear. If the chain is too long it will be too slack when it is on smaller gears and may jump off. If it is too short you may be able to shift to the big rear cog but not to the biggest chainwheel or even to the middle chainwheel.

4. Shift the chain so it's on the largest freewheel sprocket and the largest chainwheel. The rear derailleur should now be almost parallel to

Fig. 4-13: Use this Quick-Link tool to hold the chain together while you reattach the chain pin.

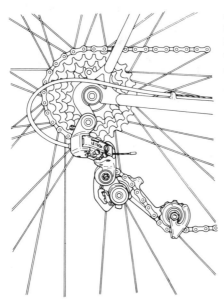

Fig. 4-14: Chain is the correct length when it is on the big rear cog and the big chainwheel, and the derailleur cage is nearly parallel to the chain stay.

the chain stay (Fig. 4-14). If you can't shift the chain to the biggest freewheel cog and to the largest chainwheel, you may have a super-low gear setup, such as a 34- or 38-teeth rear cog, for which the chain is too short. In this case don't add links to the chain because if you do, the chain will be dangerously loose when you shift to the smallest freewheel sprocket. Console yourself that you have a super-low granny gear for steep hills. If, on the other hand, your biggest freewheel cog has 32 teeth or less, you should be able to shift so the chain is on that sprocket and on the large chainwheel. If not, add chain links as needed.

5. Shift the chain to the smallest freewheel sprocket and the smallest chainwheel. The rear derailleur should be about vertical to the ground (Fig. 4-15). If not, remove one or two links.

6. Shift the chain to the largest freewheel sprocket and the largest chainwheel. Try the "pinch" test (Fig. 4-16). If you can squeeze the chain as shown, chain length is okay.

7. Check and adjust chain wraparound as described in Chapter 2.

8. If you replaced a short cage derailleur (Fig. 4-17) with a long cage derailleur (Fig. 4-18) because you changed from short- to wide-ratio gearing, you will have to install a longer chain. I discourage just adding

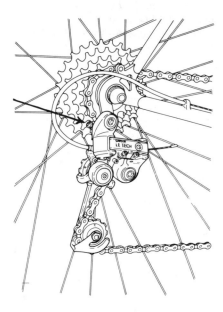

Fig. 4-15: Chain is the correct length when it is on the small rear cog and the small chainwheel and the derailleur is perpendicular to the ground, as shown.

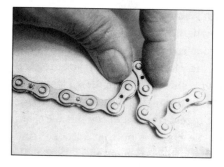

Fig. 4-16: Another test for correct chain length. If you can pinch four links as shown with the chain on the big cog and big chainwheel, chain length is okay.

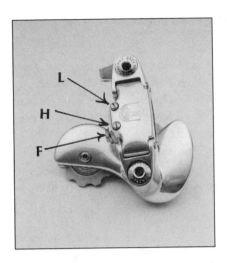

Fig. 4-17: Short cage derailleur for use with narrow-range gearing.

Fig. 4-18: Long cage derailleur for use with wide-range gearing for touring, hill climbing, and riding a loaded bike on safari.

links to your old chain, because then you will have four or five new links along with old links on the rest of the chain. You could have erratic chain action.

I recommend installing a plastic self-adhering chain guard on your chain stay, to prevent occasional chain rub from damaging its finish. Clean the stay before installing the guard.

A WORD ABOUT NEW CHAIN DESIGNS

New makes of chains require special installation consideration. SunTour Superbe Pro chains have "high arch" inner links (Fig. 4-19). When you replace the SunTour chain, be sure the arched part of the outer link goes over the gear teeth (Fig. 4-20). For comparison purposes, a conventional chain design is shown in Fig. 4-21.

For *index systems,* it is especially important that you use the same make and model chain that came on the bike. Some chains are narrower than others. For example, a 7-speed freewheel usually requires a narrow-design chain. A normal-width chain will just not work.

Fig. 4-19: SunTour chain has high-arch inner links.

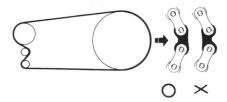

Fig. 4-20: Install a SunTour chain with high-arch inner links so these links always face toward the gear teeth, as shown.

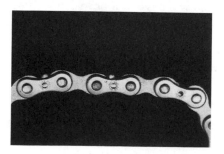

Fig. 4-21 Conventional chain design.

The new Shimano Hyperglide ultra-narrow HG chain (Fig. 4-22) takes a special pin every time you take it apart. These pins are available in bike shops. I can report that my standard, garden-variety chain tool worked just fine with this chain. You must cut (remove the rivet) from a new Hyperglide chain at only a black rivet. If you cut it at any other place you damage the chain. This also holds true for newer Regina chains and, eventually, I suppose, for many other makes. Check instructions that come with your new chain. If you lengthen or shorten this chain, or remove it for cleaning, use the special reinforced pin to replace the pin (rivet) you removed. Break off the excess part of this pin with a pair of pliers (Fig. 4-23). Your bike shop should have a supply of these pins.

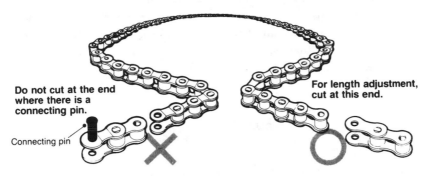

Do not cut at the end where there is a connecting pin.

Connecting pin

For length adjustment, cut at this end.

Fig. 4-22: *The new Shimano HG chain has a black connecting pin (arrow) which should* never *be pushed out or removed. Remove any other pin but the black one.* Courtesy Shimano.

■**How to use the reinforced special pin**

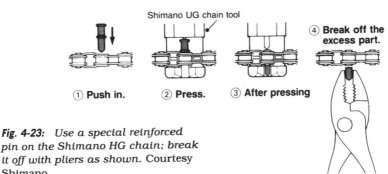

Shimano UG chain tool

④ **Break off the excess part.**

① **Push in.**   ② **Press.**   ③ **After pressing**

Fig. 4-23: *Use a special reinforced pin on the Shimano HG chain; break it off with pliers as shown.* Courtesy Shimano.

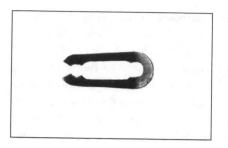

Fig. 4-24: Replace link clip on coaster-brake hub bikes with the open end facing toward the rear of the bicycle.

I have tried putting this chain back together. It is not easy. You have to press the old pin all the way out of the chain. Then you have to fight to get the new, special pin back in the chain side plate. You can do it, but it's a time-consuming pain. Again, never remove the original black pin that connected the chain when the chain was brand-new. Push out any other pin but that one and use the special new pin instead. The Park Superchain tool makes this job easier.

COASTER BRAKE CHAINS

Bicycles with coaster-brake hubs use wider chains that won't fit derailleur bicycles. Remove the connecting link to take this chain apart. Be sure to face this link *with the open end facing toward the rear of the bicycle* (Fig. 4-24).

In the next chapter I will review maintenance and cog-changing techniques on freewheels, including the cassette-hub design.

5

All About Your Freewheel

I t's infrequent, but it happens. You start pedaling—and nothing, nada, zilch. Cranks turn, pedals spin, but the bike stays put. A piece of dirt has found its devious way into the innards of the freewheel body. Once there, it has lodged between the pawls and the ratchet body. Now the pawls are held closed. This lets the freewheel spin around uselessly, as though you were backpedaling forward. The purpose of the pawls is to let the freewheel turn in one direction, as when you are coasting, but not in the other direction, as when you are pedaling. If you are on the road and the pawls get stuck, bum some kerosene or some sort of nonflammable solvent and flush out the freewheel. Don't get any on the tire. Spin the freewheel until the pawls work free and catch. If they don't work free, you may have a broken pawl spring. Some freewheels have only one spring, others have a tiny phosphor bronze spring behind each pawl. In any case, now you will need a replacement freewheel. I hope this does not happen when you are far from a bike shop. Otherwise you will have to thumb a ride or walk back to the last town you passed. If you are near a town of any size, the local bike shop can fix the freewheel for you or, of course, furnish a replacement.

STEPS IN BASIC FREEWHEEL MAINTENANCE

The maintenance steps below apply *only* to conventional freewheels (Fig. 5-1). For *freehub cassette* maintenance, where the freewheel is an integral part of the hub (Fig. 5-2), follow the lubrication and cleaning procedures below. For freehub-bearing maintenance, please see Chapter 7.

Every 60 days, more often if you ride a lot, follow these steps:

1. Leave the rear wheel on the bike.

2. Squirt light oil (3-1 sewing machine oil, for example) into both sides of the freewheel to lubricate the bearings. Be careful not to drip oil on the tire or wheel rim. Some oils eat some tires. Oil on the wheel rim reduces braking to a dangerously low level, so be *sure* to remove any lubricant from the rim with a rag dipped in solvent such as kerosene and dry the rim thoroughly with a clean rag.

3. Clean each freewheel cog with a tool such as the Park cog cleaner (Fig. 5-3). Remove all dirt, gunk, and accumulated hardened oil from the chain. An old toothbrush works well for this.

Fig. 5-1: Here are just a few of the many designs of freewheel remover tools for conventional hubs.

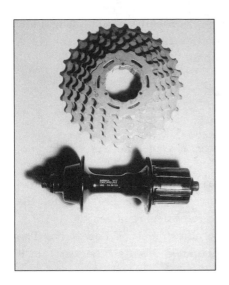

Fig. 5-2: *Freehub has cassette cluster that fits over splines in the freehub body.*

At least once a year, remove the freewheel for more serious cleaning.

Tools You Will Need

1. Freewheel remover. Buy one that fits your freewheel. At last count, there were 23 different styles of this tool to fit that many freewheels, and no other. Fig. 5-1 shows just a few configurations.

Fig. 5-3: *Clean freewheel teeth with this Park cleaning tool.*

2. Cog remover (Fig. 5-4), if you replace worn ones or change gear ratios (see Chapter 6 for information on gearing).

3. Freewheel vise (Fig. 5-5), optional.

Steps to Remove the Freewheel

1. Remove the wheel from the bicycle.

2. Remove the quick-release unit or, if your bike has a solid axle, the axle bolt on the freewheel side.

3. Insert the correct size and style remover (Figs. 5-1 and 5-6, showing a few of the 23 variations) in the freewheel (Fig. 5-4). Tighten the quick-release or axle bolt so it locks the freewheel remover in place (Fig. 5-7). (See Chapter 7 on quick-release adjustments, if necessary.) The quick-release or bolt should not be tightened down all the way. Set it

Fig. 5-4: *Chain-type conventional freewheel remover.*

Fig. 5-5: *Freewheel vise, shown here fitted onto a freewheel. It holds the freewheel in place, in a vise, when you are removing cogs on a conventional freewheel.*

Fig. 5-6: *More freewheel remover tools for conventional freewheels.*

Fig. 5-7: *With the freewheel remover held loosely by the quick-release (or axle bolts), turn the tool counterclockwise to remove the freewheel from the wheel hub.*

just close enough so it will let you turn the freewheel remover counter-clockwise a half to one full turn with a wrench (Fig. 5-7). You could also hold the freewheel tool in a vise and turn the wheel counterclockwise.

4. When the freewheel breaks loose, remove the quick-release or the axle bolt.

5. Finish removing the freewheel by turning the freewheel tool by hand. As the freewheel approaches the last few threads, hold it firmly so it comes off the hub without harming the softer aluminum hub threads.

6. Agitate the freewheel in kerosene. With a brush and rag, clean each cog.

7. Dry the freewheel with an airhose, if available, to remove the solvent.

8. Squirt *light* oil into both sides of the freewheel.

9. Resist the temptation to take the freewheel apart. There are dozens of minuscule ball bearings inside which, once free from the confines of the freewheel, will flee pell-mell to the floor and hide themselves away, never to be seen or found again. Not to mention the teensy little springs and pawls. Oh well, if you have the talent of a watchmaker or locksmith, and if the exploded view of a freewheel (Fig. 5-8) doesn't scare you, go ahead. The only reason I can think of for dismantling a freewheel would be to replace broken springs or pawls. If the little balls wear out, you would have some minor side-to-side play of the freewheel

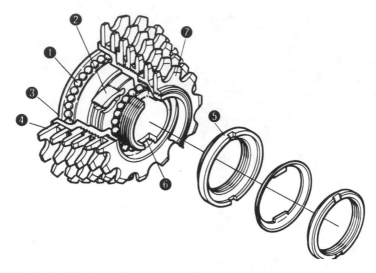

Fig. 5-8: *Exploded view of conventional freewheel. Parts are: (1) bearing raceways on inner and outer ends, where you should apply very light oil; (2) heat-treated pawl; (3) body; (4) sprocket teeth; (5) adjustable cone; (6) inner freewheel body; (7) cogs. Not recommended for disassembly unless you are a watchmaker.*

which could cause chain skip. I'd eliminate all the other causes of chain skip first, though, such as worn freewheel cogs, chainwheels, and chain, and needed derailleur adjustments. Again, you will need a special tool unique to your freewheel to dismantle it. It's much easier to take the bloody thing to your bike shop, and probably cheaper just to buy a new one. If you have any form of index shifting you will need an exact replacement freewheel.

10. With the freewheel removed, look for spoke cracks that foretell spoke breakage (Fig. 5-9). If the chain has slipped off the big rear cog at any time it may very well have cut into one or more spokes. In fact, in testing a bike sent by the manufacturer for this purpose, the rear derailleur low-gear maladjustment permitted chain override down into the spokes. Instantly the chain chopped three spokes as though with a pair of cutting pliers. If this happens to you on the road, far from a bike shop, you will have to remove the freewheel in order to replace any cut spokes. As you can see from the freewheel removal instructions above, removal without a heavy crescent wrench and the remover tool would be very difficult.

Fig. 5-9: *The arrows point to spokes that have been cut by the chain as it overrode the big cog. These spokes are on the way to failure.*

To Remove the Freewheel on the Road

There is a light (two ounces), new compact tool, however, that makes on-the-road or trail freehub cog removal relatively easy. These tools do not remove the freewheel itself, nor can they be used to remove cogs on conventional freewheels. With cogs out of the way, you have access to the spokes on the freewheel side of the hub, so you can replace damaged spokes on that side. The tool is also useful for changing to different size cogs. It works on conventional freewheels and on freehubs where the outer pocket is threaded. It's called a Cassette-Cracker (Fig. 5-10), available from your bike shop for about $9.50. Primary application

Fig. 5-10: *On the road, remove freehub cogs with this Cassette-Cracker to replace broken spokes.*

is on Shimano and SunTour freehubs. Use it like this:

1. Place the hook end of this tool on the chain stay, or seat stay (Figs. 5-11 and 5-12. Wrap the Cassette-Cracker's chain around the smallest freewheel cog (as shown in Fig. 5-11).

2. Push down (forward) on the pedal. It helps if the bike chain is on the smallest chainweel. Be sure to have extra spokes of the correct length for your bike along, though, and a spoke wrench. See Chapter 11 for wheel-truing instructions.

The Cassette-Cracker won't work on Shimano HyperGlide freehubs with a threaded lockring. For those hubs, the people that made the Cassette-Cracker also have a Hyper-Cracker (Fig. 5-13). Use it like the Cassette-Cracker, except:

1. Remove the rear wheel.
2. Engage the Hyper-Cracker in the HyperGlide lockring.

Fig. 5-11: Cassette-Cracker chain goes under small cog; clip end goes on chain stay.

Fig. 5-12: At right, removing freehub cogs. At left, replacing cogs, using Cassette-Cracker.

Fig. 5-13: *Hyper-Cracker for Shimano HyperGlide freehubs.*

3. Reinstall the wheel.

4. Put the Hyper-Cracker's lever on the seat stay (left in Fig. 5-14).

5. Apply forward pedal pressure to loosen the lockring.

6. Remove the wheel.

7. Pull the cogs off the cassette hub.

8. Replace broken spoke(s). Retrue the wheel.

9. Replace cogs and thread on the lockring.

10. Engage the Hyper-Cracker in the HyperGlide lockring.

11. Reinstall the wheel.

12. Place the Hyper-Cracker's lever on the chain stay (as shown at right in Fig. 5-14).

Fig. 5-14: *Left, removing HyperGlide cogs with Hyper-Cracker. Right, replacing the cog using this tool.*

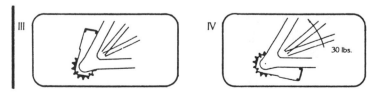

13. Apply about 30 pounds of tangential pressure by hand-pulling the tire backward to tighten the lockring. (Do not use the bike chain for this step.)

Replacing (Conventional) Freewheel Cogs

1. Remove the freewheel as described above.
2. Place the freewheel in a freewheel vise (Figs. 5-5 and 5-15).
3. Place the freewheel-laden vise in a bench vise. If you don't have a special freewheel vise tool, do what I do. Drill two holes in your wood workbench to hold two bolts, spaced to fit the holes in the large freewheel cog (Fig. 5-16).

Fig. 5-15: Conventional freewheel vise holds freewheel, so it, in turn, can be clamped in a machinist's vise.

Fig. 5-16: Use two bolts in your workbench to hold freewheel, in lieu of vise tool shown in Fig. 5-15.

4. Use the cog remover (Figs. 5-4 and 5-17) to turn the small free-wheel cog counterclockwise. Remove it. On most freewheels only the small cog is threaded on. If the second cog is also threaded on, remove it the same way. Now you can slide off the remaining cogs and their spacers. As you remove these parts, make a note of which spacers go where, because some may be thinner than others (Fig. 5-18). If the space between any two cogs is too wide or too narrow, the chain may slip when you shift, and cause an accident.

5. Replace worn cog(s) (Fig. 5-19) and/or install cogs which have a different number of teeth. For example, if you want a lower, hill-climbing

Fig. 5-17: *Turn small freewheel cog (conventional freewheel) counterclockwise with a chain tool to remove cogs.*

Fig. 5-18: *Cogs removed from conventional freewheel, Note spacers, which must go back in the same place and order.*

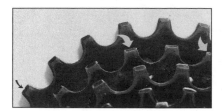

Fig. 5-19: *Arrows point to worn cog teeth. To avoid chain skip replace cogs that look like this.*

granny gear, replace the big cog with a 32- or 34-tooth cog. Years ago SunTour made a 38-tooth cog. If you call enough bike shops you may find such a super-low gear cog on the freewheel board. Before you go this route, please review Chapter 6 on gears and gearing, especially the data on rear derailleur capacity. Any cogs you replace must also be compatible with the old cogs and with whatever shift system and chain you use. See your bike shop for specific fit help. Note also that if you go to a bigger rear cog you will have to install a longer chain. Don't just add new links to your old chain. They won't be worn the same way as the old links, so you could have chain skip. Review Chapter 4 for more data on chains.

A Word About Threading Freewheels

When you purchase a freewheel to mount on your good aluminum alloy hub, you need to remember two things. First, the hub boss, where the threads are located, is aluminum (Fig. 5-20). Again, I repeat, these threads are a-l-u-m-i-n-u-m. They are very soft compared to the hardened steel of the freewheel threads.

Never put a freewheel on a hub unless you are sure you can get it off. Because once you pedal, you really tighten down on the freewheel where it threads onto the hub boss. The threads must be compatible. For example, English-threaded hubs are 1.370 inches by 24 threads per inch. Some Italian-threaded hubs are 35 millimeters by 24 threads per inch (TPI). Now if you multiply 1.370 × 25.4 to transform the English to metric, you come up with an English hub in metric terms of 34.798 millimeters, very close to the 35 millimeters of the Italian hub threading. Because the TPI is the same, but the Italian hub is 0.202 millimeters bigger than the English hub, it is reasonable to assume that an Italian-

Fig. 5-20: *Hub threads are aluminum, freewheel threads are steel. Avoid cross-threading when replacing conventional freewheel back on the hub.*

threaded freewheel will fit, albeit somewhat loosely, on the 0.202-millimeter smaller English-threaded hub. It will fit and work okay.

Going the other way, if you bought an Italian bike on your last trip to Milan, and the hub is threaded Italian, and now you want to put an English-threaded freewheel on that hub, will it fit? The answer is, maybe. It's yes if you are terribly careful not to start threading the freewheel on cocked. Make sure you get it on straight. You will have some slight forcing to do, because you will be cutting 0.202-millimeter deeper threads on the softer aluminum Italian-threaded hub with the hard steel of the slightly smaller English-threaded freewheel, but you can do it. I don't recommend the practice, but this is out of sheer perfectionism, not because it isn't fairly easy to do.

You also have to make sure that the freewheel will clear the shoulder of the hub flange. Some flange bosses have a wider or deeper shoulder (the raised part just behind the threads) than others, and when you tighten down the freewheel it rubs on the shoulder, sometimes so tightly the freewheel can't turn. In any case, the freewheel must rotate freely and not rub on anything. Some combinations of freewheels and hubs just won't work for this reason. I can't give you particular combinations, there are so many; just be aware that the problem does exist.

FREEHUB MAINTENANCE

Freehubs combine the hub and the freewheel in one piece. As you can see in Fig. 5-2, the cogs are mounted on splines and held in place by the small freewheel cog which is threaded on. The freehub permits a stronger wheel because the rim does not have to be dished as much as it does for a conventional hub (see Chapter 11 for an explanation of dishing). Also, a freehub axle is stronger because it extends all the way out to the end of the freewheel. This means that the bearings are at the extreme right-hand side of the hub, rather than at the right side of the hub body. Hub bearing surface wear is less and hub strength is greater. In fact, many makes of top-of-the-line all-terrain bikes now come with the freehub. Racing cylists also prefer them. Note: Hollow rear hub axles (equipped with a quick-release) are bendable under wheel impact. Freehubs minimize this problem. Solid bolt-on axles minimize it still further.

To remove a freehub cassette, you will need special tools. There are many models and makes of these hubs. New models, requiring new special tools, seem to be announced monthly. I see no reason to remove the entire freehub cassette from the hub body, unless it is totally worn out. This is a shop job, so if you feel you need to replace the cassette, I recommend you let the shop, with its special tools, do this work. To remove freehub cogs, see on-the-road cog removal instructions above.

ABOUT COG INTERCHANGEABILITY

If you change cogs on your freewheel or freehub cassette, be sure to use compatible new cogs. Check this out with your bike shop. The new, narrower chains may not work on older freewheel cogs, and vice versa.

Some 6-speed freewheels will fit on a normal 120-mm locknut-to-locknut hub, made for a 5-speed freewheel. This means you can switch over to a 6-speed cluster with this freewheel without having to change to a longer axle. Bikes built for five speeds have 120 mm between the inner surfaces of the dropouts. Frames built for six speeds usually have 125- or 126-mm spacing between the inner surfaces of the dropouts (Fig. 5-20). Frames built for 7-speed freewheels have a still wider distance, from 130 to 140 mm. The narrower freewheel-and-chain combinations now let you increase your choice of gears without having to buy a new frame. If you have a long touring frame you usually won't have to worry about chain clearance between the chain and the inside of the chain stay. However, some bikes have rounded chain stays, rather than flattened, which can cause chain rub on the small (high-speed) cog. You can sometimes get by with a spacer: simply remove the spacer from between the left-side locknut washer and cone nut, and move it over to the freewheel side on the axle. If adding spacers to the axle means you have to force the stays apart so the axle will fit in, don't do it if you have a fine frame. And don't let anyone else do it. If the chain stay is flattened where the high-gear cog rotates (a very slight flattening), you will probably have clearance for the wider freewheel with more cogs. The SunTour Ultra-Six freewheel is 26.5 mm between cogs, so it will fit onto a 120-mm axle where your 5-speed freewheel now resides. The Ultra-Six weighs 510 grams (18 ounces) and has cogs from 14 to 32 teeth. The model I tested has cogs of 13, 15, 17, 21, 26, and 32 teeth.

Now let's go to Chapter 6, where you will learn the basics of gear selection and how it affects your pedaling and hill climbing.

6
Gears and Gearing

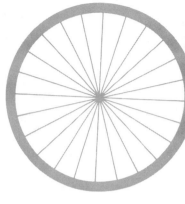

Most of us ordinary tourists need granny gears to help us pedal an equipment-laden bike up steep hills. Granny gears are big, big rear cogs, such as a 34-tooth freewheel cog, combined with a small 24- or 28-tooth chainwheel. SunTour used to make a 38-tooth freewheel cog (Fig. 6-1), but no more. You may, if you're lucky, find such a cog still hanging on the cog display board in your bike shop. I have one on both my ATB and road bikes. I hope

Fig. 6-1: A 38-tooth freewheel cog.

they never wear out. With the chain on these gears I can ride up most hills. It's slow, but a lot better than walking and pushing the bike uphill. However, there are grades over 15 percent even racing cyclists have to walk up.

You pay a penalty for such a wide gear selection. The penalty is that you won't be able to use all gear combinations. But if you already have 18 or 21 gear selections, who cares? For example, the rear derailleur won't handle a shift to the 38-tooth cog *and* to the largest chainwheel. Well, it will if you make the chain longer. But then the chain is going to be so long it will flop around when it's on smaller gears and may jump off a cog or a chainwheel as you bounce downhill or shift inaccurately. As noted above, there are some hills you just have to get off your bike and walk up. Because some hills are graded in degrees and others in percent grade, Table 6-1 converts from one to the other. For me, even in my lowest 24-inch gear, any hill over 15 percent grade is one I walk up.

Table 6-1 CONVERSION FROM DEGREES OF GRADE TO PERCENT OF GRADE

Degrees	Percent
1	1.7
2	3.5
3	5.2
4	7.0
5	8.8
6	10.5
7	12.3
8	14.1
9	15.8
10	17.6

Table 6-1: The steepness (grade) of a hill is expressed in degrees by engineers and in percent by the rest of us. For example, Michelin maps of European countries commonly have a V or similar symbol to indicate grade. Each V symbolizes a 5-percent grade. I hit a couple triple V grades in the south of France and I can report they are not real friendly. Especially if you are lugging 35 or 45 pounds of gear.

TWO WAYS TO BEEF UP YOUR GEARS

There are two ways you can beef up your gearing. You can install bigger
cogs on your freewheel. You can also go to a smaller chainwheel, or
convert to a triple chainwheel setup with a small 24-tooth chainwheel.
In this chapter I will discuss how to select and design your own gearing.
Please see Chapter 3 for technical data on chainwheel changes, Chapter
5 for freewheel changes, and Chapter 4 for both. I have stressed going
to bigger gears thus far. You can, of course, also change to smaller
freewheel cogs and bigger chainwheels if you want to go faster and have
the muscles to back up that desire. Back to granny gears. Any set of
gears that lets you reach the top of steep hills without going into cardiac
arrest is just dandy. You can even have 21 speeds, 7 cogs in the back,
3 up front. However, the step-by-step gear shifting you need to feel
comfortable at various hill gradients can be amply met with at most 18
speeds; for me, 15 is plenty.

ABOUT THOSE GEAR RATIOS

For the past 100 years or so the bicycle fraternity has referred to gear
ratios in "inches" of gear. The gear-inch usage is a throwback to the pre-
1900 high-wheel bicycle (Fig. 6-2) when the gear ratio of a bicycle was
simply the diameter of the big front wheel in inches. These high wheelers
did not have gears. The pedals and cranks were attached to the front
wheel. The bigger the wheel, the faster you could go. All you needed
were legs long enough to reach the pedals. This concept was translated
to modern multi-geared bicycles by a leap of the imagination, a love of
bicycle lore, and some simple math.

To arrive at the "inches" of gear for any combination of front chainwheel and rear freewheel cog, use this simple two-step formula. Count
the number of teeth of the freewheel cog of your choice. Do the same
for the chainwheel of your choice. Find the *gear ratio* between these two
gears by dividing the number of teeth in the chainwheel by the number
of teeth in the freewheel cog. For example, say you counted 48 teeth in
the chainwheel and 32 teeth in the freewheel cog. Then $48 \div 32 =$
1.5, which is the *gear ratio of this combination*. The second step in finding
the gear *inches* is to multiply this *gear ratio* by the diameter of the rear

Fig. 6-2: *High-wheeler of the 1890s. This is a direct-drive machine. What you pedal is what you get in mph. Speed is a function of the diameter of the big wheel and the cadence (pedal rpm) exerted by the rider. The wheel diameter is a function of the rider's leg length.*

wheel, which on an ATB is 26 inches and on road bikes either 27 inches or 700 centimeters. For example, 26 × 1.5 = 39 inches, rounded off. That is the number of inches of this gear combination. That would be, in 1890s bike parlance, equivalent to a high wheeler with a 3.25 foot diameter front wheel (39 ÷ 12 = 3.25). At the other extreme, a free-wheel 13-tooth cog and a chainwheel with 54 teeth would be a gear ratio of 54 ÷ 13 = 4.2. Translated into "inches," that would be 4.2 × 26 = 109 inches. It would take a 9-foot highwheeler front wheel to achieve this gear (109 ÷ 12 = 9.1). (I have rounded all results to the nearest

Table 6-2: *Gear chart for a road bike with 27-inch or 700-cm wheels. To find the gear for any combination of chainwheel and freewheel teeth from this table: a. Count the teeth in the chainwheel. b. Count the teeth in the free-wheel. c. Find the number of chainwheel teeth you counted in the top (hori-zontal) row of the table. d. Find the number of freewheel teeth you counted in the left (vertical row) of the table. e. Draw an imaginary line to where the numbers for the chainwheel teeth and the freewheel teeth you counted inter-sect. For example, say you have a 48-tooth chainwheel and a 14-tooth free-wheel. From the table, you can see that the "gear" you would be in with the chain on this combination of freewheel and chainwheel teeth would be 93.*

NUMBER OF TEETH IN REAR SPROCKET

Table 6-2 NUMBER OF TEETH IN CHAINWHEEL
(For 27-inch and 700-centimeter wheels only)

Sprocket ↓ \ Chainwheel →	24	25	26	27	28	29	30	31	32	33	34	35	36	37	38	39	40	41	42	43	44	45	46	47	48	49	50	51	52	53	54
12	54	56	59	61	63	65	68	70	72	74	77	79	81	83	86	88	90	92	95	97	99	101	104	106	108	110	113	115	117	119	122
13	50	52	54	56	58	60	62	64	66	69	71	73	75	77	79	81	83	85	87	89	91	93	96	98	100	102	104	106	108	110	112
14	46	48	50	52	54	56	58	60	62	64	66	68	69	71	73	75	77	79	81	83	85	87	89	91	93	95	96	98	100	102	104
15	43	45	47	49	50	52	54	56	58	59	61	63	65	67	68	70	72	74	76	77	79	81	83	85	86	88	90	92	94	95	97
16	41	42	44	46	47	49	51	52	54	56	57	59	61	62	64	66	68	69	71	73	74	76	78	79	81	83	84	86	88	89	91
17	38	40	41	43	45	46	48	49	51	52	54	56	57	59	60	62	64	65	67	68	70	72	73	75	76	78	79	81	83	84	86
18	36	38	39	41	42	44	45	47	48	50	51	53	54	56	57	59	60	62	63	65	66	68	69	71	72	74	75	77	78	80	81
19	34	36	37	38	40	41	43	44	45	47	48	50	51	53	54	55	57	58	60	61	63	64	65	67	68	70	71	72	74	75	77
20	32	34	35	36	38	39	41	42	43	45	46	47	49	50	51	53	54	55	57	58	59	61	62	63	65	66	68	69	70	72	73
21	31	32	33	35	36	37	39	40	41	42	44	45	46	48	49	50	51	53	54	55	57	58	59	60	62	63	64	66	67	68	69
22	29	31	32	33	34	36	37	38	39	41	42	43	44	45	47	48	49	50	52	53	54	55	56	58	59	60	61	63	64	65	66
23	28	29	31	32	33	34	35	36	38	39	40	41	42	43	45	46	47	48	49	51	52	53	54	55	56	58	59	60	61	62	63
24	27	28	29	30	32	33	34	35	36	37	38	39	41	42	43	44	45	46	47	48	50	51	52	53	54	55	56	57	59	60	61
25	26	27	28	29	30	31	32	33	35	36	37	38	39	40	41	42	43	44	45	46	48	49	50	51	52	53	54	55	56	57	58
26	25	26	27	28	29	30	31	32	33	34	35	36	37	38	39	41	42	43	44	45	46	47	48	49	50	51	52	53	54	55	56
27	24	25	26	27	28	29	30	31	32	33	34	35	36	37	38	39	40	41	42	43	44	45	46	47	48	49	50	51	52	53	54
28	23	24	25	26	27	28	29	30	31	32	33	34	35	36	37	38	39	40	41	41	42	43	44	45	46	47	48	49	50	51	52
29	22	23	24	25	26	27	28	29	30	31	32	33	34	34	35	36	37	38	39	40	41	42	43	44	45	46	47	47	48	49	50
30	22	23	23	24	25	26	27	28	29	30	31	32	32	33	34	35	36	37	38	39	40	41	41	42	43	44	45	46	47	48	49
31	21	22	23	24	24	25	26	27	28	29	30	30	31	32	33	34	35	36	37	37	38	39	40	41	42	43	44	44	45	46	47
32	20	21	22	23	24	24	25	26	27	28	29	30	30	31	32	33	34	35	35	36	37	38	39	40	41	41	42	43	44	45	46
33	20	20	21	22	23	24	25	25	26	27	28	29	29	30	31	32	33	34	34	35	36	37	38	38	39	40	41	42	43	43	44
34	19	20	21	21	22	23	24	25	25	26	27	28	29	29	30	31	32	33	33	34	35	36	37	37	38	39	40	41	41	42	43
35	19	19	20	21	22	22	23	24	25	25	26	27	28	29	29	30	31	32	32	33	34	35	35	36	37	38	39	39	40	41	42
36	18	19	20	20	21	22	23	23	24	25	26	26	27	28	29	29	30	31	32	32	33	34	35	35	36	37	38	38	39	40	41
37	18	18	19	20	20	21	22	23	23	24	25	26	26	27	28	28	29	30	31	31	32	33	34	34	35	36	36	37	38	39	39
38	17	18	18	19	20	21	21	22	23	23	24	25	26	26	27	28	28	29	30	31	31	32	33	33	34	35	36	36	37	38	38

whole number.) This means the pedal, attached to, say, a 7-inch crank, would be about 64 inches below the circumference of the wheel when at the bottom of its stroke ($109 \div 2 + 7 = 61.5$). That's an inseam length worthy of a Paul Bunyan, or maybe Bigfoot. But it does show you that technology can engineer a bike with all the speed advantages of a 9-foot direct-drive wheel in a bike that a five-foot person could ride today.

Let's go to the other extreme and find a super low, low gear in the archaic "inch" terminology (we're stuck with it). Say you have a rear cog with 38 teeth (which is as big as they come) and a small chainwheel with 24 teeth (as small as they come). Put these two gears together and what do you have? $24 \div 38 = 0.6$ (a negative gear ratio). Then $0.6 \times$ your 26-inch wheel diameter gives you an *inch* equivalent gear of 16, which is truly a wall-climber.

One problem you may have in selecting your own gears is that so many combinations are either duplicates or so close as to be duplicates. I have computed gear tables for bikes with 26-inch wheels and for bikes with 27-inch wheels. The difference in diameter between 27 inches and 700 cm is minuscule for purposes of gear calculation. If you have 700-cm rims, use the 27-inch Table 6-2. If you have 26-inch rims, use Table 6-3. In these tables you will see many, many repetitions. For example, in Table 6-3, a 45-inch gear appears seven times, with seven different gear combinations. In selecting gears, the idea is to arrive at a minimum of such useless combinations.

Workable gear combinations are, for a 15-speed (triple chainwheel, 5 freewheel cogs): 26-, 38-, and 40-tooth chainwheels and 13-, 16-, 20-, 28-, and 32-tooth freewheel cogs. This combination gives a low gear of 22 and a high gear of 83. For an 18-speed (triple chainwheel, 6 freewheel cogs), good combinations are: 28-, 36-, and 46-tooth chainwheels and 14-, 17-, 21-, 24-, 28-, and 34-tooth freewheels. Table 6-4 shows a gear combination for an 18-speed touring bike. Note that only 15 out of the 18 gears are usable. But you will have excellent gearing for hill climbing. Table 6-5 shows the actual gear selections for this bicycle.

HOW FAST CAN YOU GO?

Your speed depends on your strength and endurance, of course. But the strongest cyclist in the world won't go very fast when the chain is on a

Table 6-3 GEAR TABLE FOR ALL-TERRAIN BICYCLES WITH 26-INCH WHEELS*

Number of Freewheel Teeth	Number of Chainwheel Teeth									
	24	26	28	36	38	40	46	48	50	52
13	48	52	56	72	76	80	92	96	100	104
14	45	48	52	67	71	74	85	89	93	97
15	42	45	49	62	66	69	80	83	87	90
16	39	42	46	59	62	65	75	78	81	85
17	37	40	43	55	58	61	70	73	76	80
18	35	38	40	52	55	58	66	69	72	75
19	33	36	38	49	52	55	63	66	68	71
21	30	32	35	45	47	50	57	59	62	64
22	28	31	33	43	45	47	54	57	59	61
23	27	29	32	41	43	45	52	54	57	59
24	26	28	30	39	41	43	50	52	54	56
28	22	24	26	33	35	37	43	45	46	48
30	21	23	24	31	33	35	40	42	43	45
32	20	21	23	29	31	33	37	39	41	42
34	18	20	21	28	29	31	35	37	38	40
38	16	18	19	25	26	27	31	33	34	36

*Gear tabulations are rounded off to the nearest whole number. Differences in the diameters of 1.50″, 1.75″, and 2.125″ tires have not been calcualted because they are so small. Note that there are repetitions of gears in this table, which you can avoid by selecting gears that do not include them. For example, a 45-inch gear occurs in five places in this table.

Table 6-3: *Gear chart for an all-terrain bicycle with 26-inch wheels. See Table 6-2 caption for instructions.*

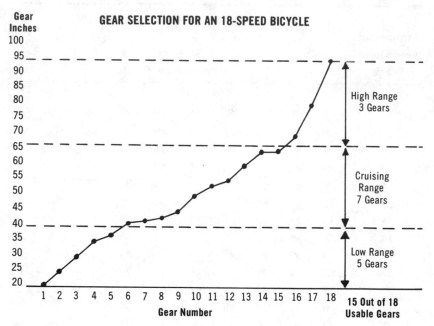

Table 6-4: *High, cruising, and low gear ranges for an 18-speed bicycle. From this table you can chart the gears that will provide ample ratios in each speed category.*

26-tooth rear cog and 25-tooth chainwheel. There is a limit as to how fast any human being can twirl the pedals (called cadence). For example, Table 6-6 shows inches of gear, crank rpm (cadence), and miles per hour. From Table 6-2, the rider with a 26-tooth rear cog and 25-tooth chainwheel is in a 26-inch gear.Now, look at Table 6-6. Find the inch-gear in column one. Look at the horizontal column labeled "Revolutions per minute of the crank arm." At the dizzy cadence of 160 crank rpm, the rider would only be going 12.38 mph if he could spin that fast. Now, let's go back to Table 6-2 and find the inch-gear when the chain is on a 13-tooth rear cog and a 56-tooth chainwheel. Want to find the inch-gear? Let's call it 116 inches. Now find the 116-inch gear in Table 6-6. At a cadence of 160 rpm, you'd be traveling 55.22 mph. Of course, I

Table 6-5 GEAR COMBINATIONS FOR AN 18-SPEED TOURING BICYCLE

Gear No.	Number of Teeth in Freewheel	Number of Teeth in Chainwheel	Gear, Inches
1	32	24	20.3
2	26	24	24.9
3	22	24	29.5
4	32	40	33.8
5	19	24	34.1
6	16	24	40.5
7	26	40	41.5
8	32	50	42.2
9	14	24	46.3
10	22	40	49.1
11	26	50	51.9
12	19	40	56.8
13	22	50	58.7
14	16	40	67.5
15	19	50	67.5
16	14	40	77.1
17	16	50	84.4
18	14	50	96.4

Table 6-5: These are the gears from which Table 6-4 was derived. Make up your own gear table based on the gears on your bike, or the gears you would like on your bike.

know, I know. You have to factor in the wind velocity and direction, the grade of the road, tire pressure, and tire tread design, to name a few parameters. But you don't, really. These tables say nothing about those factors. They just tell you the gear-inches and how fast you would be going *if* you maintained a specific cadence. Whether the wind resistance, road grade, and other factors will *let* you maintain the cadence you desire is not the tables' problem.

Make up your own speed chart from these tables. Table 6-7 is just such a chart. If you don't find the speed listed in Table 6-6, compute your own, using this formula: Speed in mph = pi × the gear inches × the crank rpm × 60 divided by 63.36.

Table 6-6 SPEED CHART

The Speed in MPH Equals pi Times the Gear Times the Crank RPM Times 60 Divided by 63.360

Gear	Revolutions per Minute of the Crank Arm										
	60	70	80	90	100	110	120	130	140	150	160
26	4.64	5.41	6.19	6.96	7.73	8.51	9.28	10.06	10.83	11.60	12.38 MPH
27	4.82	5.62	6.43	7.23	8.03	8.84	9.64	10.44	11.25	12.05	12.85 MPH
28	5.00	5.83	6.66	7.50	8.33	9.16	10.00	10.83	11.66	12.49	13.33 MPH
29	5.18	6.04	6.90	7.76	8.63	9.49	10.35	11.22	12.08	12.94	13.80 MPH
30	5.35	6.25	7.14	8.03	8.92	9.82	10.71	11.60	12.49	13.39	14.28 MPH
31	5.53	6.46	7.38	8.30	9.22	10.14	11.07	11.99	12.91	13.83	14.76 MPH
32	5.71	6.66	7.62	8.57	9.52	10.47	11.42	12.38	13.33	14.28	15.23 MPH
33	5.89	6.87	7.85	8.84	9.82	10.80	11.78	12.76	13.74	14.73	15.71 MPH
34	6.07	7.08	8.09	9.10	10.11	11.13	12.14	13.15	14.16	15.17	16.18 MPH
35	6.25	7.29	8.33	9.37	10.41	11.45	12.49	13.54	14.58	15.62	16.66 MPH
36	6.43	7.50	8.57	9.64	10.71	11.78	12.85	13.92	14.99	16.06	17.14 MPH
37	6.60	7.71	8.81	9.91	11.01	12.11	13.21	14.31	15.41	16.51	17.61 MPH
38	6.78	7.91	9.04	10.17	11.30	12.44	13.57	14.70	15.83	16.96	18.09 MPH
39	6.96	8.12	9.28	10.44	11.60	12.76	13.92	15.08	16.24	17.40	18.56 MPH
40	7.14	8.33	9.52	10.71	11.90	13.09	14.28	15.47	16.66	17.85	19.04 MPH
41	7.32	8.54	9.76	10.98	12.20	13.42	14.64	15.86	17.08	18.30	19.52 MPH
42	7.50	8.75	10.00	11.25	12.49	13.74	14.99	16.24	17.49	18.74	19.99 MPH
43	7.68	8.95	10.23	11.51	12.79	14.07	15.35	16.63	17.91	19.19	20.47 MPH
44	7.85	9.16	10.47	11.78	13.09	14.40	15.71	17.02	18.33	19.63	20.94 MPH
45	8.03	9.37	10.71	12.05	13.39	14.73	16.06	17.40	18.74	20.08	21.42 MPH
46	8.21	9.58	10.95	12.32	13.68	15.05	16.42	17.79	19.16	20.53	21.90 MPH
47	8.39	9.79	11.19	12.58	13.98	15.38	16.78	18.18	19.58	20.97	22.37 MPH
48	8.57	10.00	11.42	12.85	14.28	15.71	17.14	18.56	19.99	21.42	22.85 MPH
49	8.75	10.20	11.66	13.12	14.58	16.04	17.49	18.95	20.41	21.87	23.32 MPH
50	8.92	10.41	11.90	13.39	14.87	16.36	17.85	19.34	20.82	22.31	23.80 MPH
51	9.10	10.62	12.14	13.66	15.17	16.69	18.21	19.72	21.24	22.76	24.28 MPH
52	9.28	10.83	12.38	13.92	15.47	17.02	18.56	20.11	21.66	23.20	24.75 MPH
53	9.46	11.04	12.61	14.19	15.77	17.34	18.92	20.50	22.07	23.65	25.23 MPH
54	9.64	11.25	12.85	14.46	16.06	17.67	19.28	20.88	22.49	24.10	25.70 MPH
55	9.82	11.45	13.09	14.73	16.36	18.00	19.63	21.27	22.91	24.54	26.18 MPH
56	10.00	11.66	13.33	14.99	16.66	18.33	19.99	21.66	23.32	24.99	26.66 MPH
57	10.17	11.87	13.57	15.26	16.96	18.65	20.35	22.04	23.74	25.44	27.13 MPH
58	10.35	12.08	13.80	15.53	17.25	18.98	20.71	22.43	24.16	25.88	27.61 MPH
59	10.53	12.29	14.04	15.80	17.55	19.31	21.06	22.82	24.57	26.33	28.08 MPH
60	10.71	12.49	14.28	16.06	17.85	19.63	21.42	23.20	24.99	26.77	28.56 MPH
61	10.89	12.70	14.52	16.33	18.15	19.96	21.78	23.59	25.41	27.22	29.04 MPH
62	11.07	12.91	14.76	16.60	18.44	20.29	22.13	23.98	25.82	27.67	29.51 MPH
63	11.25	13.12	14.99	16.87	18.74	20.62	22.49	24.37	26.24	28.11	29.99 MPH
64	11.42	13.33	15.23	17.14	19.04	20.94	22.85	24.75	26.66	28.56	30.46 MPH
65	11.60	13.54	15.47	17.40	19.34	21.27	23.20	25.14	27.07	29.01	30.94 MPH
66	11.78	13.74	15.71	17.67	19.63	21.60	23.56	25.53	27.49	29.45	31.42 MPH
67	11.96	13.95	15.95	17.94	19.93	21.93	23.92	25.91	27.91	29.90	31.89 MPH
68	12.14	14.16	16.18	18.21	20.23	22.25	24.28	26.30	28.32	30.34	32.37 MPH
69	12.32	14.37	16.42	18.47	20.53	22.58	24.63	26.69	28.74	30.79	32.84 MPH
70	12.49	14.58	16.66	18.74	20.82	22.91	24.99	27.07	29.15	31.24	33.32 MPH
71	12.67	14.79	16.90	19.01	21.12	23.23	25.35	27.46	29.57	31.68	33.80 MPH
72	12.85	14.99	17.14	19.28	21.42	23.56	25.70	27.85	29.99	32.13	34.27 MPH
73	13.03	15.20	17.37	19.55	21.72	23.89	26.06	28.23	30.40	32.58	34.75 MPH
74	13.21	15.41	17.61	19.81	22.01	24.22	26.42	28.62	30.82	33.02	35.22 MPH
75	13.39	15.62	17.85	20.08	22.31	24.54	26.77	29.01	31.24	33.47	35.70 MPH

Table 6-6 SPEED CHART

The Speed in MPH Equals pi Times the Gear Times the Crank RPM Times 60 Divided by 63.360

Gear	Revolutions per Minute of the Crank Arm										
	60	70	80	90	100	110	120	130	140	150	160
76	13.57	15.83	18.09	20.35	22.61	24.87	27.13	29.39	31.65	33.91	36.18 MPH
77	13.74	16.04	18.33	20.62	22.91	25.20	27.49	29.78	32.07	34.36	36.65 MPH
78	13.92	16.24	18.56	20.88	23.20	25.53	27.85	30.17	32.49	34.81	37.13 MPH
79	14.10	16.45	18.80	21.15	23.50	25.85	28.20	30.55	32.90	35.25	37.60 MPH
80	14.28	16.66	19.04	21.42	23.80	26.18	28.56	30.94	33.32	35.70	38.08 MPH
81	14.46	16.87	19.28	21.69	24.10	26.51	28.92	31.33	33.74	36.15	38.56 MPH
82	14.64	17.08	19.52	21.96	24.39	26.83	29.27	31.71	34.15	36.59	39.03 MPH
83	14.82	17.28	19.75	22.22	24.69	27.16	29.63	32.10	34.57	37.04	39.51 MPH
84	14.99	17.49	19.99	22.49	24.99	27.49	29.99	32.49	34.99	37.48	39.98 MPH
85	15.17	17.70	20.23	22.76	25.29	27.82	30.34	32.87	35.40	37.93	40.46 MPH
86	15.35	17.91	20.47	23.03	25.58	28.14	30.70	33.26	35.82	38.38	40.94 MPH
87	15.53	18.12	20.71	23.29	25.88	28.47	31.06	33.65	36.24	38.82	41.41 MPH
88	15.71	18.33	20.94	23.56	26.18	28.80	31.42	34.03	36.65	39.27	41.89 MPH
89	15.89	18.53	21.18	23.83	26.48	29.13	31.77	34.42	37.07	39.72	42.36 MPH
90	16.06	18.74	21.42	24.10	26.77	29.45	32.13	34.81	37.48	40.16	42.84 MPH
91	16.24	18.95	21.66	24.37	27.07	29.78	32.49	35.19	37.90	40.61	43.32 MPH
92	16.42	19.16	21.90	24.63	27.37	30.11	32.84	35.58	38.32	41.05	43.79 MPH
93	16.60	19.37	22.13	24.90	27.67	30.43	33.20	35.97	38.73	41.50	44.27 MPH
94	16.78	19.58	22.37	25.17	27.96	30.76	33.56	36.35	39.15	41.95	44.74 MPH
95	16.96	19.78	22.61	25.44	28.26	31.09	33.91	36.74	39.57	42.39	45.22 MPH
96	17.14	19.99	22.85	25.70	28.56	31.42	34.27	37.13	39.98	42.84	45.70 MPH
97	17.31	20.20	23.09	25.97	28.86	31.74	34.63	37.51	40.40	43.29	46.17 MPH
98	17.49	20.41	23.32	26.24	29.15	32.07	34.99	37.90	40.82	43.73	46.65 MPH
99	17.67	20.62	23.56	26.51	29.45	32.40	35.34	38.29	41.23	44.18	47.12 MPH
100	17.85	20.82	23.80	26.77	29.75	32.72	35.70	38.67	41.65	44.62	47.60 MPH
101	18.03	21.03	24.04	27.04	30.05	33.05	36.06	39.06	42.07	45.07	48.08 MPH
102	18.21	21.24	24.28	27.31	30.34	33.38	36.41	39.45	42.48	45.52	48.55 MPH
103	18.39	21.45	24.51	27.58	30.64	33.71	36.77	39.84	42.90	45.96	49.03 MPH
104	18.56	21.66	24.75	27.85	30.94	34.03	37.13	40.22	43.32	46.41	49.50 MPH
105	18.74	21.87	24.99	28.11	31.24	34.36	37.48	40.61	43.73	46.86	49.98 MPH
106	18.92	22.07	25.23	28.38	31.53	34.69	37.84	41.00	44.15	47.30	50.46 MPH
107	19.10	22.28	25.47	28.65	31.83	35.02	38.20	41.38	44.57	47.75	50.93 MPH
108	19.28	22.49	25.70	28.92	32.13	35.34	38.56	41.77	44.98	48.19	51.41 MPH
109	19.46	22.70	25.94	29.18	32.43	35.67	38.91	42.16	45.40	48.64	51.88 MPH
110	19.63	22.91	26.18	29.45	32.72	36.00	39.27	42.54	45.81	49.09	52.36 MPH
111	19.81	23.12	26.42	29.72	33.02	36.32	39.63	42.93	46.23	49.53	52.84 MPH
112	19.99	23.32	26.66	29.99	33.32	36.65	39.98	43.32	46.65	49.98	53.31 MPH
113	20.17	23.53	26.89	30.26	33.62	36.98	40.34	43.70	47.06	50.43	53.79 MPH
114	20.35	23.74	27.13	30.52	33.91	37.31	40.70	44.09	47.48	50.87	54.26 MPH
115	20.53	23.95	27.37	30.79	34.21	37.63	41.05	44.48	47.90	51.32	54.74 MPH
116	20.71	24.16	27.61	31.06	34.51	37.96	41.41	44.86	48.31	51.76	55.22 MPH

Calibrated by an IBM 360 and Programmed by Sam Rhoads

Table 6-6: *This table lets you calculate how fast you could go in a given gear, at a given pedal cadence.*

Table 6-7 SAMPLE INDIVIDUALIZED SPEED CHART*

	Number of Teeth in Rear Sprocket				
	14	17	22	28	34
Chainwheel T 54					
Gear (Inches Eq.)	104.1	85.8	66.3	52	42.9
MPH Speed	21.45	17.88	13.8	10.83	8.8
Chainwheel T 49					
Gear (Inches Eq.)	94.5	77.8	60.1	47.3	38.9
MPH Speed	19.35	16.8	12.5	9.8	8.0
Chainwheel T 36					
Gear (Inches Eq.)	69.4	57.1	44.2	34.7	28.6
MPH Speed	14.9	11.89	9.2	7.1	5.9

*Based on 72-rpm cadence. You'll probably be going a lot faster downhill, so you may want to gradually increase the cadence for fast runs downhill or before the wind. Or you can make up several charts, say one foot for a cadence of 72, one for 80, one for 85, etc., so you can pull out a 3- × 5-card for every road condition. And you may be pedaling a lot slower than 72 rpm up steep hills. Because the gear inches did not correspond exactly to the cadence chart, we made our own interpolations, which is why the speeds, or some of them, don't correspond exactly to speeds on the cadence chart.

Table 6-7: Here is a table you can make up for your own gear combination. Keep it on top of your bar bag as you count your cadence in a gear, to figure your speed (unless, of course, you have a velometer).

A bit simpler approach to calculating how fast at what cadence is shown in Table 6-8.

A WORD ABOUT DERAILLEUR CAPACITY

It's important to know how derailleur capacity is arrived at and what it means to you. For example, you may be unhappy with the gear ratios you have now. You want a lower gear, let's say, to ease your way when your bike is gear-laden and the hills are steep. To change to lower gears

Table 6-8 SPEED IN MILES PER HOUR

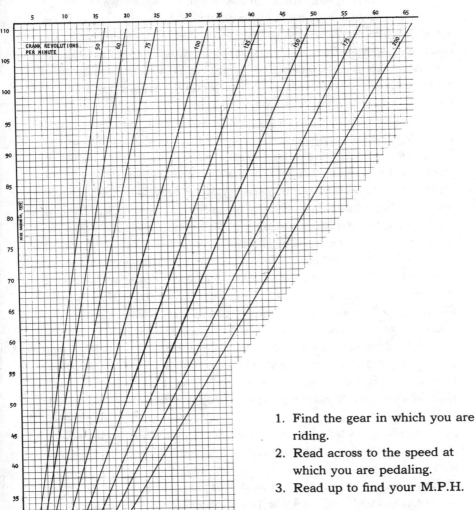

1. Find the gear in which you are riding.
2. Read across to the speed at which you are pedaling.
3. Read up to find your M.P.H.

To calculate the gear number, divide the number of teeth on the rear cog into the number of teeth on the front cog. Multiply this answer by the diameter of the rear wheel in inches.

Table 6-8: *A simplified speed table. Find the intersection of your gear-inch and cadence, and go up to the top horizontal line to find mph. Let me hear from you if you crank a 200 cadence in a 110-inch gear. The Guinness people may be interested. So would your cardiologist. And the highway patrol.*

you will, of course, have to change your low freewheel gear to one with more teeth, or change the small chainwheel to one with fewer teeth. Or, you could change the chainwheel setup from a double to a triple chainwheel set with a smaller chainwheel at the low end. In either or both cases, you will need front and rear derailleurs with the capacity to handle the larger gears you plan to install on your bike. Derailleur manufacturers list the capacity, but it needs some interpretation. Here's how to determine what derailleur capacity you need.

To compute derailleur capacity, simply subtract the number of teeth in the smallest rear cog from the number of teeth in the largest rear cog. Then you subtract the number of teeth in the smallest chainwheel up front from the number of teeth in the largest chainwheel. Then you add these two numbers for the total capacity of the derailleur. For example, one of my bikes has a super-wide-range-gear freewheel gear of 13 teeth on the small cog and 38 on the big cog. Therefore, $38 - 13 = 25$. The small chainwheel has 24 teeth and the big one has 48 teeth. Then $48 - 24 = 24$. Adding these, $25 + 24 = 49$. That's the capacity of the rear derailleur I am supposed to be using. I say "supposed" because there is not a derailleur on the market rated at 49 teeth. Not, at least, the last time I looked. The penalty I pay for this wall-climbing set of gears is that I can't use the biggest (low-gear) freewheel cog and the biggest (high-wheel) chainwheel at the same time. To me this is no penalty at all. I positively, absolutely love the hill-climbing low gear I get with this combination. Sometimes I believe I could walk up hills faster than when my chain is on the 38-tooth freewheel and on the 24-tooth chainwheel, but when I try I soon discover that, slow as it seems, *riding* uphill is a whole lot easier and more comfortable than walking and shoving the bike along, especially when the bike is loaded down with camping gear.

However, remember that adding gears (changing from a 5- to a 6- or 7-speed freewheel, or from a dual to a triple chainwheel) may and probably will render your index shifters unworkable. Single- and dual-lever index shifters are designed for a specific number of gears. A 5-gear rear index shifter won't work on a 6-gear setup, nor will a 6-gear index shifter handle a 7-speed freewheel. The same goes for dual to triple chainwheel conversions. If you lust for a granny hill-climbing gear, you may either have to return to good old reliable friction shifting, or install a new index shifting system that's compatible with your new gearing.

If you want bigger (granny) gears than your bike now has, I can recommend either the SunTour AG Tech or the SunTour MounTech (or the current version of these derailleurs). When they are equipped with a super long cage, the capacity of these derailleurs is 40 teeth. Bring your old SunTour derailleur to the dealer and have him fit the longer cage on it. Another excellent derailleur, also rated at 40 teeth, is Shimano's Model RD-525-SGS. The SGS means "super long cage."

7

Hubs and Quick-Releases—
Maintenance and Adjustment

I was on a road trip in Vermont. We had pedaled over dirt and sandy roads to get into state parks at night. One evening, after dinner, I decided to check my hubs. Spinning a bike wheel, I heard a grinding noise coming from my precision-machined, costly Campagnolo rear hub, a gritty sound that penetrated to the very depths of my wallet. Sand had worked its destructive way into the bearings. Fortunately I had a set of hub wrenches along, and some grease. When I disassembled the hub I did indeed find sand, but no damage. I was lucky. So, my suggestion is to make the following daily check on a bike trip, or make it at least monthly if you do more casual day riding:

1. Clean and relube conventional non-sealed bearing hubs after every extensive trip, or every two weeks on a road or trail trip if you have biked through water or over sandy trails.

2. Turn the bike upside down. Spin each wheel.

3. Feel for grittiness with your fingertips on the hub body (be careful you don't catch fingers in the spokes), listen for grating sounds from the hub. Relube by following the instructions below. If all seems okay, you may be able to get by for a longer period. But, if you have forded streams, or cycled over sand a lot, I do urge you to up the relube frequency. These instructions apply to freehubs (with an integral freewheel) as well as to conventional hubs.

Tools and Supplies You Will Need

1. Thin hub cone wrenches, 13, 14, 15, 16 and 17 mm, depending on size of hub locknuts and adjustable cones (Fig. 7-1).

2. 13-, 14-, or 15-mm socket, for an inch/pound torque wrench (Fig. 1-2). Review the section on use of the torque wrench in Chapter 1.

3. Axle vise to protect axle threads (Fig. 7-2), optional. Note: This vise also fits pedal axles, as discussed in the pedal section in this chapter.

4. Water-resistant grease. I like boat-trailer wheel-bearing grease.

5. Torque wrench (Fig. 1-2). Also please review use of a torque wrench, discussed in Chapter 1.

Table 7-1 TORQUE SPECIFICATIONS FOR HUBS

(inch/pounds of torque)

Part	Torque
Closing quick-release lever	80–105
Locknut for quick-release axle	88–220
Solid axle nuts	300–320

Maintenance Steps

1. Remove the wheel from the bicycle (see Chapter 1).

2. If the wheel is held by axle bolts, remove them. Or remove the quick-release mechanism. Hold the quick-release adjusting nut (see the section on operation and adjustment of the quick-release mechanism

Fig. 7-1: You need thin cone wrenches to work on your ball-bearing hubs.

Fig. 7-2: The hub axle vise grips the axle threads without harming them, holds the wheel in the bench vise, and eases the job of dismantling the hub.

following Step 29, below) while you turn the quick-release lever counterclockwise until the adjusting nut comes all the way off the skewer threads. Grasp the quick-release lever and pull the skewer out of the hollow axle. Catch the little springs ("2" in Fig. 7-4) so you don't lose them. Put the springs and the adjusting nut back on the skewer for safekeeping. On a rear wheel, remove the freewheel (as described in Chapter 5) so you can get at the bearings on the freewheel side. You do not have to remove the freewheel on freehubs, though, because the bearings on the freewheel side are reachable once the axle is withdrawn.

3. From here on out, you can simply lay the wheel on the bench and remove the bearings. However, the axle vise (Fig. 7-2), held in a bench vise as shown, makes life a lot easier. The axle vise holds the axle by its threads, so they won't strip. Or you can hold the locknut in a bench vise.

4. Hold the adjustable cone with one cone wrench and turn the locknut counterclockwise with the other cone wrench (Fig. 7-3). Remove the locknut and the spacing washer.

5. With the cone wrench, turn the adjustable cone a few turns counterclockwise. You should now be able to unscrew it by hand. Remove it from the axle.

6. Lay a rag out on the workbench next to the wheel. Hold the axle

Fig. 7-3: *Remove cones, loose bearings, and axle by holding the cup with one wrench while loosening the locknut (the one on top) with another wrench.*

end facing you with one hand, and with the other hand loosen the vise just enough to remove the wheel. Still holding the axle securely in the hub, carefully lay the wheel on the rag.

7. Lift the wheel off the rag enough so you can pull the axle out. You should still have an adjustable cone, washer, and locknut on one end of the hub axle. Leave them on the axle. Be ready to catch loose ball bearings as they fall out of the hub.

8. With a screwdriver, carefully pry off both dust caps ("9" in Fig. 7-4).

9. Remove any bearings still in the hub.

10. Roll the loose balls around in a cup of kerosene to remove old grease and dirt. Carefully spread them out on the rag and dry off the kerosene.

11. Clean both hub cups, the adjustable cones, the dust caps, and the axle.

12. Examine the hub cups and the adjustable cones ("13" in Fig. 7-4) for signs of galling and brinelling. Replace worn cones. If the hub cup(s) are worn, it's time for a new hub.

13. Examine the loose ball bearings for wear. If you've had the bike for three or four years, I recommend you replace these balls. Take a sample ball bearing to your bike shop to make sure you get the right size. Buy a couple of extra balls in case you drop one on the floor and lose it.

14. Hold the axle in the axle vise (Fig. 7-2), a case where the axle vise really helps. Hold the other adjustable cone with the cone wrench and remove the remaining locknut, washer, and adjustable cone.

15. Check the axle alignment. Roll it on a smooth, flat surface, such as an old piece of plate glass. Replace it if it's bent. Take the axle to your bike shop for an exact replacement.

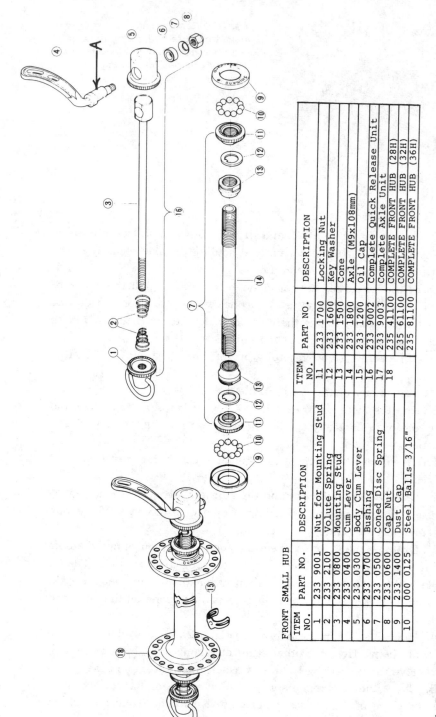

FRONT SMALL HUB

ITEM NO.	PART NO.	DESCRIPTION
1	233 9001	Nut for Mounting Stud
2	233 2100	Volute Spring
3	233 0800	Mounting Stud
4	233 0400	Cum Lever
5	233 0300	Body Cum Lever
6	233 0700	Bushing
7	233 0500	Coned Disc Spring
8	233 0600	Cap Nut
9	233 1400	Dust Cap
10	000 0125	Steel Balls 3/16"

ITEM NO.	PART NO.	DESCRIPTION
11	233 1700	Locking Nut
12	233 1600	Key Washer
13	233 1500	Cone
14	233 1800	Axle (M9x108mm)
15	233 1200	Oil Cap
16	233 9002	Complete Quick Release Unit
17	233 9003	Complete Axle Unit
18	235 41100	COMPLETE FRONT HUB (28H)
	235 61100	COMPLETE FRONT HUB (32H)
	235 81100	COMPLETE FRONT HUB (36H)

Fig. 74: Exploded view of a typical loose ball-bearing–type hub. Courtesy Shimano.

16. Cover the loose balls in grease. Layer in grease in both hub cups and on the adjustable cones.

17. Thread the adjustable cone, washer, and locknut on one end of the axle to about where they were before you removed them. Hold the adjustable cone with a hub wrench and tighten the locknut with another hub wrench. Then look at both ends of the axle. About ¼ inch of threads should be left where the axle fits into the dropouts. If not, adjust the cones and locknuts as necessary. If you are working on the front wheel, for example, both ends of the axle should show the same number of threads when you replace the other adjustable cone.

18. Insert the ball bearings in one side of the hub. Layer more grease on top of the balls.

19. Replace the dust cap on that side.

20. Insert the axle with adjustable cone, washer, and locknut into the hub side that has the bearings in place. Be careful not to dislodge bearings.

21. Hold the axle up while you turn the wheel over and lay it down on the bench.

22. Replace bearings in the other side of the hub, cover with more grease.

23. Replace the dust cap.

24. Thread on the adjustable cone, replace the washer, thread on the locknut. Again, check to make sure the same number of axle threads show on both sides of the hub. On a rear hub, the same number of threads should show outside the freewheel as on the other side of the hub.

25. Hold the adjustable cone with one wrench while you tighten the locknut with another wrench. The cone and locknut on the facing side of the hub should still only be hand-tight.

26. Hold the adjustable cone you tightened in Step 25 above with one wrench. Tighten the other adjustable cone just barely snug. Back the cone off, counterclockwise, a half turn.

27. Now, hold that second cone with one wrench and tighten its locknut with another wrench.

28. With the wheel still out of the bike, spin the axle between your thumb and forefinger. If it feels tight, if you sense that the axle is binding, hold the cone with one wrench and loosen the locknut a turn with the other wrench. Then tighten the cone about a quarter turn, hold it with the wrench, and tighten the locknut. Repeat until the axle runs silky smooth.

29. Replace the quick-release in the hub axle. Before I go any farther I want to stop and review how to adjust the quick-release. After this review I will finish the hub *bearing maintenance* section, starting with Step 30. But first, for your own safety, I want to make sure you understand how the quick-release works.

Adjusting the Quick-Release Mechanism

Your safety depends on proper, safe, and correct use of the quick-release mechanism. If the quick-release is not safely tightened, the wheel could pop out of the fork, for example, and cause an accident. Once you understand how to use a quick-release, always check its tightness before you ride the bike. This check should become a habit. If you left the bike someplace, the quick-release could have been tampered with. If it fell over in the garage, it could be loosened. If you don't check it before you get on the bike, the bike could be in a dangerous condition. Looking at the quick-release lever isn't good enough. Just because the lever is pointing in the closed position, as described below, doesn't mean it's safely tight, for two reasons. First, the quick-release skewer ("3" in Fig. 7-4) eventually stretches, which can cause the quick-release to loosen. The skewer may also break, due to metal fatigue and over-tightening (Fig. 7-5). Second, someone may have tampered with the quick-release adjuster nut (see below) and changed the original tightness adjustment.

Before I give you details on use of the quick-release, it's vital you understand that *this is NOT a nut-and-bolt device*. It is a cam action mechanism. The cam (Fig. 7-6) is eccentric and offset, and attached to the lever. The cam turns when the lever turns and tightens or loosens the quick-release mechanism, depending on which way the lever is turned. *Never try to tighten just the adjustment nut alone, either with*

Fig. 7-5: Quick-release skewers have been known to break. Here the skewer has snapped off at the control lever. Check yours to make sure it's intact.

Fig. 7-6: A quick-release is a cam-actuated *device,* not *a nut-and-bolt mechanism. See text for details.*

your fingers or with a tool! The adjustment nut ("1" in Fig. 7-4) will *never* hold the wheel securely in place all by itself. On the other hand, pull tests made by Schwinn in their lab show that it takes 500 foot/pounds of pressure to pull a properly tightened quick-release mechanism wheel out of the bike frame. For example, in some twenty years of cycling, I have had two accidents involving the front wheel. In one, the front wheel caught in a bridge grating. The bike stopped instantly, the frame broke in half, but the *wheel stayed in the fork.* In another accident, a driver suddenly stopped in front of me. My front wheel hit the car's rear bumper at about 15 mph. The frame was totaled, yet the front wheel did not budge out of the fork dropouts.

Tightening the Quick-Release

1. Turn the quick-release lever so it is pointing toward the front of the bike (Figs. 7-7 and 7-8). The word OPEN should be visible.

Fig. 7-7: Turn the quick-release lever to the OPEN *position to remove the wheel.*

Fig. 7-8: The quick-release lever is in the open position when the word OPEN *faces you and the lever points toward the front of the bike.*

Fig. 7-9: Adjust the quick-release by holding the lever with one hand while you tighten the adjuster nut with the other hand, as shown here.

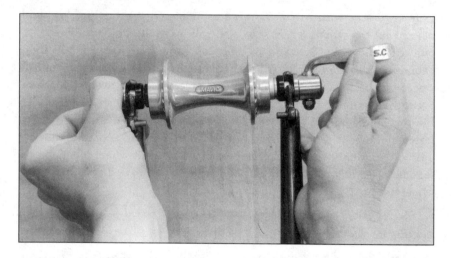

Fig. 7-10: Quick-release adjustment is correct when you feel considerable turning resistance from the control lever as it approaches the twelve o'clock position.

2. Hold the quick-release lever with one hand while you tighten the adjuster nut counterclockwise with the other hand (Fig. 7-9) as far as possible.

3. As you turn the quick-release lever toward the rear of the bike, you should feel resistance to turning when the lever is about at the twelve o'clock position, at a right angle to the frame of the bike (Fig. 7-10).

4. From the twelve o'clock position it should take *considerable* muscle to turn the lever all the way to the closed position, where the lever is pointing toward the rear of the bike (Fig. 7-11). The word CLOSE should be clearly visible (Fig. 7-12).

Fig. 7-11: *Turn the quick-release lever all the way toward the rear of the bike to close it.*

Fig. 7-12: *The word* CLOSE *shows, facing you, when the control lever is closed and turned toward the rear of the bike.*

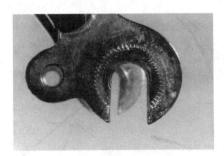

Fig. 7-13: *Sharp serrated teeth of the quick-release adjuster bolt (or a solid axle bolt) and hub cone locknut grip the axle dropouts when the quick-release is correctly adjusted, or solid axle bolts are tightened to 300 to 320 inch/pounds.*

5. Check tightness of the quick-release this way:

a. Turn the lever to the OPEN position (Fig. 7-7). Remove the front wheel (see Chapter 1 on brake adjustment; make sure that the tire will clear the brake shoes as you remove the wheel).

b. Inspect the dropouts. They should have indents on all four sides of the dropouts that look that those in Fig. 7-13. The sharp sawtooth edges of the quick-release (Fig. 7-14) (or the axle bolts) and the hub locknuts

Fig. 7-14: "Teeth"-mark bites from serrations noted in Fig. 7-13 must show if the quick-release or solid axle bolts are safely tight. These bites should overlap when the wheel has been removed and replaced more than once.

("11" in Fig. 7-4) should have made these indentations. If the wheel has been removed more than once, you should see multiple overlapping indentations. If you do not see these indentations, readjust the quick-release as above.

c. Replace the wheel. Replace the crossover brake cable in the brake arm. Make sure the wheel is evenly centered between the fork blades, then turn the quick-release to the closed position.

A Note About Wheel Retention Devices

The Consumer Products Safety Commission requires a wheel retention device on bolted-on front wheels but not on quick-release–held front wheels. Since quick-release hubs are more prone to accidental release than bolted-in ones, to me it makes absolutely no sense that retention devices are required only on bolted-on hubs. Recognizing this problem, responsible manufacturers now have front-wheel retention devices on quick-release hubs as well as on their bolted-on hubs. Schwinn has far and away the best front-wheel retention device on the market. To remove the wheel, press the tab end (Fig. 7-15) toward the wheel, and push the retent lever downward. When the wheel is replaced, just pull the retent lever upward (Fig. 7-16) until it clicks into place over the stud on the inside of the fork blade (Fig. 7-17).

Fig. 7-15: *Schwinn's excellent safety retention device holds the wheel in place even if the quick-release is not safely tight. The wheel will wobble if it's loose, of course. That's your signal to stop, readjust the quick-release, and tighten it. To unfasten the retention unit, push the lever toward the wheel. Pull the lever back to the position shown here.*

Fig. 7-16: *To replace the Schwinn detention device, push it toward the fork until it snaps into place.*

Fig. 7-17: *Here the Schwinn detention device is snapped in place, as you see from this view, looking toward the inside of the left fork blade.*

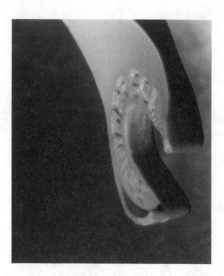

Fig. 7-18: *Another detention idea is a depression on the inside face of the fork dropout. To remove the wheel, turn the quick-release lever to the open position, then loosen the quick-release adjuster nut four or five turns until you can pull the wheel out of the dropouts.*

Yet another type of wheel retention device is actually molded into the dropout (Fig. 7-18). If the quick-release should open or is too loose, it will still be held by the outer lip of each dropout. You can't remove a wheel from this type of dropout unless you loosen the quick-release adjuster nut so the quick-release will clear the dropout lip as you remove the wheel. I like this idea, because when you replace the wheel you *have* to readjust the quick-release (see above for instructions).

Back to Hub Maintenance

Picking up from where I left off from Step 29 above:

30. Replace the wheel in the frame dropouts.

31. Adjust the quick-release lever to its safe operating tightness as described in Step 29, above.

32. Or, if you have a solid axle, thread on the bolts and tighten them to 300 to 350 inch/pounds.

Note: When you tighten the axle in the bicycle frame dropouts, with the quick-release or with the bolts, the hub cones will tighten up due to thread play.

33. Turn the wheel so the tire valve is at the three o'clock position. Let go of the wheel. The weight of the tire valve should be enough to let the wheel turn slowly by itself. Or, spin the wheel and watch it come

to a stop. If it stops very gradually, that's fine. If it stops suddenly, in midrevolution, the adjustable cone is too tight. Readjust as in Step 28 above.

34. Remove the wheel. Push the axle in and out and up and down, without turning it. If the axle moves, the cone is too loose. Readjust the cone as in Step 28 above, except tighten the cone a quarter turn.

35. Replace the wheel, close the quick-release, or tighten the axle bolts. Move the wheel left and right, without spinning it. If the wheel wobbles or moves from side to side, the cone is still too loose. Readjust as in Step 27, except tighten the cone a quarter turn, then tighten the locknut as described above. Close the quick-release or tighten the axle nuts again. Repeat this step until the axle spins smoothly.

Note: The quick-release is just that. It's quick for you, and quick for crooks. One way to have the benefits of a quick-release without the hazard of theft is to install a Qwik Cam (Fig. 7-19). It replaces the lever with a standard Allen wrench.

SEALED-BEARING HUBS

All modern bearings have some degree of seal. My definition of a true sealed bearing, however, is that it's one which uses sealed cartridge

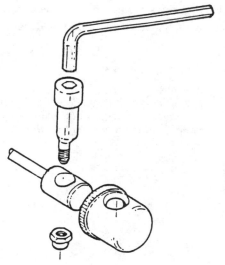

Fig. 7-19: *Deter theft of quick-re-lease—held wheels. Replace the quick-release lever cam with this cam that uses an Allen wrench to turn it. Carry the Allen wrench in your pocket.*

Fig. 7-20: *Sealed-bearing hubs use industrial-type cartridge bearings.*

bearings (Fig. 7-20) as opposed to those using ball bearings either loose or in a retainer (Fig. 7-4). Cartridge bearings are removable but only with special tools, although they do have an effective seal against water and abrasives. I suggest you relube cartridge bearings every 1,000 miles, non-cartridge more often, depending on use, as noted below:

1. Remove the wheel, quick-release, or axle bolts.
2. Remove the split washer (circlip) if there is one.
3. *Carefully* pry off the fragile seal (Fig. 7-21) with a thin-bladed knife.
4. With your fingers, force grease into the bearing cartridges. Be generous.
5. Replace the seal. Remember, the seal is fairly fragile. If bent it won't seal well. Press it back evenly all around the edges.

Eventually even sealed cartridge bearings wear out and need replacement. As I said earlier, this requires special tools and should be a bicycle shop job.

Fig. 7-21: *Pry off the seal on cartridge bearings with a thin-bladed knife. Stuff in grease, replace the seal.*

A new sealed-bearing hub, introduced just as I was finishing this book, has *four* sets of industrial-type sealed bearings. These are probably the strongest hubs you can buy, but are rather pricey at $330 a pair (front and rear). However, these would be the hubs of my choice were I to embark on a cross-country safari. The manufacturer says the bearings, even the two inboard ones (Fig. 7-22), are reachable for greasing and/ or replacement. See your dealer. They are called Hugi-Technik, are made in Switzerland and imported by BikeLab Limited, 1001 Bridgeway #623, Sausalito, CA 94965. Cogs are available from 12 to 30 teeth on the rear hub. There are rear hubs to fit 126 mm and 130 mm for road bikes and 7- to 8-speed cassettes for 135- and 140-mm spacings on ATBs.

3-SPEED INTERNAL-GEARED REAR HUBS

These hubs are a rather complicated assemblage of gears and mechanisms. (If Fig. 7-23 doesn't scare you off, nothing will!) Many require special tools to assemble or disassemble, and the majority of bicycle dealers are competent enough to deal with most of them.

This section, therefore, will be limited to routine hub maintenance, adjustment, and tips on correct usage. If you follow these instructions, your hub should last the life of the bicycle and seldom, if ever, need to be taken apart. However, if you really want to disassemble your rear hub, either out of curiosity or because you can't find a bicycle mechanic who knows how to fix it, you can obtain step-by-step illustrated assembly and disassembly instructions, complete with a list of spare parts, from the hub manufacturer or the bicycle manufacturer.

Fig. 7-22: *This Hugi-Technik, Swiss-made hub has four sets of cartridge bearings for strength.*

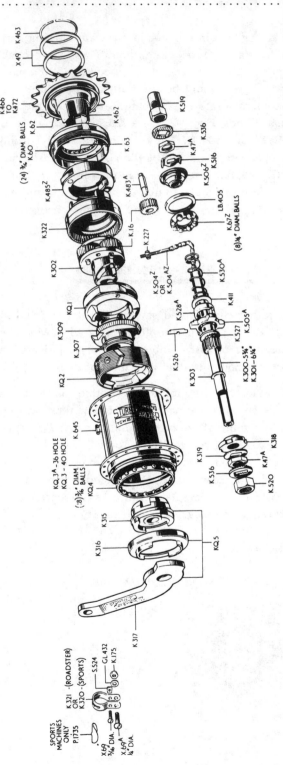

Fig. 7-23: *Sturmey-Archer 3-speed hub and coaster-brake combination. This drawing is shown here to convince you not to take any 3-speed hub apart. Let your bicycle dealer fix these. Of course, if things mechanical pose a challenge to you, go right ahead, take it apart, but save the pieces.*

Shifting

Stop pedaling, and coast while you move the shift lever to the gear you want. Resume pedaling after shifting. Note: This is a reverse procedure from shifting externally geared hubs.

Lubrication

Because all the working parts are inside, these hubs don't require much maintenance, beyond regular lubrication about every month and after long trips. Use a fairly light oil, equivalent to No. 20 SAE viscosity motor oil. Squirt about a teaspoonful into the hub through the hub hole provided for this purpose. Once a year you should take the bicycle into the dealer and have him disassemble and regrease the hub and check for any worn or broken parts.

Adjusting the Gear Shift

1. Put the gearshift lever in the No. 2 position.
2. Unscrew the locknut ("A," Fig. 7-24).
3. Adjust the knurled section of the cable until the end of the indicator rod is exactly level with the end of the axle ("B," Fig. 7-25). Check the location of the indicator rod through the "window" in the long nut on the axle ("B," Fig. 7-24).
4. Tighten the locknut.

Fig. 7-24: *Cable adjustments for typical 3-speed internally geared hub. "A," locknut; "B" indicator rod. Adjustment is correct when indicator is in the position shown.*

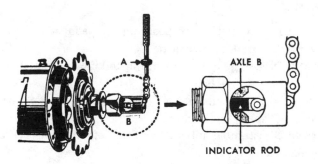

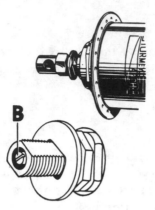

Fig. 7-25: Three-speed hub cable is also correctly adjusted when the adjuster rod, "B," is aligned with the face of the axle, as shown.

5. If you can't obtain enough adjustment with the cable connection at the hub, unscrew the nut and bolt holding the cable on the top tube and move the cable forward or rearward, as required. This step is known as "changing the fulcrum point" of the cable.

6. On some Shimano hubs, the adjustment for both the twistgrip and the lever-type control should start with the shift in the "N" position. At this position, the red "N" on the bellcrank should be centered in the "window" of the bellcrank or, on older models of this hub, the arrow indicator should be centered over the indicating line on the bellcrank.

7. If the centering in Step 5 cannot be made, move the fulcrum stop on the top tube forward or backward, as necessary, to make more or less cable slack as needed, then readjust at the bellcrank end by loosening the cable locknut and screwing the cable ferrule in or out as required. This step applies for both twistgrip and lever-type controls.

Troubleshooting

1. PROBLEM: In the "H" shift position, the pedal skips or won't turn. Pawl is worn or installed backward.

SOLUTION: Disassemble the hub and install new pawl and pawl spring (a job for the bicycle mechanic).

2. PROBLEM: Pedal skips at "N" position. Planet cage pawl worn or broken, or pawl spring broken.

SOLUTION: Disassemble hub and replace defective parts (a job for the bicycle mechanic.)

3. PROBLEM: Gears are stuck or do not change smoothly. Broken parts are caught up in hub mechanism.

SOLUTION: Complete hub overhaul (a job for the bicycle mechanic).

4. PROBLEM: Hub is noisy. Rusty mechanism due to lack of oil.

SOLUTION: If rust has proceeded far enough, a new hub may have to be installed. Try oiling the hub first. If this doesn't work, disassemble the hub and look for the rusted part. Install new parts as needed (a job for the bicycle mechanic).

5. PROBLEM: Erratic shifting. Control cable not set correctly.

SOLUTION: Adjust as described above.

8

Headset Maintenance

T he headset (Fig. 8-1) takes a terrific beating, especially on rough roads. The lower set of balls is under thrust stress, the upper set is under radial stress. Thrust stress is force applied toward or away from an object, like the reactive force on the springs of a car on a rough road, or when you strike a nail with a hammer. Radial stress is force spread outward, like the ripples a pebble makes when it's dropped in a pond. Road shock tends to flatten bearings. The bottom set takes most of the beating. Road shock will also wear grooves in the headset cups and cones, and flatten the bearings, especially on all-terrain bikes and camping gear–laden touring bikes. When bearings and cups wear, the headset becomes loose.

Loose headsets are the cause of many wheel shimmy accidents. Once started, shimmy is difficult or impossible to stop. You can easily lose control and go for a spill. Headsets work loose more often in all-terrain bicycles than in other bike types. This is because trail shock ultimately flattens the headset just a fraction of a thousandth of an inch, which loosens the headset. The flattening effect comes sooner if the headset is already loose. It always creeps up on you, gradually, unnoticeably. Sometimes the headset locknut and adjustable cup work loose as bearings wear down. Sometimes the adjustable cup is loose to begin with, right out of the bike factory. Then, one day, at speed, down a rough, steep hill, the front wheel assumes a quick left-right-left life of its own, known as wheel shimmy.

Fig. 8-1: *Headset components: The headset at right is the new, larger Fisher Evolution design. The headset at the left is the Shimano 600 model.* Courtesy Fisher MountainBikes.

I have even found five balls missing from the retainer (Fig. 8-2) in one ATB accident I investigated, an accident involving wheel shimmy and serious, permanent injury to the rider. This particular ATB was an el cheapo, part of a stable of similar inexpensive (spell that under $200) bikes for loan to guests of a mountain resort inn. We can glean two lessons here. First, loaner bikes may be dangerous. Two, cheap bikes have poor metallurgy, steel parts that wear down fast on impact. In this accident, the bike involved had a headset with grooves worn in cups (Fig. 8-3) and cones, *plus* missing ball bearings.

Even expensive bikes may have loose headsets. For example, a few years ago, on a bike trip in Puget Sound's San Juan Islands, I made a random check of headsets of bikes parked (captive audience) on the ferry

Fig. 8-2: *A brand-new bike came with* five *missing ball bearings, as this retainer shows. The moral is, prevent undue bearing wear. Take your headset apart now to make sure all bearings are in place.*

Fig. 8-3: *Check for worn headset cups and cones. This cup has a groove indicating much wear, and should be replaced.*

en route from island to island. Many of these bikes had been rented from bike shops on the mainland, or had been provided by a bike tour agency. I must have checked a hundred bikes during these island hopping ferry rides. About one in every four bikes I checked had dangerously loose headsets.

HEADSET SAFETY CHECKS

Make these two checks for headset adjustment every few months if you ride a lot.

    1. Straddle the bike, both feet on the ground. Squeeze the front brake lever hard, and rock the bike back and forth. Watch the headset locknut as you do so. If you feel looseness, if the locknut moves in any direction, or if it's so loose you can turn it by hand, readjust the headset bearings to prevent hazardous wheel shimmy, as described below.

    2. Lift the front wheel off the floor. Turn the bike so the handlebars are free to flop from side to side. The handlebars should turn or move without binding. Readjust headset bearings if necessary, as described below.

    Disassemble, clean, and readjust the headset every four to six months and install new bearings every year. Here's how to do it.

Fig. 8-4: *Park Tool makes excellent headset wrenches in both 32-mm and 36-mm sizes.*

Tools You Will Need

1. Pair of headset wrenches that fit Campagnolo, SunTour, and older Shimano headset locknuts and adjustable cups. The new larger headsets take a 36-mm wrench. Fisher ATBs take a 40-mm wrench. Older bikes take a 32-mm wrench (Fig. 8-4). Park Tools make lightweight take-along versions of these wrenches which you can bolt to the frame (Fig. 8-5). Mavic headsets take *two* sizes, one wrench for the locknut, a bigger one for the adjustable cup. These wrenches (Fig. 8-6) are very special and

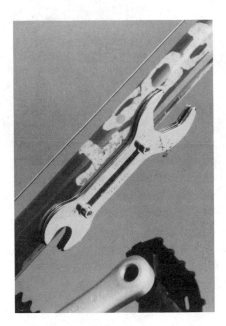

Fig. 8-5: *Park Tool headset wrenches are light and compact, and can be fitted to water bottle cage bosses, so you can readjust your headset on the road.*

Fig. 8-6: Mavic headsets take special wrenches. One wrench fits the lock-nut, the other fits the adjustable cup. You need them both.

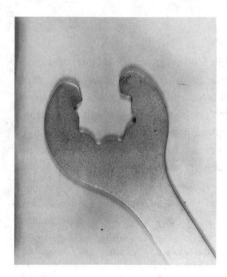

Fig. 8-7: This headset wrench fits Shimano headsets.

won't fit anything else. I miss the good old days when just a few tools would fit everything on all bikes. I think too many design engineers have been spawned. They don't have enough to do. They justify their existence by coming up with ridiculously complex products and nonstandard part sizes for a simple product, a bike. Shimano has special headset wrenches (Fig. 8-7), but they had the good sense to make the headset locknut and adjustable cup also take a standard 32-mm wrench.

2. A 5- or 6-mm Allen wrench or a 10-mm open-end wrench to fit your stem binder bolt (Fig. 8-8).

Fig. 8-8: Use an Allen wrench, as shown here, or a 10-mm wrench to loosen stem binder bolts.

Follow These Steps for Headset Maintenance

1. Remove the front wheel.

2. If you are working on an all-terrain bike, mark the stem where it comes out of the locknut with chalk, so you can replace it at the same height. This is important, because if you change the stem height, you will have to readjust the front brake shoe-to-rim clearance, as I noted in Chapter 1.

Fig. 8-9: The stem at left fits the large steering tube fork on Fisher ATBs. The stem at the right fits all other bikes.

3. Loosen the stem binder bolt about six turns with the Allen wrench or a 10-, 11-, or 12-mm wrench, but do not remove it all the way. The expansion bolt has a nut that expands against an angle cut in the stem (Figs. 8-9 and 8-10). As it's tightened, the expansion bolt wedges the stem tightly inside the fork steering tube. The stem bolt must be tapped down to break this wedge lock. Tap this bolt down with a hammer over a block of wood (Fig. 8-11). One firm tap should break it loose.

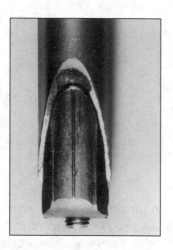

Fig. 8-10: *Stem binder bolts wedge against the fork steering tube and hold the stem firmly when this bolt is tightened.*

Fig. 8-11: *Remove the stem by loosening the stem binder bolt six or seven turns, then tapping it down with a block of wood and a hammer, as shown, to break the wedge fit.*

4. Remove the handlebars and stem (Fig. 8-12). Drape them over the top tube, out of the way.

5. Hold the adjustable cup with one wrench while you loosen the locknut with another wrench (Fig. 8-13). Remove the locknut and the washer under the locknut.

6. Loosen the adjustable cup (a.k.a. upper hand cup) until you can turn it by hand. Hold the fork in the bike frame with one hand while you unscrew and remove the adjustable cup. Carefully remove the fork. Most bikes these days have bearings in a retainer. However, in case the bearings are not in a retainer, be ready to catch loose bearings. Put a rag on the work bench, put the bike on it, and catch loose balls as you withdraw the fork.

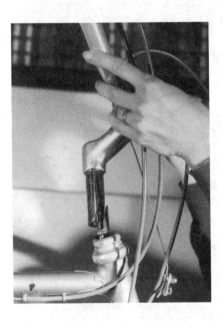

Fig. 8-12: Once the stem wedge fit is loosened, the stem and handlebars can be pulled up out of the steering tube and placed across the top tube, while you work on the headset bearings.

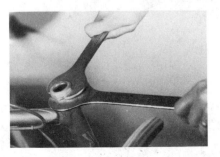

Fig. 8-13: To get at the bearings, hold the adjustable cup with one wrench (bottom) while you turn the locknut with the other wrench (top).

7. If the headset has a dust shield (Fig. 8-14), remove it so you can remove the ball bearings.

8. Remove the bearings. Clean off the old grease. If the bearings are in a retainer, check retainer and bearing wear. If the bearings easily fall out of the retainer, it's time to replace them, as noted below. In fact, I

Fig. 8-14: *Exploded view of a headset. Note that the ball retainer should be placed so its curvature follows the curvature of the cone or cup involved. Courtesy Shimano.*

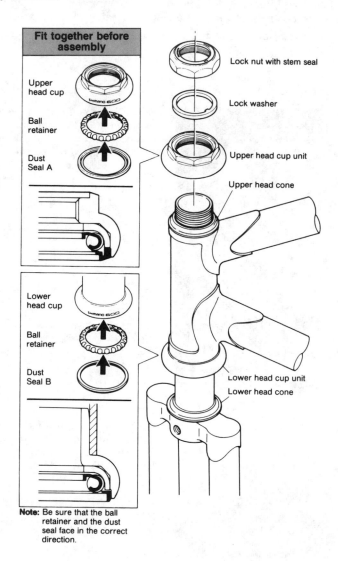

recommend always replacing headset balls every time you disassemble the headset. Balls are cheap; headset parts and labor are not.

9. Clean the old grease out of the adjustable cup, and the top and bottom cones and cup.

10. Examine the cups (Fig. 8-15) and cones (Fig. 8-16) for grooves, rust, or wear. If you see grooves or dents in the cups or cones, take your bike to the bike shop and have them replaced. Don't do this yourself; it's too complicated. For example, before replacing the entire headset, including fixed cones, you need to know the exact internal diameter (ID) of the head tube and the outside diameter (OD) of the steering tube. You also need to know the stack height, which is the steering tube length minus the head tube length. Headsets come in 37-, 40-, and 42.5-mm

Fig. 8-15: *If you see grooves worn in an adjustable cup, like this one, take your bike to the shop for a replacement cup.*

Fig. 8-16: *If grooves are worn in a cone, have the shop replace it.*

stack heights. Before installing a new headset, it is very important that the head tube be reamed with a head tube reamer tool. The fixed cone and cup must be aligned. These procedures require special tools and skills. A special press tool (Fig. 8-17) is used to install the fixed cone and cup. Have your bike shop check the seats (Fig. 8-18, 8-19, and 8-20) where the cones and cups fit, to make sure the factory has accurately machined them. If not, have them remachined so that the cups and cones seat accurately. This permits the bearings to absorb road shock evenly

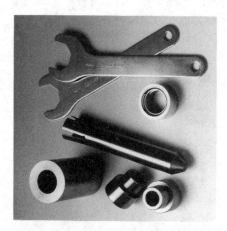

Fig. 8-17: Fixed headset cups and cone replacement is a job for the bike shop. Special tools, such as those shown here, and special skills are needed. The 40-mm wrenches at the top are for Fisher ATBs only. Courtesy Fisher Mountain Bikes

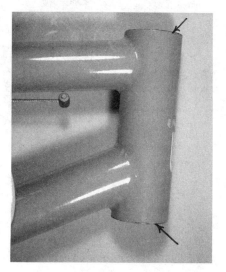

Fig. 8-18: The top and bottom surfaces of the head tube (arrows) must be specially machined for the cup (bottom) and cone (top) to seat accurately. In this photo, cup and cone are not installed.

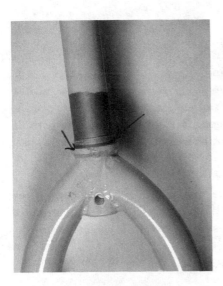

Fig. 8-19: The bottom cone fits over the base of the fork. This area (arrows) must be accurately machined to assure correct alignment of the headset components.

Fig. 8-20: An example of excellent bottom cone fit. The bottom cone takes a major share of road shock.

and wear uniformly. Uneven bearing wear can loosen the headset and cause wheel shimmy. Note: Fisher ATB headsets take a 40-mm wrench for the headset locknut and adjustable cone (Fig. 8-17). This size is unique to Fisher. At this writing, at least, no other bike uses 40-mm locknuts and adjustable cups.

Headset Reassembly

1. Headset bearings are inexpensive. But they can play a major role in safe bicycle handling, in avoiding wheel shimmy. My advice is to install new balls. Forget the retainer. Buy enough of the same size to replace the number of balls in the retainer plus two or three more. As you can see in Fig. 8-21, you can get more balls, at least two more, in the same space without the retainer. More balls means greater headset life and improved protection against bearing wear.

2. Reassemble the headset. Grease the bearings, cups (Fig. 8-22), and cones. Replace any seals. Note: If you leave the bearings in the retainer, be sure you replace the retainer correctly. The curvature of the retainer must be matched to the curvature of the cone (as shown in Fig. 8-14).

Fig. 8-21: Discard the retainer. You can fit an additional two or three balls (depending on headset size) for longer life. The bearing set at left is in a retainer. The cup at right holds bearings removed from the retainer at left. You can see there is room for two or three additional loose balls.

Fig. 8-22: Be generous with grease when replacing bearings. Use boat-trailer wheel-bearing grease, which resists water washout.

3. Place the bottom set of bearings in the bottom cup with enough grease to hold them in place. Replace any seals you have removed.

4. Put a lot of grease in the adjustable cup (Fig. 8-22). Replace ball bearings in the cup.

5. Replace the fork. Be careful not to knock any balls off the bottom cup. Hold the fork in place while you thread on the adjustable cup by hand, as far as possible.

6. Tighten the adjustable cup with a wrench until it is snug, then back it off a quarter turn.

7. Install the washer over the adjustable cup.

8. Thread on the locknut. Hold the adjustable cup with one wrench and tighten the locknut with the other wrench (Fig. 8-13).

9. Replace the handlebars. The stem should be at the height marked earlier. Remember, if you don't replace an ATB stem at the original height, you will have to readjust brake-shoe clearance, for which please see Chapter 1. Also, and this is very important, at least 2½ inches of the stem *must be inside the steering tube* (Fig. 8-23)! Otherwise the stem could snap under the stress of hard riding (Fig. 24), which is definitely an unhealthy situation.

10. Tighten the expander bolt to 175 to 260 inch/pounds.

11. Replace the front wheel.

Fig. 8-23: *Be sure at least 2½ inches of the stem (arrows) is inside the steering tube. Most stems have a safety scribe line which must not show above the headset locknut.*

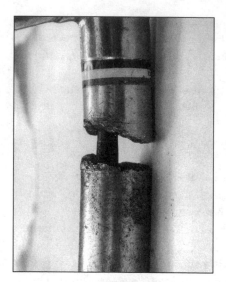

Fig. 8-24: *Stems can break and snap if not fitted far enough into the steering tube.*

12. Check the headset adjustable cup setting: Headset adjustment is so important I am going to repeat the instructions given earlier in this chapter:

a. Check for looseness. Mount the bike, both feet on the ground. Hold the front brake lever tightly closed. Rock the bike back and forth. If the fork feels loose, hold the adjustable cup with one wrench and turn the locknut counterclockwise one turn. Turn the adjustable cup clockwise a quarter turn, hold it with the wrench, and tighten the locknut. Repeat until the fork has no free play.

b. Check the headset for tightness. Lift the front heel off the ground and turn the handlebars in both directions. Tilt the bike so the handlebars move freely by gravity, without binding or tightness. If the handlebars stick or bind, hold the adjustable cup with a wrench, loosen the locknut, then loosen the adjustable cup a quarter turn and hold it with a wrench while you tighten the locknut. Repeat until the fork turns freely.

c. Check the stem binder bolt for tightness. Hold the front wheel between your knees. Try to twist the handlebars. If the handlebars turn but wheels do not, retighten the binder bolt. This is a very important safety check!

A good way to keep the headset from working loose is to install a SunTour headset clamp (Fig. 8-25). This unit prevents the locknut from loosening. Or install a Max System Bulldog Brace head and stem. This

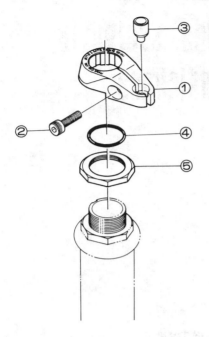

Fig. 8-25: Install a SunTour special lockring that keeps the headset from loosening under road shock. Courtesy SunTour.

headset lock has a set-screw lock plus tapered prongs and a clamping ring that locks the prongs against the handlebar stem. If your bike shop does not have this set, write to Cariberia Imports, Nevada 306, San Gerardo, Rio Piedras, Puerto Rico 00926, or phone 1-809-764-8422.

9

Pedals, Saddles, Seatposts, and Handlebars

PEDAL MAINTENANCE

The pedals on your bike sit closer to the ground than any other part except tires, so they take heavy wear from dust, dirt, and water. Their tiny ball bearings are subjected to pressure of 50 pounds in moderate pedaling, 170 pounds when racing, and 350 pounds by strong riders straining uphill. So pedals require periodic cleaning and lubrication, especially after hard riding over dusty roads or in rainy weather.

Here's how to maintain your ball-bearing–type pedals (Fig. 9-1) (for cartridge-type bearings see separate instructions later in this section).

Tools You Will Need

1. 8-, 10-, 11-, and 15-mm wrenches.
2. Special wrenches for your pedals if they don't take the tools above. See your bike shop.
3. Pedal vise (Fig. 7-2). (Same as the hub axle vise; has separate, smaller opening for pedal axles.)
4. 5- and 6-mm Allen wrenches for some Shimano pedals.
5. Special wrench for Shimano Dura-Ace pedals (Fig. 9-2) and some older Shimano pedals (Fig. 9-3).

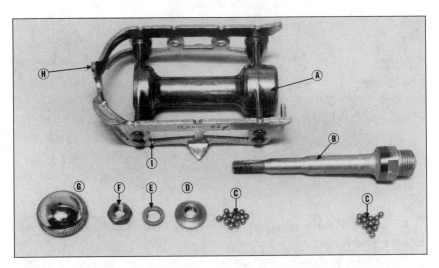

Fig. 9-1: *Conventional loose ball-bearing pedal. "A," pedal body; "B," axle; "C," ball bearings; "D," adjustable cone; "E," washer; "F," locknut; "G," dust cap; "H," rattrap.*

Fig. 9-2: *Exploded view of road pedal. "1," axle; "2," needle bearing set; "3," locknut; "4," spacer; "5," cup; "6," ball bearings; "7," body; "8," cleat holder nuts; "9," toe clip retainer plate; "10," toe clip; "11," cup; "12," special tool.* Courtesy Shimano.

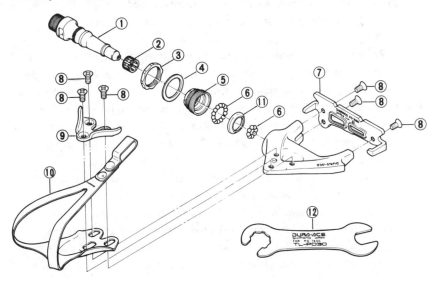

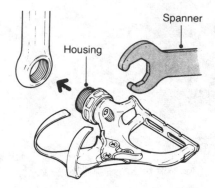

Fig. 9-3: Special wrench for pedal installation in crank. For some Shimano pedals. Courtesy Shimano.

6. Circlip (split washer) pliers for some makes of sealed cartridge bearing pedals.

7. Grease, preferably boat-trailer wheel-bearing grease.

Table 9-1 TORQUE REQUIREMENTS FOR PEDALS

Part	Torque (inch/pounds)
Pedal axle to crank	350
Adjustable cone locknut	70–130
Toe clip cage fixing bolts	22

Maintenance is straightforward. It simply involves getting access to the bearings, then removing, cleaning, and replacing them. Here's how:

1. Remove both pedals. Most pedal axle flats take a 15-mm wrench. A few makes use a 6-mm Allen wrench on the inside end of the axle. I don't want to get you all bogged down with right- and left-hand thread instructions. Just remember this: *pedals always thread on in the direction of crank rotation and, of course, thread off in the direction opposite crank rotation.* If you keep this in mind you can't go wrong. Also remember that most pedals have an "R" and an "L" stamped on the axle.

2. Put the threaded end of the pedal axle in a pedal vise (Fig. 7-2), and put that vise in a bench vise. (Note: this vise has a small-diameter hole for the pedal axle, a larger one for the hub axle.) Now you are ready to work on the pedal. You could skip using the pedal vise and just hold the pedal by the axle flats, the part you turn with a wrench. But the vise is much handier and eliminates the potential for thread damage.

3. Remove the dust cap (Fig. 9-1). You may need a special tool for this. To even get at the dust cap on some pedals, you have to remove the cage. Most take a 2-mm Allen wrench (Fig. 9-4).

4. With a 9-, 10-, or 11-mm wrench, turn the axle locknut (Fig. 9-5) counterclockwise and remove it and the washer (Fig. 9-6) under it.

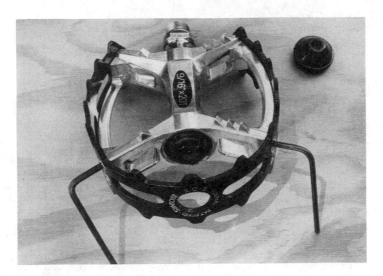

Fig. 9-4: *Use 2-mm Allen wrenches to remove rattrap section of the body, so you can get at the dust cap and other pedal parts.*

Fig. 9-5: *With dust cap removed, remove the locknut. This one takes a 10-mm wrench.*

Fig. 9-6: Remove the washer.

5. Remove the pedal from the axle vise and lay the pedal on a rag on the workbench, ready to catch the small, loose ball bearings.

6. Turn the adjustable cone (Fig. 9-7) counterclockwise and remove it.

7. Pull the axle out of the pedal body. Remove all the bearings (Fig. 9-8).

Fig. 9-7: Use a small screwdriver to remove the adjustable cone.

Fig. 9-8: Remove the bearings.

8. Clean the bearings, cones, and axle bearing faces.

9. Put a generous layer of grease on both cups in the pedal body.

10. Replace the balls in both pedal body cups.

11. Insert the axle in the pedal body. Be careful not to knock any balls out of the cups as the axle goes in.

12. Thread on the adjustable cone, hand-tight, as far as possible.

13. Replace the pedal in the axle vise.

14. Replace the washer and thread on the locknut.

15. Tighten the locknut while you hold the adjustable cup to keep it from turning.

16. Remove the pedal from the vise. Twist the axle between your thumb and forefinger. If it feels tight, loosen the locknut, back the adjustable cup off a quarter turn, and retighten the locknut as in Step 15 above. Now push the axle in and out and from side to side. If you feel play, loosen the locknut, tighten the adjustable cup a quarter turn, and retighten the locknut. Repeat these steps until the axle turns smoothly, without binding or looseness.

17. Replace the pedal cages.

18. Replace the pedals on the cranks. Start threads straight, so you don't cross-thread and strip them. Remember, the cranks are aluminum alloy, the pedal axles are steel. If you mangle the threads, have the bike shop rethread them with a tap (Fig. 9-9).

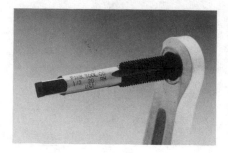

Fig. 9-9: Retap crank threads if they have been stripped. Pray a lot. If the threads are badly stripped, you may need a new crank.

Special Ball-Bearing Pedals

Some older Shimano pedals have a spindle diameter of 25 mm, versus 14 mm for conventional pedals. They fit only Shimano cranks with a 25-mm threaded bore. Maintenance procedures are a bit different from conventional loose ball-bearing pedals. If you have these pedals, here is how to maintain them:

1. Remove the strap. Remove the toe clips by unscrewing the three Phillips head screws (Fig. 9-10). There is just no way you are going to take this pedal apart conveniently without these steps.

2. Remove the pedal from the crank with a 30-mm wrench (Fig. 9-10). (*Install* the pedal with a 6-mm Allen wrench, *but do not remove it with that wrench.*)

3. There are, according to my count, fourteen 5/32-inch (2.5 mm) balls in the inner cone and eighteen in the outer cone. With a 5-mm Allen wrench in the locknut (refer to Fig. 9-2) and a 6-mm Allen wrench holding the cone (outer side), turn the locknut clockwise and remove it.

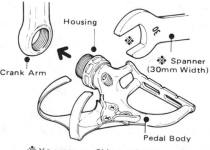

Housing

Crank Arm

Spanner (30mm Width)

Pedal Body

❖ You may use Shimano EX Head Parts exclusive tool (Model XB-420) when tightening.

Fig. 9-10: Use the 30-mm wrench to remove some older Shimano pedals from the crank.

Catch the tiny spacing washer ("6" in Fig. 9-2) as the locknut comes out. Don't lose it; your dealer will have a tough time replacing it until Shimano stocks build up on this new pedal. (If you do lose it, it will help if you ask for Shimano part number 461 0800.)

4. The locknut ("2" in figure 9-2) holds the whole shebang together. Hold the cone with the 6-mm Allen wrench and turn the locknut counterclockwise one or two turns, just enough to take pressure off the cone threads ("4" in Fig. 9-2). Fig. 9-11 illustrates the position of the two Allen wrenches. The locknut is going to be very tight, believe me, so use some muscle on it. You may have to put the 6-mm wrench in a vise. Once the locknut is loose, back out on the cone with the 6-mm Allen wrench, and the works will come apart (Fig. 9-12). Be ready to catch the balls. Clean and regrease them.

5. Stick the balls back in a layer of grease in the right-side housing ("4," Fig. 9-2). Now, you may think you can do the same with the left side of the housing, but you can't, because the cone won't go in that way. You have to stick the balls back in a layer of grease on the cone itself and reassemble as follows.

Reassembly Steps

1. Refer to Figure 9-2 and to the set of fourteen balls at the left, next to the cone, part "4." These are the balls you have to stick on the cone. Okay, now we have balls on the cone and inside the housing; fourteen on the cone, eighteen in the housing. Now, holding the pedal body (platform) in one hand (left hand if you are right-handed), put the left-side housing back onto the right-side housing, holding the pedal upright with your other hand. Still holding the pedal, take the cone with the balls held by grease and with the flat washer on the end held with grease, and put it inside the housing (part "4"). Gently, by hand, turn the cone clockwise until it is hand-tightened. With the 6-mm Allen wrench, tighten the cone so that it is just snug. Then tighten the locknut. Check for binding or looseness. *Adjustment of the cone does not depend on adjustment of the locknut.* Adjust the cone to remove any binding or looseness, then tighten the locknut. The locknut holds whatever adjustment you have made on the cone. Reinstall the toe clip.

2. Install the toe strap. The strap should have its Velcro fixing system facing outward. When you replace the toe clip, remember that the front plate ("12," Fig. 9-2) goes on top of the toe clip. (If you lose one of these special beveled screws, reference to Shimano part number 000 1900

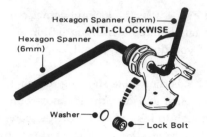

Fig. 9-11: Use a 5-mm Allen wrench to adjust the bearings on this type of Shimano pedal.

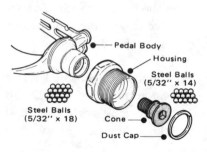

Fig. 9-12: Bearings are located on both sides of the pedal housing.

Fig. 9-13: Pedal housing.

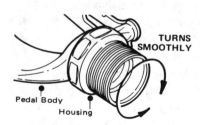

Fig. 9-14: Adjust housing so bearings do not bind, or are not too loose.

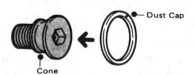

Fig. 9-15: Replace the cone and its dust cap.

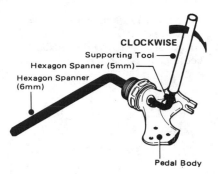

Fig. 9-16: *Use 5-mm and 6-mm Allen wrenches to adjust bearing play.*

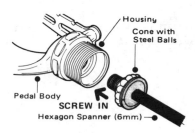

Fig. 9-17: *Hold outboard bearings in place with grease while you install the race.* Figs. 9-10 to 9-17, courtesy Shimano.

will help your dealer order more.) Figs. 9-11 to 9-17 illustrate major steps in assembly and disassembly. A final word about bearing adjustment: if you have binding or looseness, you have to back off on the locknut before making any adjustments. Then retighten the locknut.

Cartridge-Type Bearings

These bearings use standard industrial cartridge bearings, available from a bearing supply house or from a small electrical motor repair shop (if your bike shop doesn't stock them). Figs. 9-18 and 9-19 show cutaway views of these pedals.

You can't get at the bearings on Phil Wood pedals, so forget about maintaining them. When they go dry and get cranky, you could return the pedals to Phil (see your bike shop) for bearing replacement, which takes special tools.

Cartridge Bearing Maintenance

1. Remove the pedals.
2. Remove the cage (Fig. 9-4).

Fig. 9-18: Cutaway view of a sealed housing pedal. Note that there is a circlip (split washer) that holds the bearings in place.

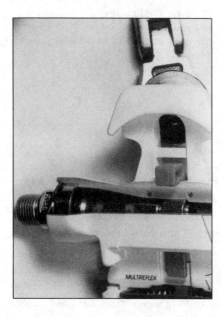

Fig. 9-19: Another make of sealed bearing pedal.

3. Remove the axle bearing retainer bolt.

4. Carefully tap the axle out of the pedal body.

5. Carefully pry off the bearing seals with a thin-bladed knife.

6. Stuff lots of grease into the bearings (Fig. 9-20) and press the seals back in place. Replace the circlip (split washer) if one is used.

7. Carefully tap the axle back into the pedal body.

8. Replace the pedals on the cranks.

Fig. 9-20: *Sealed bearing pedal with dust cap pried off.*

ABOUT SADDLES, SELECTION AND ADJUSTMENTS

What you sit on and steer with are both major contributors to cycling comfort—or pain. When it comes to saddles, I prefer one made of leather, preferably one with springs that absorb road shock (Fig. 9-21). A leather saddle will have give because the leather shapes and molds itself to your anatomy. As it conforms to you, the leather saddle offers support where you need it most.

A plastic saddle, on the other hand, will never shape itself to you. The plastic has little give or bounce. Even gel-filled plastic saddles, or saddle covers, cannot, in my opinion, begin to challenge the comfort of a leather saddle. Ask any cowpoke or equestrian or mounted cop.

Excellent high-quality leather saddles have been made by Brooks since the early 1900s. The Brooks Conquest two-wire dual spring saddle (Fig. 9-21) costs about $39.95 from any good bike shop. This is the rugged, comfortable model I recommend for trail or road riding. It weighs 30.3 ounces. A 16.7-ounce version, the Brooks Team Professional, without springs, costs the same. I prefer the spring-loaded comfort of the

Fig. 9-21: *A leather saddle will shape itself to your special anatomy. This is a four-rail saddle held by an adapter in a seat post designed for a two-rail saddle.*

Conquest, or the current two-wire version of this four-wire springed saddle. It surely does reduce fatigue on long, bumpy rides.

Leather Saddle Selection and Care

Keep your fine leather saddle (I'll cover other saddle materials below) in shape for years of riding comfort. Here's how:

1. *Break-in:* Time and miles are the only way to break in a new leather saddle. It takes at least 500 miles of riding to make a new saddle pliable enough to fit your anatomy. It's worth it. You could also ride your leather saddle on a bike exerciser, which is how I break in my own leather saddles.

Don't try to break in a new leather saddle by soaking it in neat's-foot oil. This will over-soften the leather, so that it will become swaybacked.

2. *Leather preservation:*

a. first, brush the saddle with a soft, dry cloth.

b. For a new saddle, apply a light coat of a good leather preservative, such as Brooks Proofide, to the top portion of the saddle. Use a soft cloth.

c. Let the preservative dry, preferably overnight, so it soaks into the leather.

d. Polish the saddle with a soft cloth.

e. Apply the preservative after every ride through rain. This is especially important if your bike does not have fenders to keep water and dirt off your saddle.

f. Never apply heat to the saddle to dry the preservative. If the saddle is water-soaked, dry it at room temperature before applying preservative. Note: Some leather saddles, such as the Brooks Team Pro Special, are prestretched and dressed with preservative, so the initial dressing is unnecessary.

3. *Saddle adjustments:* A leather saddle will stretch. If you can depress the saddle by pushing hard on it, it's time to take out the stretch. Remove this stretch by turning the stretch adjuster, located at the nose of the saddle ("B" in Fig. 9-22).

Four-Wire Adapter

If you have one of the older Brooks saddles, the kind with four rails (Fig. 9-23), you should install an adapter (Fig. 9-24) to keep the wires from bending. Modern seat posts are made for two-wire saddles. The

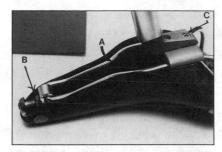

Fig. 9-22: *Remove leather saddle stretch at the adjuster bolt, "B." "A" shows the rails, "C" shows the seat post tilt adjuster bolt.*

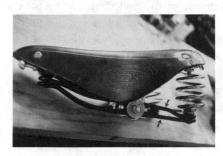

Fig. 9-23: *This four-rail saddle is held in a seat-post clamp designed for it. Use an adapter on other types of seat posts so you do not bend a rail.*

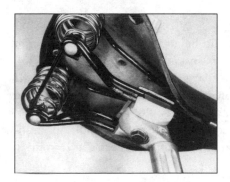

Fig. 9-24: *This adapter holds a four-rail saddle in a two-rail seat post. Your bike shop should have this adapter in stock.*

new two-wire model can be installed on any standard seat post. If you install a four-wire rail saddle on a seat post built for two rails, the wire can bend, especially if you are a heavyweight. When the saddle wire bends, the saddle will tilt off-center. You can prevent this by using an adapter, which costs about $9.95. Insert the adapter so it clamps all four saddle rails (Fig. 9-24). The adapter comes with a longer seat post clamp bolt because the four-wire saddles are wider. The adapter fits Campagnolo Gran Sport and Nuevo Record, Sugino and S.R. twin bolt, LaPrade, and many other makes of seat posts.

Wider leather saddles are available for women, as a woman's pelvic area is a bit wider than a man's, and these saddles can be more comfortable.

Non-Leather Saddles

Plastic saddles, even foam-filled models, will never shape to your anatomy. On the other hand, they don't need breaking in, won't stretch, are immune to water, dust, and dirt, and require little or no maintenance. Because they're lighter (as low as 9 ounces for the Selle San Italia Turbo, the model with alloy wires, for $25) in contrast to leather saddles (16.6 ounces for the Brooks Team Pro, $35.96), racing cyclists like them. A combination leather-and-gel saddle holds promise. It's the Vetta Leather Gel Turbo. It weighs 14 ounces and costs $34.95. Wider plastic saddles for women, such as the Avocet GelFlex ($30), are also available. If you like your saddle but it's a pain on long rides, you could cover it with a Spenco elastic polymer pad that distributes pressure more evenly and absorbs road shocks. It costs about $23.

Saddle Adjustments

The first cardinal rule about saddle height is *always make sure that at least 2½ inches of the seat post is inside the seat tube* (Fig. 9-25). Otherwise you risk breaking off the seat post or the seat post cluster. If the seat post is too short, install a longer one (Fig. 9-26). Seat posts come 300-mm long, and in 25.4-, 25.8-, 26-, 26.2-, 26.4-, 26.6-, 26.8-, 27-, and 27.2-mm widths (to convert millimeters to inches, multiply millimeters by .03937). For fat tube aluminum bikes, there's a 25-mm × 250-mm seat post.

Saddle Tilt

Adjust saddle tilt by loosening the saddle clamp bolt (Figs. 9-27 and 9-28). (These bolts differ in size and type, according to make of seat post.) Move the nose of the saddle up or down and retighten the clamp bolt to 175 to 350 inch/pounds. Most people seem to find a comfortable saddle tilt to be just slightly nose down, about 10 degrees from horizontal. If the saddle is tilted too far down, your body is thrust forward and too much weight is placed on the arms. The result is sore arm muscles and pain in the palm of your hands. If the saddle tilt is too far upward, you

Fig. 9-25: Keep at least 2½ inches of the seat post inside the seat tube. Otherwise the seat-post cluster could break, especially on an aluminum frame, or the seat post itself could snap.

Fig. 9-26: Install a longer seat post if you can't keep 2½ inches of the seat post inside the seat tube. The spring gadget is for all-terrain bikes. Once adjusted to your normal riding height, it lets you shove the saddle down for safe runs downhill. At the top, releasing the quick-release pops the saddle up to normal height again.

Fig. 9-27: Adjust saddle tilt and fore-and-aft distance from the handlebars by adjusting the height of each of these two seat-post bolts.

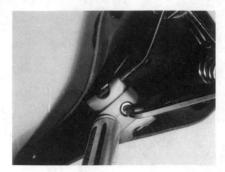

Fig. 9-28: *One Allen wrench is all it takes to adjust saddle tilt and fore-and-aft position on this modern seat post.*

tend to slip backward on the saddle and have arm strain from holding onto the handlebars to keep from this slip. You also can have NCP, a.k.a. numb crotch pain. (No, that's not a contradiction. Numbness can be a form of pain.)

You can also move the saddle closer to or farther away from the handlebars to suit your upper torso and arm length. However, this is a very limited option. If your bike is badly sized to you, moving the saddle in any direction won't compensate. But if the bike fits you, back and forth saddle adjustment may make the difference between arm strain and comfort. The ideal saddle position is when the nose of the saddle is directly above a plumb line intersecting the middle of the bottom bracket. Don't worry too much about this adjustment. All that counts is that the saddle-to-handlebar distance is comfortable for you. And that's a decision only you can make. Make this adjustment by loosening the saddle clamp binder bolt and moving the saddle farther from or closer to the handlebars. Do this in increments of a half inch until you find the position most comfortable for you.

ABOUT SEAT POSTS

High-quality bikes have a precision seat tube that allows the seat post to smoothly slide up and down when you wish to readjust saddle height. Grease the seat post to make saddle height adjustments easier. Your bike shop can ream out your seat tube if the seat post won't slide easily inside it.

Do not force a seat post that doesn't quite fit, or use one that fits *loosely!* Hammering down an oversize seat post only destroys the bike frame, or leads to major bike shop surgery to remove it. Too small a seat post may not be held securely by the seat post quick-release (Fig. 9-29) or binder bolt (please review the data on how to use a quick-release in Chapter 7). As a result, the saddle may move down when you least expect it. The seat post must slide snugly, but smoothly, up and down in the seat tube.

A recent innovation, a hydraulic seat post (Fig. 9-30), is claimed to reduce road shock to your upper body, make unnecessary a change of rider position or style when meeting rough terrain, and improve braking and handling on descents. Called a HydraPost, it comes in the stock sizes noted above, weighs 25 ounces, and costs about $74.95. A titanium version weighs 18 ounces, but the price is not available at this writing. Get it from your bike shop, or write Knapp Engineering, 1081 Graham Ave., Kent, Ohio 44240, or call 1-800-343-7951. Also, a spring-loaded seat post is made by Sakae.

Fig. 9-29: *Seat-post quick-release works just like a wheel quick-release. See Chapter 7 for details.*

Fig. 9-30: *A hydraulic seat post absorbs the slings and arrows of discomfort on rough roads and trails.*

HANDLEBARS: FLAT VS. DOWNTURNED, AND OTHER TYPES

Flat handlebars permit a more upright riding stance, and a better road view than downturned handlebars, which is a safety factor in city cycling. The wide, flat bars also provide high leverage for muscling the front wheel straight while traversing stubborn rocky and potholed terrain which tries to wrest steering control from you.

The downturned bars give you four places to rest your hands. You can put your hands in two places on top of the bars, halfway down the curve, and at the bottom end of the curve where it aims back at you.

All-Terrain Handlebars

Tailor flat bars to your reach. Twist them in the stem, if you have a separate stem and bars. Or, you could clamp Onza bar extenders on your flat handlebars for $36.95. For ATB bikes, the Scott AT-4 bar (Fig. 9-31) fits most ATB stems, gives you a much wider range of hand positions, costs $42.95, and replaces the flat handlebars. The Profile XCR Bar Extension (Fig. 9-32), $59.95, fits onto the ends of flat handlebars to give you many more hand positions for when you ride on the road to get to the trail. Or just on the road.

New Road-Bike Handlebars

You can clip the Mavic aero bar, $109.95, on your downturned bars. Adjust both overall bar length and elevated elbow pads. Fine-tune the pad cups to your elbow position. The Profile Aero I racing bar (Fig. 9-

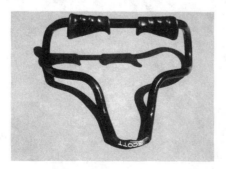

Fig. 9-31: For more hand positions, replace flat handlebars with this Scott AT-4 handlebar.

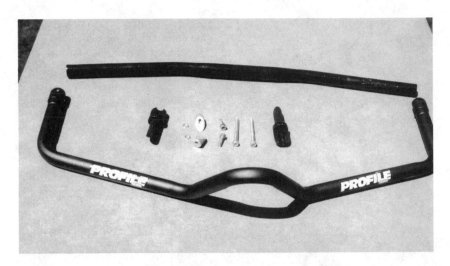

Fig. 9-32: *Snap this Profile XCB Bar Extension into the ends of your existing flat handlebars for a wider range of handlebar positions.*

33), $79.95, comes in three reach sizes. The Aero II clip-on bar (Fig. 9-34), $64.95, can be fastened to your regular handlebars. Ideal for time trials, the Scott DH handlebar, $69.95, has grip pads and allows eight different hand positions. The Scott/LeMond clip-on bar (Fig. 9-35), $59.95, is easily clipped onto or removed from downturned handlebars, and comes in three lengths.

I am indebted to Performance Bike Shop for the data on the new ATB and road-bike handlebar designs above. They have a terrific catalog. See the appendix for more information.

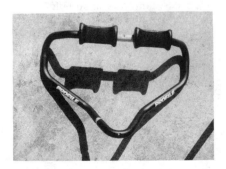

Fig. 9-33: *Replace downturned handlebars with this Profile Aero I racing bar. Comes in 18 inch or "long reach" for folks with longer arms and/or upper torso.*

Fig. 9-34: Clamp this Profile Aero II onto your downturned handlebars. It has padded elbow rests and adjustable reach.

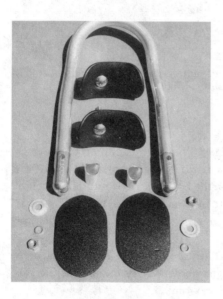

Fig. 9-35: Scott clip-on handlebar is the one Greg LeMond used in his Tour de France victory. Pads are adjustable, and it fits all downturned handlebars.

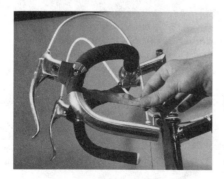

Fig. 9-36: Start taping downturned handlebars about an inch from the stem. Loop a couple of turns around the brake lever body, as shown.

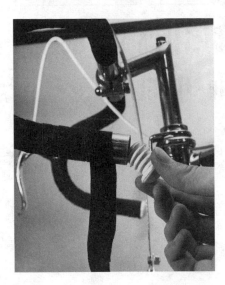

Fig. 9-37: Finish taping handlebars down to the end of the drop. Leave two inches of the tape to stuff into the ends of the handlebars. Shove the bar end plug in with the tape.

Handlebar Padding

Until a few years ago, canvas tape was the preferred cover padding for handlebars. It has the advantage of allowing a firm grip for accurate steering control. Now tape also comes in Lycra polypropylene, imitation leather that's self-adhesive, and cushioned vinyl tape. I prefer the Cinelli cork ribbon self-adhesive tape. To apply the tape, start at the top, near the stem. Overlap each layer and wrap a few turns around the brake body (as shown in Fig. 9-36). Leave an inch or so loose to stuff into the handlebar end (Fig. 9-37), and shove in a plug at each end. For a foam-type pad, install Grab-on Maxi grips.

Install a hydraulic steering damper if you have trouble controlling steering on bumpy terrain. It's made by Odyssey, and I can report that it does work. It's adjustable for the amount of turning resistance you need for the terrain you're on. See your bike dealer or write Odyssey, 17101 S. Central Ave., #G, Carson, CA 90746.

10

Care and Repair of Tires for Road, Trail, and Track

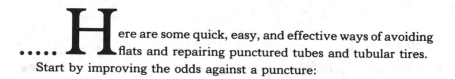

H ere are some quick, easy, and effective ways of avoiding flats and repairing punctured tubes and tubular tires. Start by improving the odds against a puncture:

1. *Reduce impact on your tires* and the chance of a blowout as you come to an obstruction, such as a pothole. Pull back on the handlebars as the front wheel comes to a tire-threatening obstacle. Move forward on the saddle as the rear wheel does the same.

2. *Protect your tubes from punctures by street debris.* Install a heavy-duty plastic tire liner, such as Mr. Tuffy, between the tire and the tube. This liner comes in sizes to fit most tires. In areas where barbed thorns can cause many flats, such as the Southwest, use a thicker, thorn-resistant tube. You could also switch to a semisolid tire called the Poly-Air. It has no inner tube so it is immune to punctures. If you can't find them at your bike shop, write Poly-Air Tires, Inc., 205, 259 Midpark Way, S.E., Calgary, Alberta, Canada T2X 1M2; phone: 403-256-9562. I can report that these tires offer the same, or nearly the same, comfort as pneumatic tires.

3. *Remove anything stuck in your tires,* such as glass shards, nails, thorns, and small stones in the tread, before each ride.

4. *Replace worn tires and those with weather-cracked sidewalls.* The cost of new tires is a small price to pay to avoid accident-causing tire failure.

5. *Alternate braking between front and rear wheels* on long downhill runs, to avoid heat buildup that could cause a blowout.

6. *Match a new tire to your rim width.* ATB tire tread widths vary from 2.25 inches to 1.5 inches. Bead widths of these tires can vary even within the same sizes. Wheel rim widths are more or less standardized to .669, .834, and .992 inches. As a general rule, use the wider tires with the wider rims. If you put a wide tire on a narrow rim you risk a bead pop-out with a blowout.

7. *Keep tires inflated to the correct pressure.* For trail, off-road rides, keep at least 35 p.s.i. in the tire. For road use you increase the pressure to 50 to 75 p.s.i., depending on the make of tire. Tire sidewalls usually give safe pressure ranges. An underinflated tire can bottom out and puncture; an overinflated tire can pop off the rim.

8. *Scan the road ahead.* Watch for anything on the road immediately in front of your bike that could cause a puncture. Be ready to take evasive action.

Always carry a patch kit and tire levers. Bring a roll of duct tape (ask your hardware store clerk). Use it to patch slits and large holes in the tire that would cut the tube and make another puncture. The duct tape can get you home, where you can replace the tire. Spare tubes keep you on the move. Patch the punctured tube later, around the campfire. Fold-up tires spell security. Stow them in your bike bag or strap them on your carrier or under your seat. If you destroy a tire on a razor-sharp rock, the spare tire will keep you going.

Tools You Will Need

1. Patch kit.
2. Duct tape for emergency tire-casing repair.
3. Piece of chalk (carry it in your patch kit to mark leak location).

Steps in Tire Repair

1. Release remaining air from the tube by holding down the valve core. Use a twig or pencil on a Schraeder valve (the fat kind like those on automobile tires), or unscrew its core (Fig. 10-1). Unscrew a Presta valve core and hold it down (Fig. 10-2).

2. Remove the wheel from the bicycle.

3. Squeeze both sides of the tire together, all the way around the wheel, to break the bond between the tire bead and the rim. Remove the valve nut from a Presta valve.

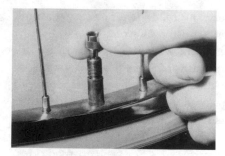

Fig. 10-1: Remove air from a Schrae-der valve by holding down, or remov-ing, the valve core.

Fig. 10-2: Remove air from a Presta valve by unscrewing the valve core, then holding it down.

4. Remove the tire from the rim, starting on the side opposite the valve. If the tire is stubborn, use two tire levers, one to hold the tire off the rim, and the other to separate the tire bead from the rim (Fig. 10-3). Once you get about ten inches of the bead off, you should be able to remove the rest of the bead with one lever or with your fingers.

5. Remove the tire. Remove the tube from the tire.

6. Pump air into the tube so you can find the leak (Fig. 10-4).

7. Use one of these three ways to find the leak:

a. Dunk the tube in water. Watch for the source of air bubbles (Fig. 10-5).

Fig. 10-3: *Start tire removal on side opposite the valve.*

Fig. 10-4: *Pump up the tube to check for location of leak.*

Fig. 10-5: *Dunk the tube in water, watch for bubbles that tell location of puncture.*

   b. If water isn't available, try listening for the hiss of escaping air.

   c. Or put the tube next to your cheek to feel escaping air (Fig. 10-6).

   d. Circle the leak(s) with chalk, a pen, or anything that will leave a mark on the tube (Fig. 10-7).

   8. Roughen the area around the puncture with the sandpaper (Fig. 10-8) that came with your patch kit. Don't use a metal scraper; it can weaken the tube.

Fig. 10-6: Or put the tube next to your cheek, feel escaping air.

Fig. 10-7: Circle puncture location with chalk.

Fig. 10-8: Scrape area around puncture with fine sandpaper.

9. Put a few drops of patch rubber cement around the puncture area (Fig. 10-9). Spread it out with the nozzle of the glue tube and wait a minute until it gets tacky.

10. Peel the backing paper off a patch (Fig. 10-10). Put the patch on the puncture and press it down firmly with your fingers.

11. Pump up the tube and check it again for punctures and leaks as above. Moisten the top of the valve to make sure the valve core is seated. If you see bubbles, tighten the valve core. If the valve still leaks on a Schraeder valve, buy a new valve core from your bike shop or a

Fig. 10-9: *Apply glue sparingly around puncture, let it get tacky.*

Fig. 10-10: *Peel backing off patch, apply patch to puncture.*

service station. Presta valve cores aren't replaceable. If the Presta valve is damaged, you will need a new tube.

12. Thoroughly inspect the inside of the tire casing, sidewalls, and tread for whatever caused the puncture. Remove all foreign embedments. If you find a slit in the tire casing, roughen the cut area on the inside of the tire with sandpaper. Cover that area with patch cement. When the cement dries, cover the cut with a piece of duct tape. Otherwise the slit can puncture the tube. Replace a slit tire as soon as possible.

13. If you have a major cut in the tube and no spare tube, put multiple patches over the slit, then apply duct tape around the patches. Pray a lot. If you're lucky you may have a slow leak but can make it home.

14. If you don't have a tire lever, remove the quick-release unit from the hub and use its lever (Fig. 10-11). It works. I know.

15. Check your patch kit every so often to make sure an already-opened tube of rubber cement hasn't dried out. Keep a couple of extra patch kits in your bike bag.

16. Remove the rim strip (Fig. 10-12). Snip off any spokes that protrude from the nipples and could puncture the tube. Install a new rim strip (Fig. 10-13) if necessary. Beware of rims with recessed spoke

Fig. 10-11: Use quick-release lever if you did not bring a tire lever.

Fig. 10-12: Check rim strip. If it is cut or torn, replace it.

Fig. 10-13: Use a tough rim strip, like this one.

Fig. 10-14: Note that sharp edges of recessed spoke holes can poke through rim strip and into the tube, causing a puncture.

holes (Fig. 10-14). The sharp edges of these holes can work right through a cheap rim strip and the tube, and cause a puncture. Use fiberglass or other reinforced rim strip. Get a size of rim strip that fits your rim width; they come in a wide variety of sizes.

Reassemble the Tire and Tube

1. Lay the tire on a flat surface and put the tube in (Fig. 10-15).
2. If the tire has a directional tread (check sidewall), make sure it faces the direction of wheel rotation.

Fig. 10-15: Lay tire flat, insert tube.

3. Place the tire and tube over the rim and push the valve stem through the rim hole (Fig. 10-16).

4. Place one side of the tire on the rim. Fit the tire on in both directions from the valve (Fig. 10-17). Continue until one side is fitted completely on the rim.

5. Turn the wheel over and finish fitting the tire on the rim, again working evenly from both sides of the valve (Fig. 10-18). You should be able to work by hand. If you have trouble, use the tire lever but be careful not to squeeze and puncture the tube between the tire lever and the rim.

Fig. 10-16: Lay tire, with tube, over rim. Insert valve through valve hole in rim.

Fig. 10-17: Start at the valve, push tire onto rim.

Fig. 10-18: Finish tire installation on side opposite valve.

6. Make sure the tire seats evenly in the rim, especially at the valve area (Fig. 10-19). Push the valve down into the tire about an inch, then squeeze the tire walls until the tire is seated in the rim; otherwise, the tire wall will protrude and cause a blowout.

7. Pump the tire up. If you have Presta valves, remember these are fragile and easily broken (Fig. 10-20) if you don't hold the pump steady as you use the plunger (if you use a frame-mounted pump). Hold the pump on the valve as shown in Fig. 10-21. Remove the pump from a Presta valve with a sharp downward blow from the side of your hand

Fig. 10-19: Lift tire up at the valve, inspect bead, make sure it is securely inside the rim edge before inflating.

Fig. 10-20: Presta valves are easily broken, like this one, if you wiggle the pump as you inflate the tire.

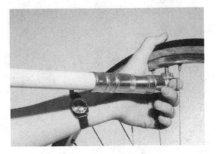

Fig. 10-21: Hold the pump tightly, as shown, especially on Presta valves, to prevent valve breakage.

(Fig. 10-22). Don't try to wiggle it off; that's a good way to bend and break the valve stem. Replace the valve nut on a Presta valve (Fig. 10-23).

8. Inspect the tire sidewalls to be sure the bead is evenly seated, all the way around, in the wheel rim. If not, deflate, reseat, and pump the tire up. Fig. 10-24 shows a tire about to blow out because of improper seating in the rim. Figs. 10-25 and 10-26 show how a tire bead is held in a rim.

Fig. 10-22: Remove pump with a sharp, straight down punch as shown. Do not wiggle the pump off a Presta valve.

Fig. 10-23: Replace the valve nut on a Presta valve, after inflating tire.

Fig. 10-24: Check that tire is inside the rim wall. Here the tire has popped out after inflation because it was not securely seated.

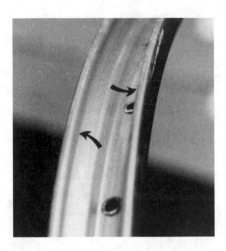

Fig. 10-25: *Arrows point to rim walls. Overhanging bead on metal rim walls hold tire in place.*

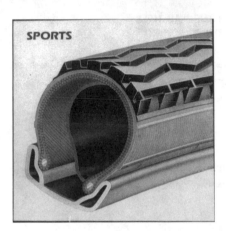

Fig. 10-26: *Here you can see how the tire bead is clamped by the rim walls.* Courtesy Michelin.

A WORD ABOUT PUMPS

A good pump is vital any time you leave home. Clip a pump to the top tube for convenient carrying on a road bike. But on an all-terrain bicycle, frame-mounted pumps can be scraped off as you negotiate a narrow, brushy trail, so a pump that also serves as the seat post on an ATB (Fig. 10-27) is handy. At least you won't have to worry about losing it. Since ATB fat tires take a lot of air, skinny road tire pumps take a long time to fill fat tires. Use a high-volume pump instead if you want to carry a

Fig. 10-27: This seat tube doubles as a tire pump.

frame-mounted pump. For home use, the double-barrel floor unit (Fig. 10-28) pumps air on both the up and down strokes of the plunger. All pumps are available with either a Schraeder or a Presta head.

HOW TO REPAIR TUBULAR TIRES

To repair tubular tires, you will have to cut a few stitches in the area where the puncture is located, repair the puncture, and restitch the tire. To repair tubulars, follow this procedure:

1. You will need a patch kit (Fig. 10-29) consisting of:

a. Special thin-tube patches (such as the ones made by Dunlop).
b. A triangular-pointed hand-sewing needle.
c. Tubular tire linen thread.
d. Rubber cement.
e. A small tube of talcum powder.
f. A small piece of yellow chalk.
g. A small screwdriver.
h. A sharp knife or razor blade.
i. A small square of *fine* sandpaper.

Bicycle mail-order houses sell a tubular tire repair kit with most of the above items. The reason for the extra-thin tube patches is that tubulars have a very thin tube. An ordinary tire patch is far too thick for this type of tube. It would cause a lump inside the tubular which would thump annoyingly on the road. Thin patches are especially needed for the lighter track-racing tubulars, which are generally handmade from silk cord and rubber latex. An old piece of tubular tube will do in an emergency.

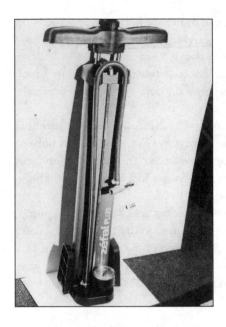

Fig. 10-28: *Double-barreled floor pump for road or ATB tires provides pressure on both up- and down-strokes of pump handle. (Also ideal for pumping up car tires.)*

Fig. 10-29: *Patch kit for tubular tire tube repair.*

2. If you have an old rim, mount the tubular on the rim, inflate it to 60 to 70 pounds of air pressure, and set the tire and rim in a half-filled washtub. Or simply remove the tubular from the wheel, inflate as above, and put it, a bit at a time, into the washtub. If you can see no puncture, you could have a loose or torn valve or a puncture at the valve area.

3. As you insert the tubular into the tub of water, you will notice that a lot of air seems to be bubbling up from around the valve stem first. The tubular is sewn and has a rubber-cemented strip over the sewing, so this is about the only place air can escape, except through the puncture itself. Rotate the tubular slowly until you come to the spot where air is seeping out through a small puncture in the tire casing. With a piece of yellow chalk, mark this area; it is also the location of the tube puncture. Deflate the tubular and remove it from the rim.

4. With the small screwdriver or another flat (but not sharp!) tool, carefully pull about 2½ inches of the tape on both sides of the puncture away from the inner circumference of the tire (Fig. 10-30).

5. With the razor or small sharp knife, carefully cut the stitching about 2 inches on either side of the puncture (Fig. 10-31). Do not cut down into the tire. Insert the knife edge under the stitching and cut upward to avoid cutting into the tube, which lies just under the stitching. Note: If you are a surgeon, you'll do well here.

6. Pull about 4 inches of the tube out gently and, with a hand pump, inflate the tube enough to find the puncture. With the yellow chalk, outline the puncture, centering it in a chalked circle about the size of a quarter. A simple way to find the puncture is to hold the tube near your lips and rotate it slowly. You should be able to feel the flow of air from

Fig. 10-30: Peel tire liner away from puncture area. Note chalk mark on sidewall showing puncture location.

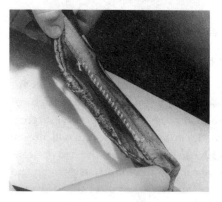

Fig. 10-31: Cut stitches with upward stroke to avoid cutting tube.

the puncture. If you can't find the puncture this way, put a drop of liquid soap in a glass, fill it with warm water, and coat the tube with this mixture until you find a bubble marking the location of the puncture.

7. Dry the tube thoroughly, if you have wet it. With the sandpaper, lightly abrade the area you have marked off around the puncture. Put a small, solid object under the tube to support it as you rub it *lightly* with the sandpaper.

8. Apply several light coatings of rubber cement to the abraded area. Let each coating dry to a hard glaze (Fig. 10-32).

9. Apply a patch of finest-grade thin rubber patch to the tube over the puncture. Note that two patches have been applied to this tube (Fig. 10-33). This is because whatever causes the flat often goes through both sides of the tube. Check the other side of the tube from where you found the first puncture to make sure that that side also hasn't been penetrated. Dust with talcum powder (Fig. 10-34) to prevent the tube from sticking to the casing.

10. Reinflate the tube slightly with the hand pump. Check the area for further punctures. Deflate the tube.

Fig. 10-32: Apply thin layer of patch cement around puncture, let it dry.

Fig. 10-33: Peel off patch cover, apply patch over puncture. Here two patches are used because the puncture penetrated through to both sides of tube.

Fig. 10-34: Squirt talcum powder over patches so tube will not stick to the tire.

11. Inspect the tire casing for damage, such as nail or glass cuts (Fig. 10-35), bruises, gouges, rips, tears, and the rare manufacturing defect. If the tire casing itself is damaged, I recommend relegating the tire to the spare-use-only category. This is because although the casing damage, if the bruise or hole is small, can be patched with a thin piece of canvas (Fig. 10-36) applied with rubber cement, even this patch will bulge and cause the tire to thump annoyingly, especially at high speeds. Tubular-

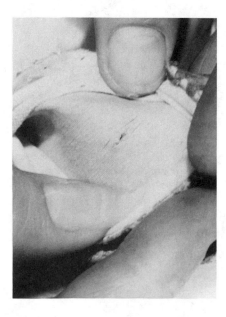

Fig. 10-35: Inspect inside of tire for cuts.

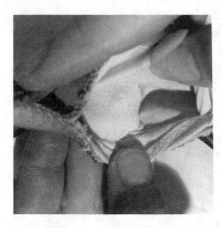

Fig. 10-36: Apply canvas patch over tire cut. Keeps cut from squeezing and puncturing tube as you ride.

tire repair kits do come with a special piece of canvas for this purpose, but I recommend its use for emergency situations only. Patched tires can, of course, serve as spares.

12. Sew up the tire, using the triangular-pointed needle (Fig. 10-37) and doubled thread. In an emergency, 12-pound-test linen thread or double thread–size fishing line will do. Nylon line won't serve the purpose; it cuts into the tire. Start by sewing back about a half inch over the cut stitching. Use a simple overhand stitch to finish the stitching. Run the thread about a half inch through existing holes left from the manufacturer's original stitching. Don't make new holes. Pull the stitches firmly (Fig. 10-38). Don't overdo it or you'll cut the tire casing.

Fig. 10-37: Stitch tire back together, using existing holes.

Fig. 10-38: Use doubled thread as stitching.

13. Apply rubber cement over the area revealed when you peeled back the protective tape over the stitching and on the tape itself (Fig. 10-39). Let it dry. Carefully lay the tape back in position.

14. Mount the tire, inflate it to riding pressure, and check again for leaks. Leave it inflated so that the rubber cement has a chance to dry thoroughly.

15. Fill in any cuts in the tread with the black rubber cement (not patch cement) that comes with your patch kit, or with black plastic rubber cement which you can buy in a hardware store.

How to Mount Tubular Tires on the Rim

Use mastic to glue road tubulars (as opposed to track tubulars) to the rim. Your bike shop should carry this type of rubber cement. It's called Tubasti, Vittoria, Clement, or Pastali rim glue. If you are fastening track tubulars you should always use shellac. Track tires have a cotton or silk nonrubberized base tape which is best cemented with shellac. Road tires have a rubberized base tape, and these are secured best on the rim with a rubber solution.

Steps for Road Tubular Tires

1. Remove all old adhesive from the rim. Use paint remover. Apply remover to the rim, wait for a couple of hours, then wipe the rim clean. Follow with a hot soap-and-water bath to remove the stripper completely.

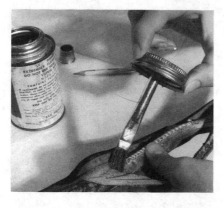

Fig. 10-39: Apply rubber cement over stitching, then smooth tire strip back in place.

2. If the rim is new or has not been scored, score it with a rough file for maximum adhesion.

3. Apply mastic to the rim. Remove any mastic that has flowed onto the sides of the rim.

4. If the road tubular has a nonrubberized cotton base tape, fill the base tape weave with a thinned-out solution of rim cement, using one of the brands noted above. Some of the base tapes of this type of tubular are sort of fluffy, and unless filled with a thin solution of rim cement, adhesion will not be secure. If the road tubular has a rubberized base tape, you need only apply the rim cement to the rim. In either case, do not wait for the cement to dry on the rim or the tubular, but fit the tubular right on the rim as soon as possible.

For Track Tubulars

1. Remove old adhesive from the rim.

2. Lightly roughen the rim surface with a file, if not already roughened.

3. Fit nipple holes with tight-fitting corks if you use very light silk tubulars. Otherwise the lighter silks may puncture just from pressure over the nipple holes. File the corks flush with the rim base so as to present a smooth, unbroken surface.

4. Apply two or three thin coats of shellac on the rim and let dry between coats. Drying time depends on temperature and humidity. What we are looking for is a smooth bed of shellac on the rim. Scrape off any shellac which has strayed over onto the rim sides.

5. Inflate the tire so it is just beginning to feel firm, with around five or six strokes of the pump. Remove any rubber solution which may have adhered to the base tape in the manufacturing process. Thin out the shellac solution and carefully brush it on the base tape and allow it to dry. What we want to do here is fill the cotton- or silk-weave base tape with shellac for proper adhesion. This is an important step, because otherwise the base tape will not adhere firmly to the shellac on the rim.

6. Go back to the rim and give it one final coat of shellac. Let it dry for from ten to forty minutes, depending on the temperature, until it gets tacky, or a bit less than tacky.

Follow These Steps in Putting All Tubulars on the Rim

1. Deflate tubular almost completely. Leave just enough air to give the tire a little body. Hold wheel in an upright position and insert valve through the valve hole in the rim (Fig. 10-40).

2. With the valve at the top of the wheel and the wheel on a soft pad on the floor, stand behind the wheel and with both hands push the tubular downward onto the rim, finishing on the side opposite the valve (Fig. 10-41). Hold the rim away from your body while you're doing this, or wear old clothes.

Fig. 10-40: Insert valve in rim. Push tire down onto rim, starting at either side of the valve.

Fig. 10-41: Continue forcing the tire onto the rim. Apply hand pressure evenly on both sides of the tire.

3. Force the remainder of the tubular onto the rim with both thumbs (Fig. 10-42).

4. True up the tubular with your fingers so that it sits evenly all the way around the rim and tension is even all the way around. Inflate the tubular partially and inspect it to make sure that it is seated evenly. Leave the tubular inflated for a few hours, if possible, before using it, to give the rim cement time to dry and become fixed.

To Replace Tubulars on the Road

So now you are on the road, in a race or just touring, and your tubular punctures. Obviously, you aren't going to sit around for a couple of hours while the rim cement dries. If you're in a race you should have someone along with a replacement wheel, so there's no fussing with changing tires. On tour, you won't want to leave the group, letting them go ahead, while you sit glumly by the side of the road waiting for cement to adhere tubular to rim. What I do is use sticky tape, a special tape made for mounting tubulars on rims. I keep this tape in a sealed plastic bag, the kind used to store food with a self-sealing top. The tape is messy, but it works, and it will get you home or to your destination. Rim tape loses some of its adhesiveness in the rain, so take it easy on cornering and high-speed downhill runs when it's raining. Another solution is to coat the tubular base tape, if rubberized, with a thin solution of rim cement and let it dry. Then I fold the tubular (Fig. 10-43) for a spare, fasten it in this position with rubber bands or a strap, put it in a plastic bag, and

Fig. 10-42: *Use thumbs to finish placing tubular tire on the rim.*

Fig. 10-43: *Proper way to fold new or repaired tubulars to carry as spares.*

put the bag in a saddle carrier. There will be enough residual molecular adhesion between the thin layer of rim cement on the base tape and the rim cement still on the rim under the punctured tubular for fair adhesion, good enough for the day's run or to get you home, but not good enough for a tough race situation. That's when you need a tire that will adhere to the rim as well as man can make it stick. If in doubt, try to roll the tubular off the rim. If it comes off easily, you have poor adhesion and you will very likely have a tubular roll off the rim in a race, and very possibly cause an accident involving not only you but others.

In the next chapter we will get into wheel tuning and wheel building.

11

How to Keep Your Wheels True to You, and Build New Ones

An untrue wheel, one that wobbles from side to side, is a safety hazard for these four reasons:

1. *Uneven brake-shoe contact* reduces braking capacity. You may not be able to stop in time to avoid an accident.

2. *Wheel shimmy* causes loss of control. Wheel wobble causes wheel shimmy. Loose or unevenly tensioned spokes also cause wheel shimmy.

3. *Spokes can break* due to metal fatigue. Metal fatigue comes from overtight or very loose spokes. Broken spokes increase the likelihood of wheel shimmy.

4. *Wobbly wheels are weaker,* more prone to collapse or to dent from impact.

On the other hand, aligned wheels with correct spoke tension permit more accurate steering. They are also incredibly strong. I know. One time a car suddenly swerved and stopped in front of me to park. My front wheel hit that car so hard my expensive Schwinn Paramount road frame crumpled and bent. I don't know which caused me more pain, my sprained wrist or my totaled frame. But the front wheel never moved out of true. Now *that's* a strong wheel!

However, spokes do stretch. A wheel true today won't stay that way forever. Get in the habit of eyeballing wheel trueness this way:

Flip the bike over, put it in a bike stand, or hang it from the garage ceiling. Spin the wheels. If the wheel does not stay the same distance from a brake shoe, through 360 degrees, it is untrue. True it up using the instructions below.

WHEEL TRUING INSTRUCTIONS, EXISTING WHEELS

1. Turn the wheel so the tire valve is opposite the chain stay. Measure the distance between the rim and the chain stay or seat stay, and from fork blades on a front wheel (Fig. 11-1).

2. Repeat on the other side of wheel, measuring at the same place on the stay or fork blade, on the other side. The measurement should be the same on both sides. If not, the wheel may be unevenly placed in the dropouts, where the axle fits.

3. Loosen the quick-release or axle bolts.

4. Reposition the wheel and check using the ruler again. If you can't get the measurements to be equal, the wheel needs to be realigned.

There are two degrees of wheel truing. The first is the simple truing you will probably have to do two or three times a year until you have removed spoke stretch and put each spoke under the same or nearly the same tension. The second and more difficult and time-consuming type of wheel truing involves making a completely new wheel from scratch, with new spokes in a new rim. In this chapter I will show you how to

Fig. 11-1: *Check wheel clearance from fork blades.*

do the casual kind of wheel truing first, because that's the kind you'll do most often. Then I'll get into wheel building and after that show you how to true a newly built wheel so it stays true—unless it's run over by a truck.

SIMPLE WHEEL TRUING IS EASY

Tools You Will Need

1. A spoke wrench (Fig. 11-2).
2. A wheel truing stand (or use your bike, as described below).
3. A bike work stand (optional).
4. If you use your bike as a truing fixture, four $^3/_{16}'' \times 1\frac{1}{2}''$ bolts, eight nuts and eight washers to fit the bolts for centerpull and sidepull brakes (Fig. 11-3). Or, for cantilever brakes, Allen wrenches (Fig. 11-4).

Fig. 11-2: *Use the correct size spoke wrench to adjust spoke tension.* Courtesy Park Tool.

Fig. 11-3: *Replace centerpull or sidepull brake shoes with bolts as shown to use bike as truing stand.*

Fig. 11-4: Replace cantilever brake shoes with Allen wrench to use bike as wheel truing stand.

If You Don't Have a Truing Fixture

1. Put your bike in a work stand, hang it from the ceiling, or turn it upside down.

2. Remove both wheels. Remove the tires, tubes, and rim strips.

3. Remove all four brake shoes (see Chapter 1).

4. Replace both wheels. Make sure the rear wheel is as far back in the dropouts as possible and that the front wheel is as far up in the fork dropouts as possible.

5. From here, truing procedure is the same for front and rear wheels. Start by spinning the wheel slowly. Find a place where each side of the rim is the same distance from the fork blades (Fig. 11-1) or the seat stays. Mark that spot with crayon on each side of the rim.

6. Put one bolt, two washers, and two nuts in each brake arm (Fig. 11-3), or an Allen wrench in a cantilever brake arm (Fig. 11-4).

7. Find the spot you marked in Step 5. Adjust the bolts so they touch each side of the rim on that spot.

If You Use a Truing Fixture (Easier and More Accurate)

1. Remove both wheels, their tires, tubes, and rim strips.

2. Put a wheel in the truing fixture.

3. Spin the wheel slowly. Find a spot on the wheel where the indicators are the same distance from each side of the rim. Mark this spot on both sides of the rim with crayon.

Follow This Truing Procedure Whether You Use Your Bike or a Truing Fixture

1. Put a drop of light oil, such as WD-40, on the top of the spoke nipples in the rim. Wipe off excess oil so it won't damage the rim strip

or tube when you replace them. This makes spoke nipple adjustment easier and helps prevent rounding off the nipple flats.

2. Check the spokes, especially on the freewheel side, where they curve up from the hub, and replace any that are bent, twisted, or cut. To replace spokes on the freewheel side, remove the freewheel. See Chapter 5 for freewheel removal instructions.

3. Note that spoke holes are staggered on a rim (Fig. 11-5). The holes alternate in closeness to one side of the rim and the other.

4. Make sure the truing indicators (on the bike or in the truing fixture) touch both sides of the rim where you marked it with crayon (Fig. 11-6). That mark is the one place where the rim is true laterally, from side to side. That's your starting point.

5. Study Fig. 11-7. Note that you can align the rim to the right by *tightening* a left spoke nipple (clockwise) or *loosening* a right spoke nipple. Try tightening a nipple first. If the nipple is already tight, loosen the nipple on the opposite side of the rim. Turn spoke nipples a quarter turn at a time.

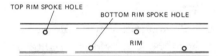

Fig. 11-5: *A bit exaggerated, this drawing shows how rim spoke holes are staggered from one side of rim to the other.*

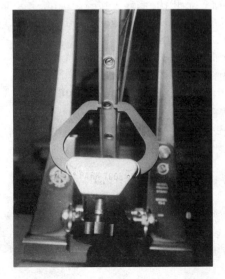

Fig. 11-6: *Adjust truing stand indicators so they touch untrue section of rim.*

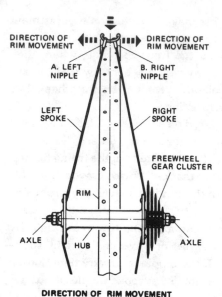

Fig. 11-7: *Move rim to the left by tightening spoke on the right, and vice versa.*

6. Rotate the rim until one side is as far away as possible from the truing indicator. Mark that spot with crayon.

7. Tighten a nipple a quarter turn on a spoke that will pull the rim toward the indicator. If the rim is too far to the left, tighten a right-side nipple.

8. Go all around the rim as above. Make rough truing adjustments on the nipple a quarter turn at a time until the rim is almost true.

9. Make final touch-up truing adjustments one eighth a nipple turn at a time until the rim is true from side to side.

10. Remember, if you can't true the rim by tightening a spoke, loosen a spoke on the opposite side a quarter turn. For example, if the rim is too far to the right, and you can't tighten a left-side spoke to pull it back, loosen a right side spoke one quarter to one eighth a turn.

11. With side-to-side (lateral) untrueness removed, now check for concentric (roundness) trueness. Look where the truing indicator meets the *top* of the rim (Fig. 11-6).

12. Spin the wheel. Note where the rim moves up or down from the indicator.

13. Correct concentric untrueness by tightening one left-side and one right-side spoke nipple one eighth turn at the high place, or loosening one right- and left-side nipple one eighth turn at the low place. *Use two* *adjacent spokes to pull the rim up or move it down. That way you keep the wheel laterally true while you correct concentric untrueness.* Repeat this step until you have removed all high and low spots and the rim is concentric.

14. Make sure *both* sides of the rim are the *same* distance from the concentric indicators (Fig. 11-6). Adjust spoke tension as needed. Otherwise one side of the rim can be pulled inward, a condition that causes uneven tire wear and, possibly, wheel shimmy.

15. Check the rim once more for side-to-side trueness, and if necessary, true it up as described above.

16. Prestretch the spokes. Start with spokes nearest the tire valve area. Squeeze two spokes together as hard as you can. Go around the wheel until you have squeezed all the spokes.

17. Check lateral and concentric alignment again. Retrue as necessary. Note: For precision wheel truing, use a dial indicator (about $69, from The Third Hand; see Appendix) that attaches by a powerful magnet to the base of the truing stand. For super precision results, use an electronic wheel truing system (Fig. 11-8). It is simple, easy and quick to use, has a liquid-crystal display, and reads wheel trueness to one-

Fig. 11-8: *An electronic truing stand for precision wheel truing.* Courtesy Digi-True.

thousandth of an inch. This Digi-True unit costs $395 from Golftek, Inc., 0203 3rd St., Lewiston, ID 83501, phone 208-743-9037.

18. Use a spoke tensionometer for accurate, even spoke tensioning. Wheelsmith makes an excellent unit (Fig. 11-9), which sells for around $79. The HKC tensionometer (Fig. 11-10) is very accurate and easy to use, and costs about $226. Both are available from The Third Hand (see Appendix).

WHEEL LACING STEPS

Let's start wheel building (a.k.a. wheel lacing) with a few basic observations about rims and hubs. Fig. 11-5 shows that rim spoke holes are drilled so that every other hole is closer to one side of the rim than to the other side. Please keep that in mind as we proceed, because we'll come back to it.

Next, study Fig. 11-11. Note that hub holes are also drilled off-center. Holes in one hub flange are offset from holes in the facing flange. If you poke a spoke down a hub hole from the top flange, straight up and down,

Fig. 11-9: Use a tensionometer for even spoke tension. Courtesy The Third Hand.

Fig. 11-10: Dial-type tensionometer for fast spoke tension adjustment. Courtesy The Third Hand.

Fig. 11-11: *Hub holes are also drilled off-center.*

it will land between the spokes in the bottom flange of the hub. Check this for yourself and bury it in your memory.

Finally, and this is also important, pick up your hub and look at the spoke holes closely. You'll notice (Fig. 11-12) that every other hub hole is countersunk. This countersinking is to permit the spoke to bend gradually and also to eliminate a sharp corner that would stress the spoke at this point and contribute to premature spoke breakage. At first, though, because we're used to inserting screw heads in countersunk holes, you may believe spoke heads should go into hub countersunk holes. Believe me, it's not so! You can bury spoke heads in countersunk holes for a

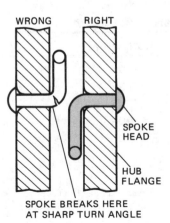

WRONG   RIGHT

SPOKE HEAD

HUB FLANGE

SPOKE BREAKS HERE AT SHARP TURN ANGLE

Fig. 11-12: *Spoke head should go into the noncountersunk side of spoke hole to avoid sharp spoke bend leading to spoke breakage.*

sexier-looking hub, but you'll have busted spokes on the road if you do so. Fig. 11-12 illustrates this point. If your hub, however, has *all* spokes countersunk, you can ignore the above instruction.

HOW TO BUILD A WHEEL

If you have dented a rim beyond repair, want to upgrade your hubs, bought a new frame and want to add your own components, or want an extra set of wheels, you have a choice of having a professional wheel builder lace (spoke) the wheels or doing it yourself. A bike shop charges about $25 to build a wheel, less the cost of spokes, rim, and hub, if you need them. You can build a wheel in about three hours, faster as you get more experience.

Every bicycle enthusiast should build his or her own wheels at least once. That way you will understand what it takes to create wheels that will see you through hell and high water. You'll appreciate your new-found skill if you ever get stuck in the boonies and have to replace a broken spoke(s) or if you live where bike shops are scarce. If you tour in Third World countries, wheel building ability is vital.

About Spokes

Spokes come in seven different lengths, as shown in Table 11-1.

Table 11-1 Available Spoke Lengths*

Inches	Millimeters
$11^{13}/_{32}$	290
$11\frac{1}{2}$	292
$11^{21}/_{32}$	295
$11^{23}/_{32}$	298
$11^{13}/_{16}$	300
12	305
$12\frac{1}{8}$	308

*Have your bike shop make up spokes to fit your combination of hub, spoke crossing, and rim diameter, if the stock spokes in this table won't fit. Many bike shops have a spoke cutter/threader machine.

Spokes also come in three gauges: 14, 15, and 15 double-butted. The lower the gauge, the thicker and so the stronger the spoke. For example, a 14-gauge spoke is 2-mm thick and a 15-gauge spoke is 1.56-mm thick, so the 14-gauge spoke is about 22 percent thicker. Number 15-gauge double-butted spokes are 14-gauge thickness for about 50 mm (two inches) at the spoke-head end, the part that goes into the hub. Use 14 gauge if you want a strong, durable wheel, 15-gauge double-butted for some sacrifice in strength to save a few ounces in weight, and 15 straight gauge for lightness at the expense of strength.

I prefer Swiss precision-made D.T. stainless-steel 14-gauge spokes. They are the strongest spokes you can buy, in my opinion. The few ounces 14-gauge spokes add to your wheels might concern a racing cyclist, but for the average touring cyclist these ounces are unimportant.

Use oval or bladed spokes, available in 15-gauge thickness, for maximum aerodynamic benefits on light 18-pound track or 22-pound road-racing bicycles. The bladed spokes offer the least wind resistance as the wheels turn. Oval spokes cost about $8 a wheel, bladed about $15 a wheel. Don't use them for anything but racing. Either type is more susceptible to side winds than the conventional round spoke.

Four-Cross vs. Three-Cross Lacing

You can lace your wheels with spokes crossed every third spoke (Fig. 11-13) or every fourth spoke (Fig. 11-14). You get a stiffer wheel with three-cross spoking, which more efficiently translates muscle power to go power. But the stiffer wheel also sends road shock back into the frame, which can be fatiguing on a long ride.

Fig. 11-13: Lace wheel in this 3-cross pattern for stiff wheels.

Fig. 11-14: Lace wheel in this 4-cross pattern for a softer bike ride.

Four-cross spoking requires longer spokes, which soak up road shock better than the stiff three-cross pattern. Use three-cross for racing, and four-cross for casual and long-distance riding and touring and for all-terrain bicycling.

Radial Lacing

You can cut a few ounces off a time trial or track bike by radially lacing the front wheel (Fig. 11-15). Spokes are shorter and so they are lighter. Radially laced wheels are far too weak for street riding or for touring. Spokes are not crossed in radial spoking; they are straight up and down, like the spokes of a wagon wheel. Some racing cyclists use radial lacing on the left side of the rear wheel and three-cross on the driving (chain) side. Never radially lace both sides of a rear wheel—it will collapse at the first thrust of your powerful leg muscles or on the first hard bump. Spokes in Fig. 11-15 are, by the way, flat for less wind resistance.

About the Number of Spokes

Hubs and rims come drilled for 28, 32, 36, and 40 spokes. Use 28- or 32-spoke hubs and rims for racing, 36 spokes for touring and ATB trail riding, and 40 spokes on tandems or on the rear wheel of a touring bike if you're a strong heavyweight spoke buster.

STEPS IN BUILDING WHEELS

1. Select the correct spoke length. There are far too many combinations of spoke crossings, rim diameters, rim widths, hub flange diameters, and spoke hole drillings in hub and rim to generate one table that gives the correct spoke length for all of them. New hub and rim designs hit the market often, so even if I designed a comprehensive spoke length table it would be obsolete in short order. Have your bicycle dealer select the correct-length spokes when you buy a new hub and rim, or take an old spoke to the bike shop for a replacement. Most bike shops have a spoke-length selector manual. This shop manual helps the bike shop match rim, hub, and spoke length.

2. Remove the freewheel gear cluster from the rear wheels; you can't poke spokes in the rear hub with the freewheel in the way (which is why

Fig. 11-15: For time trials, you can lace a front wheel radially. Spokes are not crossed. Spokes shown are aerodynamically shaped for least wind resistance. Courtesy Wheelsmith.

you should take a freewheel-removing tool as well as spare spokes on trips. See Chapter 5). You may also find it difficult or next to impossible to poke spokes through hub holes if they are drilled too small to accommodate the spoke. Use spokes of the correct diameter for hub holes— not too big, not too small.

A Few Definitions, So We're Talking the Same Language

1. *Rim* is the round steel or alloy part that the tire goes on.
2. *Spoke head* is the section of the spoke with the curved area and flat head (flat on the bottom). The other end of the spoke is threaded.
3. *Spoke nipple* is the short, tubular, internally threaded piece that holds the spoke on the rim and threads onto the spoke.
4. *Spoke head up* means that in referring to the hub, the spoke head faces up.
5. *Top rim hole* means the rim hole closest to the upper edge of the rim.

Before you start, you might consider drilling a one-inch hole in your wooden workbench to fit the axle of the hub. That way, the hub assembly will stay put as you stick spokes in the wheel. And, while I'm thinking of it and before you despair, remember that, as I said, lacing a wheel is simple. It just seems difficult; it surely is hard to write about how to do it so that it comes out sounding as easy as it really is. Since most wheels on 10-speed bikes have 36 spokes front and rear, I'll assume this is what you're about to lace. You have a naked hub and rim, and a fistful of spokes and nipples of the right diameter and length. For now, we'll stick to 36 holes with 4-cross lacing, although at one step in this procedure you will find instructions for 3-cross lacing.

Lacing

1. Grab 9 spokes, threaded ends down. Hold the hub in one hand, the spokes in the other, and stuff a spoke down *every other hole*. The spoke head must be on the countersunk side of the hub flange. Do the same for the bottom flange, with the hub in the same position as when you started. You should now have a hub that looks like Fig. 11-16.

2. Sweep up all the spokes on both flanges into two bundles. Hold them so they don't fall out while you turn the hub over and repeat Step 1. When you're through, the hub will have all 36 spokes in it, with every other spoke head alternating on each side of both hub flanges, as shown in Fig. 11-17.

3. Sweep all the spokes but one up out of the way. Take any head-up spoke from the top flange (head-up spoke means the spoke head is facing upward, on top of the flange) and put it in the first hole to the *right* of the valve hole (Fig. 11-18). This rim hole must be a top rim hole (a top rim hole is the hole closest to the top of the rim); however, some rims are drilled so that the first hole to the right of the valve is a bottom rim hole (hole closest to the bottom of the rim). If so, start lacing with the first hole to the *left* of the valve hole. On this spoke and from here on, thread a nipple four turns on each spoke as you lace it into the rim.

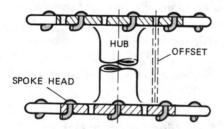

Fig. 11-16: Step 1.

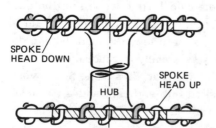

Fig. 11-17: Step 2.

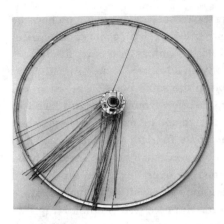

Fig. 11-18: Step 3.

4. Count off five spokes to the right (not counting the valve hole), including the hole you spoked in Step 3. This must also be a top rim hole. Into this hole put the next head-up spoke to the right of the one you spoked in Step 3. Continue this sequence until you have laced all head-up spokes in the top hub flange. The wheel will now look like Fig. 11-19, with three holes between each spoke, the center of three empty holes being a rim-top hole; the other two, rim bottom holes. (This happens to be a 32-hole rim and hub so only 8 spokes are showing. You should show 9 spokes laced into the rim.)

5. This is a critical step, so take it slowly and repeat it if you don't get it at first. Take the partially spoked rim and hub, and, keeping the same side up, *twist* the rim so the spokes are at an acute angle, just

Fig. 11-19: Step 4.

grazing the outside of their adjacent spoke holes. Depending on how the rim has been drilled, twist the rim either left or right, so no spoke crosses over the valve hole (Fig. 11-20). Hold the hub as you twist the rim.

6. Another critical step. Take any head-down spoke from the top hub flange (the wheel should still be in the same position as when you started) and, going in the *opposite direction* from the spokes laced so far, cross *over three* and *under* the fourth spoke, as shown above, then stick it in the rim and thread on a nipple four turns. Remember Step 4? You had three empty spoke holes between each spoke. Right? I hope you did, anyway. If not, stop now and go over the preceding steps to check what you did wrong. Let's assume all is well. The spoke we are lacing in Step 6 should go into a center-rim hole (top rim hole) (Fig. 11-21). You are lacing spoke "A." Note that it crosses over spokes "B," "C," "D," and under "E," and winds up in a top-rim hole. Continue lacing all head-down spokes in the top flange, cross *over* three and *under* the fourth spoke, as above. When you are finished, spokes will be in groups of two, with one bottom-rim spoke between each group of two. (If you wish to

Fig. 11-20: Step 5.

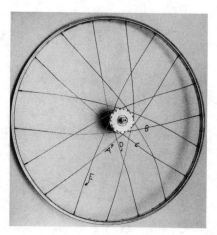

Fig. 11-21: Step 6.

Fig. 11-22: Step 7.

lace in a "cross three" pattern, pass the spoke *over* two and *under* the third spoke. Note: a three-cross pattern uses shorter spokes. Be sure to tell your bike shop which lacing pattern you will be using.)

7. This is a most critical step. Turn the wheel over, with all unlaced spokes in the top flange. Straighten spokes out, sweep all but one out of your way. Take an old spoke, put it straight up alongside any head-up spoke in the top hub flange (Fig. 11-22), with the threaded end resting

Fig. 11-23: Step 7.

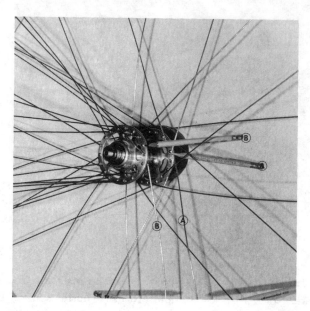

Fig. 11-24: Step 7.

on the bottom flange facing you. Notice that just to the left of this trial spoke is another head-up spoke, offset, to the left (naturally) in the bottom flange (Figs. 11-23 and 11-24). We will call the bottom reference spoke in the bottom flange spoke "A" and the spoke above and to its right, spoke "B." Bring spoke "B" parallel but angled to the left of spoke "A" below it. Put spoke "B" in the first empty rim hole to the left of spoke "A," thread on a nipple. Now you will have your first group of three spokes (Fig. 11-24), with one empty spoke hole on either side. Step 7 is so critical I have taken extra photos from various angles to demonstrate it. Figure 11-24 shows a close-up of the hub, with key spoke "A" at the bottom of the hub and key spoke "B" at the top of the hub. Fig. 11-25 shows key spokes "A" and "B" as they enter the rim. Fig. 11-24 is another view of Step 7, with pencils on spokes "A" and "B." An important point to remember is that spoke "B" is parallel to spoke "A," is offset to it, and goes next to it in the rim, just above (to the left of spoke "A"). Fig. 11-26 shows another view of this step.

8. Now, if all has gone well so far, the rest is simple. Just take the next head-up spoke, count off two *empty* spoke holes to the *left,* stick this spoke into *that* top rim hole, and thread on the nipple four turns.

Fig. 11-25: Step 7.

Fig. 11-26: Step 7.

Repeat until all head-up spokes are in the rim with nipples on. Now you will have all spokes in groups of three (Fig. 11-27), and you are ready for the final step.

9. Take any one of the remaining spokes (they will all be head down, with heads *under* the top flange) and bring it around to the right, crossing *over* three and *under* the fourth spoke, and stick it in the only hole it will fit into. If you're not sure which hole this is, please repeat Step 7, only with head-down spokes, referencing a head-down spoke in the bottom flange and being sure that the parallel head-down spoke in the top flange also goes in a direction opposite to *its* reference spoke below. Confused? Well, actually, I don't blame you. Let's take it from the top. First, find any head-down spoke in the bottom flange. Then find the first head-down spoke in the top flange offset to the right (counterclockwise) of your reference head-down spoke below, and put it in the first empty spoke hole to the right (counterclockwise) of spoke "A." Refer to Fig. 11-13 to refresh your memory as to what crossing over three and under four is all about. Continue as above, lacing up the remaining head-down spokes. Now the wheel is laced, spokes are in groups of four as shown above, and we are ready for the exacting job of "truing" the rim. Finished wheel, not trued, is shown in Fig. 11-28.

Fig. 11-27: Step 8.

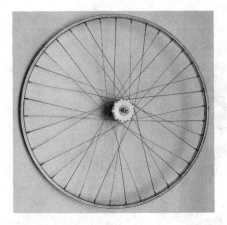

Fig. 11-28: Step 9.

STEPS IN TRUING A NEWLY BUILT WHEEL

Tools You Will Need

1. Wheel truing fixture costs about $89, a bike shop model, about $149, both from The Third Hand (See Appendix).

2. Caliper ruler (Fig. 11-1) or accurate straight ruler.

3. Spoke wrench (Fig. 11-2).

4. Dishing tool (Fig. 11-29) for centering a front wheel and dishing a rear wheel, about $28 from The Third Hand. It fits wheel sizes from 20 inches to 27 inches.

5. Tool to hold handlebars from flopping around while you work on the front wheel (Fig. 11-30). Optional, but handy, not only for wheel work but for any bike work where you want to keep the fork straight.

How to True a Newly Built Front Wheel

It's easier to true a front wheel because it doesn't have to be dished like a rear wheel. I'll explain the dishing process in the section below on truing a rear wheel. Follow these steps in truing a front wheel:

1. The hub and rim measurements that follow apply to one hub, the SunTour XC. Use these measurements as an example, but make your

Fig. 11-29: Use this dishing tool to center rim between axle locknuts. Courtesy Park Tool.

Fig. 11-30: Use this handy tool to keep handlebars from flopping around as you work on the bike. Courtesy Park Tool.

own on the hubs and rims you are using. Measure the space between locknuts. In Figs. 11-31 and 11-32 it's 10 mm or about 4 inches.

   2. Measure the width of the rim. In Fig. 11-33, it's 2.3 mm or ³⁄₁₆ inch.

   3. Subtract the rim width, 2.3 mm, from the width between the axle locknuts, 10 mm, which equals 7.7 mm.

   4. Divide the figure obtained in Step 4, 7.7 mm or 3 inches, by 2, which equals 3.85 mm or 1½ inches (to convert millimeters to inches multiply by .03937). This is the distance each side of the rim should be from each hub axle locknut when the rim is trued, in this example. In other words, the rim should be centered between the axle locknuts. This puts the rim and tire squarely centered between the fork blades (if you have put the wheel back correctly in the fork dropouts). Again, these

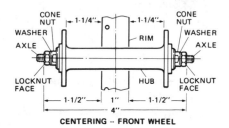

CENTERING -- FRONT WHEEL

Fig. 11-31: Wheel truing, Step 1.

Fig. 11-32: Wheel truing, Step 1.

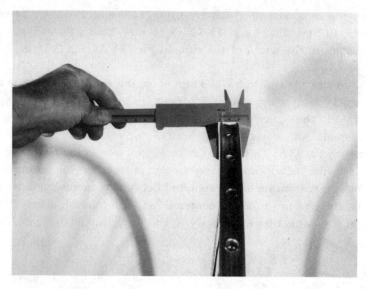

Fig. 11-33:   *Wheel truing, Step 2.*

measurements apply to one make of hub—make your own measurements on the hub/rim combination you are using.

5. Put the centering tool (Fig. 11-29) on a flat surface. Turn the measuring bolt until its bottom is 1½ inches from the flat surface.

6. Lay the wheel on the workbench and put the rim centering tool on it (Fig. 11-29).

7. Review the truing instructions given earlier in this chapter.

8. Adjust the group of four spokes nearest the rim valve hole and the four spokes across from the valve hole—on the opposite side of the rim—until the rim-centering tool's flat ends (Fig. 11-29) touch each side of the rim. Wiggle the centering tool to make sure both flats lay evenly on each rim. If not, adjust the spokes until they do.

9. Turn the front wheel over and repeat Step 8. Mark both sides of the rim where the centering gauge shows the rim is centered.

10. Put the front wheel in the truing stand. Adjust the truing stand indicators until they touch both sides of the rim where you marked it in Step 9. This is your beginning guide to truing the newly laced wheel.

11. Finish truing the front wheel as shown earlier in this chapter. Remove the wheel from the truing fixture and check side-to-side adjustment with the centering gauge a few times to make sure the rim is centered between the hub flanges and axle locknut.

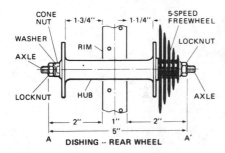

Fig. 11-34: Wheel truing, Step 12.

Fig. 11-35: Wheel truing, Step 12.

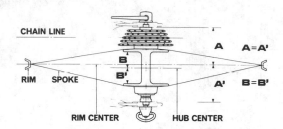

Fig. 11-36:   Wheel truing, Step 12.

12. You trued up the front wheel so the rim is centered between the axle locknuts. Do the same with the rear wheel except dish it so the rim is centered between the locknuts. You have to dish the rear wheel (except most freehubs, see Chapter 7) to center the rear wheel between the axle locknuts. As you can see in Figs. 11-34, 11-35, and 11-36, the wheel rim is *not* centered on the hub. Instead, the wheel is centered between axle locknuts. The rear wheel axle is longer to accommodate the freewheel. Dishing will be automatic as you follow Steps 1 through 11 above.

In the next chapter you will learn how to check your bike frame for bends, warps, and twists that could affect bicycle safety, and how to refinish the paint job.

12
The Frame

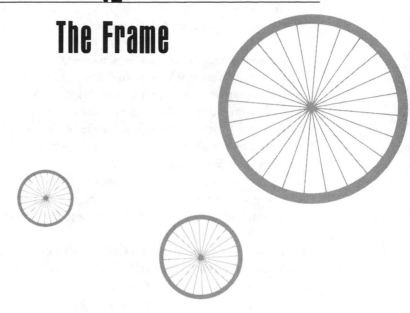

WHEEL SHIMMY

I begin this chapter with a discussion about wheel shimmy, for four reasons. One, because it's so dangerous. Two, because it can be caused by a misaligned frame or wheel. Three, because wheel shimmy is preventable. Four, because a misaligned frame can be detected.

If you have ever felt shimmy on a car, you can imagine how violent wheel shimmy on a bike can be. On a car you simply slow down until the shimmy stops. On a bike, wheel shimmy can be a life-threatening experience. Once bike wheel shimmy starts, the front wheel side-to-side movement gets faster and wilder. Before you can even think about what to do (not much except to try to control speed by braking) the bike can dump itself *and* you on the pavement. It happened to me, going down an Austrian Alpine two-lane mountain pass. To my right was a fenceless 2,000-foot drop-off, to my left, a loaded logging truck coming toward me. To my rear were some forty American tourists. I fell, and was fortunate enough to ride out the slide on top of the bike. No damage to me except for a little skin left on the pavement. Exercise-induced endorphins served as an anesthetic. The pain came later. I was lucky. Others have been seriously injured or killed due to loss of control caused by front-wheel shimmy.

Wheel shimmy can be due to one or more of these factors:

1. *Loose headset bearings.* See Chapter 8.

2. *Bent fork blade or chain stay.* Use an old axle or piece of wood between dropouts when shipping your bike, especially by plane.

3. *Out-of-line frame.* Wet down the pavement. Ride your bike straight, watch to see if wheels track evenly. Or check frame alignment, as described below. If you suspect the frame, the bike shop can make a check with their Park alignment tool.

4. *Badly balanced load.* Carry your tent, sleeping bag, clothes, and other necessities as low as possible. The higher off the ground, the greater the potential for wobble and erratic steering. Use low-rider carriers over the front wheel.

5. *Loose wheel bearings,* especially the front wheel.

6. *Misaligned wheel,* especially the front wheel. The misalignment may be caused by:

a. Bent rim, for example, from contact with a curb.

b. Bent axle.

c. Inaccurately bored hub which puts the axle off-center (rare, but it has happened).

d. Spoke stretch. Spokes loosen, and permit the rim to gradually become untrue laterally and concentrically.

e. Uneven spoke tension which can cause wheel wobble.

If your bike needs a lot of balance and steering correction to keep it going straight, you may have a bent frame or fork that can cause wheel shimmy and an accident. Check your frame and fork alignment after any hard collision with a deep pothole, a curb, or with any other obstruction. Check the frame of a secondhand bike before you buy it.

Start with the following simple checks. You can make them without disassembling the bike. Progress to the more involved inspections to be sure your bike frame is safely aligned. Do not attempt to straighten or align a bent frame. It requires special tools and alignment jigs, plus experience. An improperly aligned frame is not safe, as noted. If it can't be realigned accurately, scrap the frame, save the parts, install them on a new frame. A bent aluminum frame is usually not fixable. Check your warranty. Aluminum frame manufacturers may replace the frame at a reasonable price.

Simple Frame Alignment Checks

Study Fig. 12-1 until you are familiar with the names of the frame tubes.

Inspect the Fork

1. *Wheel alignment:* Place a pencil or a ruler on the fork blade. Rotate the wheel. If the rim moves toward and then away from the ruler, the wheel is out of line. See Chapter 11. Replace the trued wheel in the fork and repeat the check. Use the ruler to make sure the rim is centered between the fork blades. Make sure the wheel is all the way up into the dropouts (where the axle fits) and is evenly placed in the dropouts. If the trued rim stays to one side or the other, the fork may be bent. Make additional fork alignment checks as described below.

2. *Bent fork blades:* Remove the front wheel. If you have trouble fitting it back, the fork blades may be bent or the dropouts misaligned.

3. *Bent fork blades:* Remove the front brake. Attach a plumb line to the brake mounting hole in the fork crown. Measure the distance

Fig. 12-1: *Study these frame parts to better understand frame alignment.*

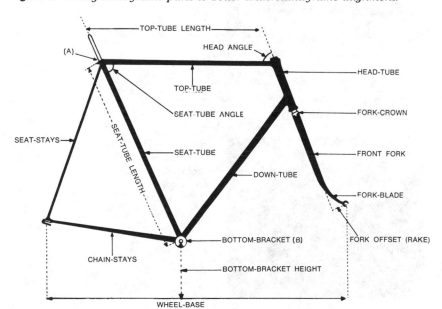

between the plumb line and the sides of both fork blades. The measurements should be the same. Have a minor misalignment cold-straightened by a bike shop. Replace the fork if one fork blade is closer to the plumb line than the other fork blade. If you ship the bike, block the fork (and rear wheel) dropouts with a piece of wood or dummy axle.

4. *Fork:* Remove the fork (see Chapter 8). Lay it on a flat surface, dropouts facing up, back of dropouts on the table (Fig. 12-2). Eyeball the flat surface under the fork ends (dropouts). If you see air, a fork blade is bent. Have it cold-straightened, if possible. A slight misalignment of the fork blades can cause a wheel shimmy and an accident.

5. *Look for wrinkled paint indicating buckled tubes* where they join other tubes. Look for bent tubes (as in Fig. 12-3). This frame was totaled. I bought a new frame for little more than the cost of replacing the bent tubes and refinishing this frame. I suggest you seriously consider this option, too.

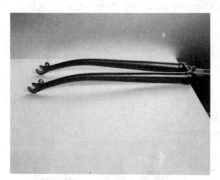

Fig. 12-2: Check fork-blade alignment on a flat surface, as shown.

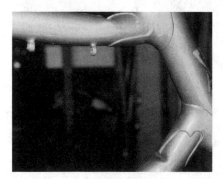

Fig. 12-3: This bike has been totaled in an accident. Frame tubes can be replaced, but a new frame may be less expensive.

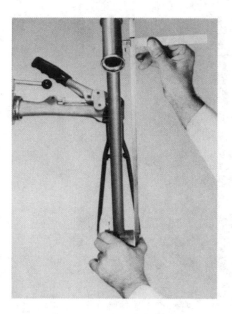

Fig. 12-4: *Check head-tube align-ment with bottom-bracket shell.* Courtesy Schwinn.

6. *Check alignment of the head tube with the bottom-bracket shell.* Place a straightedge on the bottom-bracket shell and measure the distance from it to the head tube (as shown in Fig. 12-4). Repeat this check on the other side of the head tube. Cold-straighten the head tube if both measurements are not the same.

7. *Check vertical alignment of the head tube with the rear dropouts and the seat tube.* Tie a piece of string to one of the rear dropouts, and pass the string around the head tube and back to the other rear dropout (as shown in Fig. 12-5). Measure the distance from the seat tube to the string on both sides of the seat tube. The measurements should be identical—if they are not the same, have the head tube cold-straightened.

8. *Check the head tube for twist.* Tie one end of a piece of string to a rear dropout, pass it around the *bottom* of the head tube and back to the other dropout, then from around the *top* of the head tube and back to both dropouts (as shown in Fig. 12-6). Measure the distance from the seat tube to both strings on both sides of the seat tube. All four measurements should be identical. If these measurements are not the same, the head tube is twisted. Have it cold-straightened if possible.

9. When you tighten a loose kickstand bolt, it's easy to squeeze and damage the chain stays. Remove the kickstand if it's bolted on the chain stays (Fig. 12-7), and check these stays for damage caused by over-tightening the kickstand mounting bolt. You can't do much about such

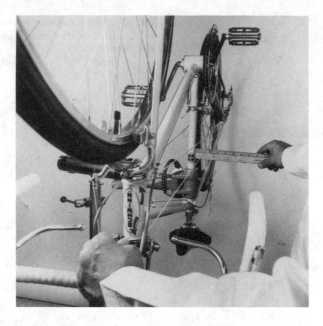

Fig. 12-5: Checking head-tube alignment. Courtesy Schwinn.

Fig. 12-6: Checking for head-tube twist (something you don't want). Courtesy Schwinn.

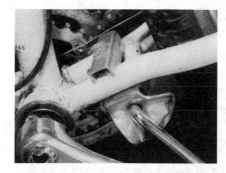

Fig. 12-7: Kickstands can damage chain stays if tightened down too hard.

damage except to throw the kickstand away. A kickstand is an unstable way to keep a bike upright, anyway. A passing child, even the wind, can knock the bike over, with possible damage to the derailleur, brake levers, and the paint finish. This is why expensive bikes are not equipped with kickstands.

   10. *Look for poor frame welds.* The bike in Figs. 12-8 and 12-9 was a very inexpensive bike, with poor welds and poor factory quality control. Stay away from cut-rate store bikes.

Fig. 12-8: This el cheapo bike fell apart at the seams. Poor, sloppy welding, plus poor quality control at the factory, spell frame disaster.

Fig. 12-9: Close-up of the bike in Fig. 12-8, showing poor welds.

11. *Check toe-to-wheel clearance.* Make sure your foot does not touch the tire or the fender (Fig. 12-10) at any point where the wheel turns.

FRAME REFINISHING

Repair minor nicks and scratches with matching paint you can buy from the bike shop. Feather the edges of the area to be retouched with fine sandpaper. Follow directions on the pressurized spray can. Make a quick circular spray in the air and then quickly spray the feathered area. Apply at least three coats, letting each coat dry before spraying the next, and sanding with fine sandpaper between coats.

Frame Touch-Up and Painting

If you have a fine bicycle, it will pain you to see the finish become nicked, scratched, and marred. Unless you keep your bicycle wrapped in cotton batting in your bedroom, nicks, scratches, or mars are the inevitable concomitants of use. Perhaps you will feel better if we call these indications of healthy use "battle scars." I know you will feel a lot better if these flaws on your beautiful, peerless machine can be removed and the finish brought back to perfection.

Removing scratches and nicks in the finish of a bicycle is virtually a fine art, and one, I must quickly admit, I am congenitally unsuited to and associate with headaches. I have, however, followed the instructions of experts and, with a great deal of internal stress and many mistakes, eventually succeeded in removing battle scars from my good bikes. I

Fig. 12-10: Make sure your foot does not contact the fender, or the wheel, in your normal riding position. Otherwise, you could steer into an accident as your foot gets knocked off the pedal or becomes jammed between the fender or wheel and the down tube.

myself am not good at fine digital movements, but you, I am sure, have the touch, the artistic taste, and the desire to bring your two-wheeled steed back to its original state. For the following instructions on scratch removal and frame finishing, I am indebted to Otis Childress, of Los Angeles, and to *Bike World* in which the following material appeared in the October 1977 and January 1979 issues. This data is from Mr. Childress's articles in those issues, reprinted by permission of both Mr. Childress and *Bike World*.

Before quoting from these articles, however, let me note that matching paint on a bike is going to be a problem. My solution is to wheel my bike into a large auto-supply store, right up to the display of pressure cans of touch-up paint, and try to select one from either the color on the top of the can (not always a reliable indication of what's inside) or from a color chart sometimes available and hanging on the rack next to the paint cans. My color-matching reliability is around − 1 on a scale of 0 to 10, so I always ask a clerk or another shopper for help, and the consensus determines which can I buy. But I have never precisely matched colors this way, although the match is close enough for my low-grade taste. Some bike manufacturers furnish spray cans of touch-up paint for current models. Okay, Otis, the rest is all yours. He says: When selecting paint, match it not only by color, but also by type: lacquer on lacquer, or enamel on enamel. Lacquer painted over enamel will lift the enamel off; enamel, however, can be painted over lacquer without causing damage.

When spraying, hold a shield half an inch to an inch away from the scrape to be repaired and spray with sweeping motions across the openings. This method is applicable to any flat, curving, or irregular surface such as around the bottom-bracket shell.

For example, let's say you're using a hand-held vignette shield (made by cutting a small hole in a piece of paper) in repairing a deep scratch. Using touch-up paint and a brush, fill in and build up the scratch above the level of the undamaged paint surface. Carefully sand until level down to the undamaged paint. Finally, after washing away the sanding residue, use the hand-held shield and spray across its opening.

Do not stop spraying while within the opening of the hand-held taped-on vignette shield or you risk having the paint run. Also, a thick layering of paint into a deep scratch may take several days to build up to allow each lower layer to dry. Do not sand paint that is not dry or you will literally roll layers of it off the area and create a gorge in the dry-to-the-touch though still-wet paint. Before painting, place a strip of masking tape on the opposite side of the frame tube, opposite the scrape, so this unprotected area will then be protected against any paint overspray. The result of overspray, when dry, is a rough texture.

Scratch Removal and Refinishing

For a "quicky" repair of scratches so they won't show at a distance, at least, follow these steps:

1. Clean the scratch with soap and water, then rub it with grade 000 steel wool to remove loosened bits of clinging paint.
2. If bare metal shows, apply a layer or two of primer and let it dry between coats for at least one hour. Brush in direction of scratch.
3. You can spray a small amount of paint into a small, clean container or onto a little piece of lint-free paper, first shaking the can. Then, with a small artist's brush, brush in the color coats. If it's just a spot dent, dab in a little paint. If the scratch is tiny, you can dabble some primer and color in it. You can also use paint sticks (Fig. 12-11). Rub the paint into the groove. Then smooth it out. Soften the paint stick with a match. Paint sticks won't work on a flat scrape where there is no groove to fill in.

Larger Scrapes, Blending In

You can fill in and blend larger scrapes with a technique known as vignetting and feathering. Mask off the damaged area with newspaper or masking tape. Follow these steps below to avoid a ridge line (Fig. 12-12) where the paint repair ends and the tape starts. Remove ridge lines

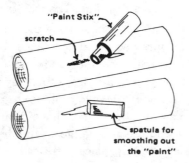

Fig. 12-11: Use paint sticks to fill in small scratches.

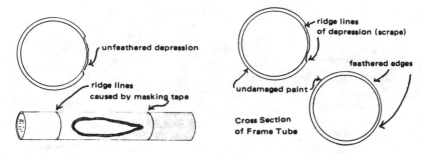

Fig. 12-12: *Try to avoid ridge lines around edges of masking tape.*

with 400-grade sandpaper or 000 steel wool and rubbing compound. However, ridge lines may still show. An alternative method of vignetting paint is to use a hand-held vignette shield. The opening should be slightly larger than the size of the scrape and should follow its general outline.

Here are steps that will help eliminate ridge lines:

1. Sand the scraped area. Feather the edges (Fig. 12-13). Start with grade 280 or 320 sandpaper (depending on toughness of the old paint). Progress to 400 or 600 sandpaper. Final sand with the paper wet to reduce abrasive action. After final sanding, wash away all residue with clear water.

2. Mask off the area of the scrape and the rest of the bike to protect it from paint overspray. Don't follow the outline of the scrape. Instead, place one or two layers of masking tape around the frame tube, perpendicular to the tube axis and two or three inches from the edges of the scrape. Masking tape is not so adhesive that it pulls off the paint when you remove it, yet it holds well enough to prevent paint seepage under the edges of the tape.

3. Build a "platform" around the masking tape already in place. Wrap extra layers of tape or a folded piece of paper around the tape. Hold it in place with a separate piece of tape. This platform should be ¼- to ½-inch thick.

4. Tear a piece of paper so it has an uneven and ragged edge. Use it as a vignette shield. The shield should be long enough to encircle the frame tube, and should overlap about ½ inch. Use paper that is lint-free and clean.

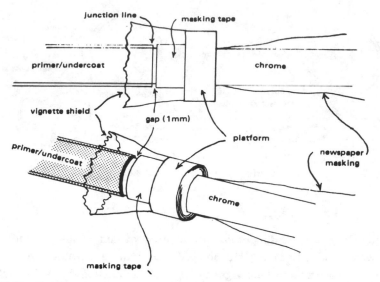

Fig. 12-13: *Feather the edges, using a shield to protect the rest of the frame.*

5. With the ragged edge toward the scrape, wrap the shield around the platform and secure it with a piece of tape (Fig. 12-13). If the shields are placed too close to the frame surface (a low platform), the paint may not be fully vignetted. This leaves a light paint line, easily removed with steel wool. To be discussed later, but worth noting now, are such variables as paint temperature and spraying distance, which also can cause paint lines and paint runs.

6. If bare metal is visible, apply two or three light coats of primer from a spray can. If only a small spot of metal is exposed, it may be covered by using a small brush. Spray, however, leaves a much smoother and more even surface. After the last primer coat has completely dried, sand lightly with grade 400 or 600 wet-type sandpaper. Steel wool (grade 0000) may be used instead of sandpaper. After sanding or steel-wooling, clean the area with a clear water solution. You may find it easier to sand and clean the area with the vignette shields removed. This way you can clear away all sanding residue and dry off all traces of water, before applying colors. Reposition the vignette shields if you do remove them. Sand each, or every other, primer coat instead of only the last.

7. If the original paint finish had an undercoat (which gives tone and depth to the outer color coats) apply two or three layers of an appropriately colored undercoat. This assures fidelity of the final color coat with the original color. To eliminate this step, especially with a large patching, would result in the repaired area having a noticeably different shade. (Howver, this can still result if the original finish is badly weathered.) Sand or steel wool each layer of undercoat or only the last as instructed in Step 6. Sand a previous coat if it dries rough, even slightly so. Otherwise the next coat will just amplify the roughness.

8. Spray on the outer color coats (four or so light ones). To assure a smooth final color coat, wet-sand the previous coat using grade 400 or 600 sandpaper or grade 0000 steel wool. The final color coat is, of course, left unsanded. Spray paints generally function best at room temperature. Submerge spray cans in warm water for ten minutes or so if necessary. If the paint temperature is too low, the spray will be too thick, or, instead of a spray, the paint will stream out; in either case, the paint will tend to run. The spray nozzle should be held 8 to 12 inches from the paint surface. The closer to room temperature the spray is, the closer to the paint surface the nozzle may be held. This is particularly important when shooting tight spots in which the nozzle must be held very close to the surface, such as around the seat cluster.

9. After the final color coat has dried, remove all the shieldings, masking tape, and so forth from the bike. After waiting a few days to a week, and especially if the patched area shows any powdered or lightly rough spots, go over the area with steel wool (grade 0000) saturated with water. If the area is gone over with dry steel wool, the gloss of the area will be removed and even waxing will not return it to a gloss matching the rest of the frame. You may want to try using rubbing compound instead of steel wool. At any rate, such rubbing should be at a minimum.

10. After the paint has completely dried (three weeks), apply wax. If paint is not allowed to dry completely and equipment is clamped on, the clamps will make an imprint into the thickness of the paint, causing it to dry bunched up instead of flat and smooth. The reader will do well to consider that a completely refinished frameset requires not less than a month to dry before waxing or clamping on components. Paint may be dry to the touch within an hour or two, but only to the touch; it will not be thoroughly dry, nor will it be durable.

CHROME FORKS AND STAYS

The second use of vignetting techniques is in the refinishing of chrome forks and stays (if the frame as a whole is being refinished).

First, if chrome is to be painted, it must be sanded, the standard preparation for painting any surface, but especially important with chromed surfaces. Second, a primer coat is a particular necessity prior to any color coat.

Paint will absolutely not "take" to a shiny chrome surface, even one clean of wax. Do not paint over chrome. Any paint over chrome can easily be removed with the lightest grade of steel wool, or actually peeled off as you might peel an orange. Yet sanding need not be too harsh. In fact, the chrome under some factory-finished forks is so undamaged that with a little buffing and polishing you can have an all-chrome fork or at least one with more chrome and less paint.

A similar problem arises from using masking tape in refinishing chrome forks and stays as with repairing scrapes and scratches: a piling up of paint into a ridge at the end of the tape. More important, in refinishing a frame, more layers of paint are used, causing a tendency for the paint to sheet-over the edge of the masking tape, forming a continuous layer (or sheet) of paint. When the paint dries and the masking tape is removed, the effect is one like tearing a sheet of paper, leaving a torn and ragged edge (Fig. 12-14). Vignetting puts a stop to such problems before they start.

Steps in Refinishing Chromed Frame Parts

The following describes the refinishing of chrome forks and stays (for simplicity, only one seat stay is described and illustrated).

1. Measure off the amount of chrome to be painted (or not to be painted) by using a taut line anchored equidistant between the stays or fork blades. The brake anchor-bolt hole is suitable for this, unless the stays or fork blades are badly misaligned (Fig. 12-15). Use a pen or pencil to mark off the distance. If the stays are misaligned, have them properly realigned (there are tools for doing this) before chroming, or if already chromed, before painting. Besides making for an ill-tracking and ill-handling bike, the misalignment may throw the above measurements off without your realizing it. If you are a bit daring, you might consider

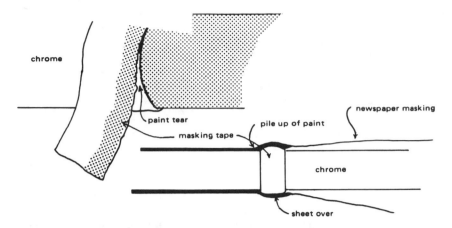

Fig. 12-14: *Torn and ragged edge,
top, can be eliminated with vignette,
bottom.*

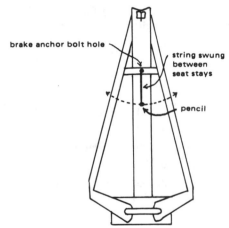

Fig. 12-15: *Measure off chromed
areas to be painted.*

having chrome only on the right, drive-side chain stay, or the drive-side chain stay and seat stay, with only the left-side dropout showing chrome. Asymmetry, if well balanced and well thought out (for example, using a dark color, particularly black), can have an unusual sort of attractiveness.

2. Using masking tape, encircle each stay. Now, with grade 400 or 320 Wet-or-Dry sandpaper, sand the stays to the edge of the masking tape, to the paint-chrome juncture line (Fig. 12-16).

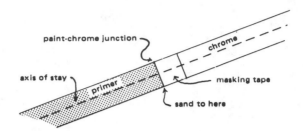

Fig. 12-16: Area to sand chromed stay.

3. After sanding, remove and replace the tape with new tape. Using no more than three encirclements of tape around each stay, be certain that the tape is straight, that is, perpendicular to the axis of the stay (Fig. 12-17). Using newspaper, mask off the chrome that is not to be painted. Mask off each stay individually, as the masking tape will be removed and replaced several times. With modification, the same procedures are used to create "spearheads" (Fig. 12-17). Masking tape is flexible enough to conform to tapering stays and chainwheel indentations.

4. Prime the complete frame (four or so light coats). After the last primer coat has dried, remove the masking tape and go over the immediate area of the juncture line with grade 0000 steel wool, in addition to wet-sanding (using grade 400 or 600) the rest of the frame. Do not sand in the area of the juncture line, or you may remove too much edge paint and scratch the chrome. If you continually sand through paint to bare metal when sanding the frame, you might want to try steel wooling the frame with grade 000 or 0000 steel wool instead of sanding it.

Fig. 12-17: Keep the tape straight around the stay.

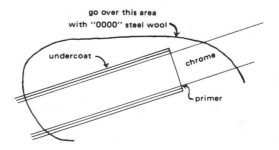

5. Replace the masking tape (from Step 4) with a new strip. Apply an undercoating (three or so coats) to the frame if you have decided to use one over the primer coat. After the last undercoating has dried, remove the masking tape, and steel-wool the area of the juncture line (as in Step 4) to remove any hint of paint buildup as you sand the rest of the frame. If at any time you suspect paint seepage under the masking tape, remove the tape and clear away the excess paint with steel wool.

6. Replace the masking tape (from Step 5) with new tape, but this time place it about one millimeter away from the juncture line (Fig. 12-18, top two figures). Now, build a platform of masking tape or folded paper behind the strip of tape already in place (Fig. 12-18).

7. Make a vignette shield from torn paper and shield off the juncture line about half an inch (Fig. 12-18).

8. Using your chosen finish color, spray the frame. The finished coat will be lightly layered (vignetted) under the vignette shield. Before spraying the last two color coats, remove the shield permanently, but leave the masking tape in place (or replace it with a new tape, still with a one millimeter gap). The final two coats, sprayed with the shields removed, will cover the drop-off at each paint-chrome juncture. When the frame is completely dry (in about a month), apply wax. After wet-sanding each color coat, it may be necessary to remove the shields in order to effectively clear away any sanding residue and water that may have rolled under the shields, in order to prevent fouling the next applied coat. Now, with the shields removed, would also be a good time to smooth out the area of the juncture line with steel wool. Remember to replace the shields. To vary the amount of spray coming through the vignette shield, alter the shield's height above the paint surface or the amount that it overlaps the juncture line. The number of coats suggested is simply that, a suggestion. Three or four coats may just as easily be five or eight light coats (but no less than three). Vignette shields can be used with each coat of paint (from the first primer to the last color coat), or only with every second or third coat (be sure to remove paint buildup between coats). An extra degree of protection may be added to the paint-chrome juncture by lining it with clear lacquer or enamel. First, using grade 000 steel wool, go over the juncture line (about one-eighth inch of paint and an equal amount of chrome). Next, using an artist's brush, trim the juncture line with two or three thin layers of the clear (which will take sufficiently to the chrome and be durable). The value of all this seemingly unnecessary concern and preparation will be seen in the results: smooth and sharply defined juncture lines, unlike some assembly-line paint jobs

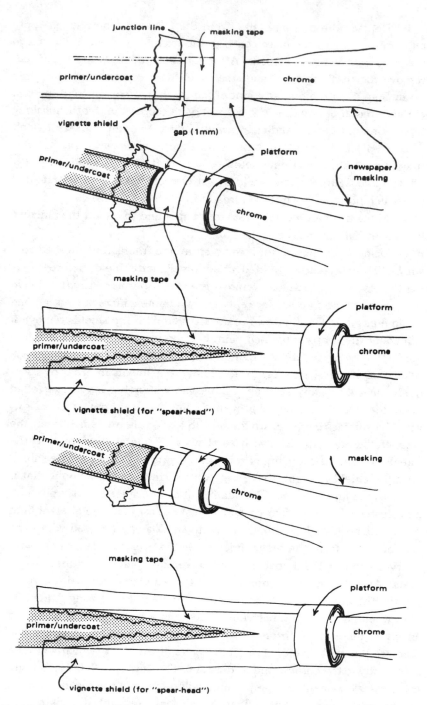

Fig. 12-18: Step 6.

that require a contrasting trim color to hide (unsuccessfully) hurried workmanship.

COLOR-CONTRASTING

The third use of vignetting is in color-contrasting the head tube color with the frame color (as the complete frame is being refinished). The preliminary steps are no different from painting the frame. In general, apply primer, then an undercoat. Next, select a color that contrasts with the chosen frame color. For illustration, orange will be the frame color, with gray as the head-tube color.

1. After the primer and undercoatings are applied and completely dried, mask off the frame, using masking tape and newspaper, about two or three inches from the lugs on the head tube. Remove the headset before painting the frame. This will allow the inside of the head tube to be cleaned thoroughly, particularly of rust. Second, if the headset is not removed, paint may seep into the thin gap between the headset and the head tube and remain wet for quite a while. Finally, painting is easier with nonessentials removed.

2. Place vignette shields around the upper and lower lugs. The opening between the shields and the lugs should be about half an inch.

3. Spray about four light coats of the chosen contrast color (gray) onto the head tube. Always spray with a sweeping motion, horizontally or vertically. When paint is dry to the touch, remove the shields. (Schwinn aluminum undercoat is a silver gray, perfect as both an undercoat and a contrast color, thus allowing Steps 1, 2, and 3 to be eliminated.)

4. After the head-tube area is completely dry, mask off the head tube only (leave the lugs, if any, unmasked). If the head tube is not allowed to dry completely (one or two weeks depending on the number and thickness of the coats), the masking tape will, when eventually removed, pull off the paint. While the frame is completely stripped of paint, a masking should be made to fit the head tube perfectly into the area between the lugs. Make a mask by placing overlapping strips of masking tape on a plastic or glass surface. Use a razor blade to cut out the masking. This is a trial-and-error proposition. Be sure to get a good fit and make an extra one. (The masking should be only one layer thick except at the overlap.) Small pieces of tape can be fitted on the head

tube along the lugs if necessary to completely mask off the head tube. Use a fingernail (or whatever) to shape the masking into a perfect fit along the edge of the lugs, where there should be no bunching.

5. Make a platform one-fourth to one-half inch high of masking tape or folded paper and place around the head tube.

6. Make a vignette shield by tearing a newspaper to the contour of the head tube, but about one-fourth of an inch larger. Place the shield around the full circumference of the head tube, and tape in place. The shield should not only overlap the lugs by at least one-fourth of an inch, but should stand off from the head tube and lugs by the same amount. Some adjustment of the shield may be necessary at the rear of the head tube (Fig. 12-19).

7. With the shield in place, apply the frame-color coats (orange in this example). After the last coat is dry to the touch, remove the shield, but do not remove the masking.

8. With the shield removed, examine the lug/head-tube juncture (where gray and orange colors meet). If the frame paint at the edge of the lugs appears to be too thin, spray on an extra-light layer or two of the frame color around the lugs (with the shield still off, but with the masking in place).

Fig. 12-19: *Design of vignette shield over a lug. (Not needed for unlugged frames, of course.)*

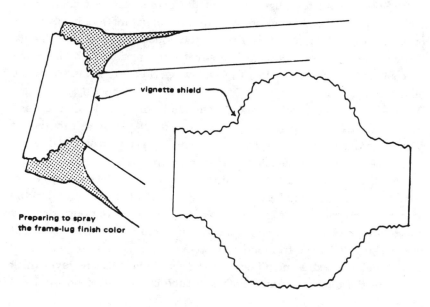

9. If satisfied with the results thus far, and after waiting about three days to a week, remove the head-tube masking. After at least a month, wax may be applied to the complete frame. If contrasting the head tube is an after-thought (after the frame has been painted one color), it may be necessary to sand away some of the paint from the lugs and head tube before beginning Step 1. If you don't do this, the extra paint of the contrast color on the head tube and the extra frame paint applied to the lugs may be so thick that it would be difficult to distinguish the lug drop-off from the head tube proper, especially with lugs thinned and tapered at the edges (Fig. 12-20).

As extra protection and as a "leveler," before waxing, you might want to line the lug/head-tube juncture with a clear lacquer or enamel using a small artist's brush. If only the head-tube masking was used (without the vignette shield), the expected piling up and sheeting-over of paint at the lug/head-tube juncture would occur. The masking would, when removed, pull and tear the lug paint, leaving a ragged edge (Fig. 12-20).

Attempting to smooth out ragged edges by sanding is frustrating at best, as it is easy to sand through to bare metal. Of course, the juncture line can be trimmed or lined with a third color and so, to a degree, can hide poor workmanship. Yet, steady hand or not, the trim line would be just a reflection of tacky workmanship.

Fig. 12-20: *Mask lugs carefully to prevent paint pileup where the lugs thin out.*

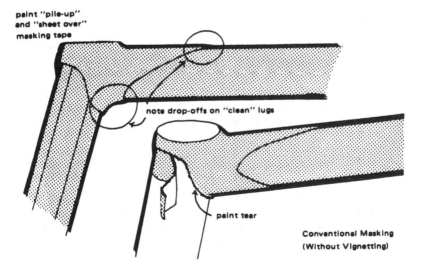

TIPS FOR INEXPENSIVE FRAME PAINTING

More often than not, we acquire experience at the expense of costly mistakes and wasted time, often only to learn a few tips, a couple of shortcuts, and several do's and don'ts. I'd like to give you some pointers on the painting of your frame.

If you have decided to repaint your bike frame but have no experience there, the following may help guide you through inexpensively. Each set of tips has been placed under appropriate headings for easy reference.

Solvents (Removers)

First, plug up the bottom-bracket shell and the head tube by tightly stuffing them with newspaper to keep solvent and water out of the frame tubes. Next, apply semi-paste solvents with a paintbrush. Then use coarse-grade steel wool to remove the solvent-loosened paint from the frame. Finally, rinse the frame clean of solvent, using water.

Keep in mind that newer paint generally dissolves more quickly and easily than older (cured) paint. Also, remember that warm, ambient temperatures will speed the dissolving action of solvents. Solvents burn, so cover exposed skin areas and have water nearby for rinsing off. Be careful. Although the fingertips may be somewhat insensitive to the burning of solvents, the sinuses, insides of the wrists, and the eyes are not.

Use paint and lacquer thinners only secondarily, as they are not primary paint removers.

Preparing the Frame

Strip off all the old paint, or at least repair all scratches, chips, and scrapes. The original paint can hide the carelessness of a frame builder. If it needs to be repainted, then it needs to be stripped.

File off all excess brazing material hiding under the original paint. If necessary, reshape the dropouts and the dropout derailleur lug. Make any needed frame realignments before painting or chroming. Remove all nonessentials such as the headset, so you can prep the frame and paint it more easily. You could remove the builder's marque and reattach it with rivets later on. Or you can leave it off and fill in the rivet holes with a filler such as one of the commercially available liquid metals.

Forget about liquid etchers. Sandpaper the bare frame to a smooth, but not slick, finish. Use coarse or medium-grade emery cloth followed by 180 or 220 Wet-or-Dry sandpaper. (As you sand, remember to always do it in one direction.) If you sandblast the old paint, be sure to use the proper grade of blasting material, mask all chrome, and repaint immediately. Sandblasted frames begin to rust very quickly. *Do not touch the frame with bare hands!* Your skin has acids that can etch into the bare, unprotected metal. Look for and remove any rust. Many times it hides in areas such as inside the seat tube.

Mask all threads before painting. Shove rolled-up newspaper into both ends of the bottom-bracket shell and head tube; leave paper sticking out. Removing paint from bottom-bracket threads without damaging the outside frame finish is not always easy. Paint has to be pried out of the threads. In addition, the front fork can and should be refinished separately from the main frame.

Painting Conditions

If you can overcome family objections, it is preferable to paint indoors in an empty, well-ventilated room in which control of dust and other conditions can be maintained. Open all windows, clear the room of furniture, or cover everything with newspaper, including the floor, and close all closets. It might be wise to wear a respirator-type mask or breathe through a wet face towel held over your mouth and nose. Keep overspray from your lungs. If you are painting outdoors, ideally you should do so on windless, dry, warm days and in the shade. If a bug lands on wet paint, remove it with a pin or needle. If the removal messes up the paint, allow the surface to dry, then sand and respray the area without masking it off.

Indoors, use well-diffused lighting. In addition to opened window curtains, use ceiling lights, repositioned table lamps (with the shades removed), and a hand-held flashlight for checking tight areas.

Remove all dust from the frame between coat applications. Use a clean paint brush for this purpose. Rags rarely are lint- or static-free. Dust particles caught under layers of paint will show through as paint blisters.

Do not create static charges by rubbing the frame tubes unnecessarily, as this tends to attract dust particles. Besides, there is no such thing as clean, oil-free hands, so hands off between coats.

Do not spray onto a cold, damp frame, or on cold damp days. Water (dampness) will bubble up or blister the paint, as I have sadly and expensively learned from personal experience. Spraying on a cold damp night can cause the paint to dry to a dull, frosty finish even though a glossy finish color is used. Maintain spraying conditions as constantly as possible from one spraying session to the next, especially if respraying only a small section of the frame. Note such spraying instructions as ". . . material and surface temperature 65–95 degrees . . . relative humidity 85% . . . recoat at 70 degrees. . . ." Keep in mind that instructions may vary among paint brands.

When cleaning up paint overspray, use a vacuum cleaner and a damp dusting cloth. Sweeping with a hand broom will only cause the overspray to become airborne and settle or resettle on furniture, shelves, and you— even worse, in your lungs.

When you finally are ready to start painting, practice on something first. Learn the spray characteristics of each spray can, and read all label instructions.

Hang the frame so that you easily can get to and spray all areas of it. Using a pipe, one end supported in a stable base and the other end inserted into the frame's seat tube (at about waist or head high), is even better. The frame should be easily rotatable on its paint stand.

Always spray with sweeping motions, except when spraying tight areas or very small spots, which are shot with quick bursts of spray. Lightly spray hard-to-get-to areas before spraying the frame, assuring that easily missed areas such as the underside of the frame tubes and around the seat and head-tube lugs are fully covered. Some manufacturers miss these areas, or the paint is so thinly applied that Comet cleanser, a dish towel, and very little elbow grease are enough to rub away the finish completely. (Use a nonabrasive cleaner for cleaning the frame.) Additionally, extra paint also should be applied to the underside of the down tube and the backside of the seat tube as extra protection against kicked-up road gravel.

Shake the spray can often to keep the paint ingredients well-mixed. Never start spraying directly onto the frame, as this may cause a paint run. Begin spraying first into the air, then with a sweeping motion move onto the frame. Conversely, stop spraying by first sweeping from the frame into the air before releasing the spray nozzle.

At some point before applying the first color coat (preferably before the first primer coat), coat the insides of the frame tubes, chain stays, and bottom-bracket shell with a rust inhibitor (Penetrol or Rust-Oleum primer) to protect from the effects of rain and condensation. Plug up one end of a frame tube and, using a funnel, fill it completely with the rust inhibitor and then empty. Do the same with the other tubes. Alternately, you might want to try using a sponge brush with a long, flexible handle.

The first two or so coats of primer, undercoat, and color coats should be misted or dusted onto the frame. They will dry slightly rough, but with successive coats and with sanding, the coats will be smoothed out. Use grade 400 or 600 Wet-or-Dry sandpaper.

A painting tip to remember is that several thin, light coats are better than one thick coat. However, spread the coat applications over time (one or two weeks). Each coat of paint will reflect the quality of the previous coat. So prepare each coat for the next one. Do not try to stop paint runs by wiping with a rag. Runs can be stopped by the following methods: soaking them up with a finger wrapped in a rag; turning the frame over to reverse the run; using quick sweeps of spray to undercut the run (but without feeding it much more paint), thus sweeping and spreading out the run; or blowing on the run to spread it out and prevent its running farther. (For a stream of air without paint, turn the spray can upside-down, aim just below the run, and depress the nozzle.)

If all else fails, allow the run to dry completely, then sand and repaint. To lessen the time needed for a thick run to dry, cut away part of it (when partially dry) with a razor blade. Do not attempt to sand wet paint, as you will only create a gorge in the thickness of the paint surface.

A coat of paint being applied over a previously applied coat may wet the previous coat, thus effectively acting as a solvent. This is one reason for not wiping away a paint run. You may wipe through the rewetted previous coat of paint and expose bare metal.

If your touch is too light, or the spray nozzle is held too far from the frame, the paint will dust-on, creating a rough or powdered texture. To smooth it out, use grade 0000 steel wool. Keep your technique controled.

Do not apply lacquer over enamel, as the former will lift off the latter. Enamel can be applied safely over lacquer without damage, but why confuse yourself? Stick with one or the other throughout.

If only a small amount of paint remains in the can, or if the nozzle is clogged, the paint will tend to spurt out, creating large paint globs (toad skin) on the frame. Either throw away these cans, or use them only with an artist's brush for small touch-up jobs. Besides, the last of the paint is never quite the same quality as the first of it. Clear the spray nozzle/ siphon tube by turning the spray can upside-down and depressing the nozzle. The nozzle itself also can be cleared by reaming it out with a pin or needle. Occasionally wipe the outside of the nozzle clean with a rag.

Epoxies and Exotics

Using "exotics" such as epoxies and the like is up to you, but learn their limitations, special preparation, and so forth. Again, practice on something first. Remember that if you choose an unusual frame color, and later must repair a large paint scrape, you may have difficulty in matching that color.

Clear lacquer (or enamel) applied over the frame color coat will give it a heightened gloss and, to a certain extent, act as a protective coat. However, a clear coat is not in the least bit necessary, and if improperly applied, may prove disastrous. If you do use a clear, practice on something before applying it to the frame.

Levelers, surfacers, and rubbing compound all have the same basic function of smoothing out scratches in the primer and finish coats. These refinishing accessories are not especially necessary, however, and you can do just as well without them. You may, however, want to try rubbing compound on the finish coats. Enamels require a different application procedure from lacquers, although some manufacturers use the same label instructions regardless of whether the paint is lacquer or enamel.

Find and stay with one supplier who has a good, no-hassle refund policy and who is knowledgeable (a salesperson who gets his or her information by reading the back label of the spray can is not knowledgeable). Finally, do not lose that receipt.

About Chrome Plating

The surface to be chromed must be absolutely smooth. Chrome plating does not fill in nor does it smooth out scratches (large, small, or tiny), it just plates them. Sand out all scratches (use grade 400 or 600 Wet-or-Dry sandpaper).

Those parts of the frame not to be chromed should be masked with plastic electrician's tape, which will conform to just about any irregular shape. It may be to your advantage to mask the frame yourself. Talk to the plater first.

Even if you want only a few inches of the lower blades chromed, have the complete front fork chromed (chrome, properly sanded, can be painted). If chroming the rear stays, chrome each stay completely, from the dropout to the seat lug or bottom-bracket shell—in general, any point where there is a bend or turn. Do so even if only partially chromed stays are desired, otherwise the chrome plating may form a ridge at the edge of the electrician's tape (depending on the thickness of the plating). Partially chromed stays (and forks) of commercially produced frames actually are completely chromed.

There are a few tight areas on a bike frame that are difficult for the plater to polish properly (a prerequisite to plating bright chrome). The result is that if you have these areas or the complete frame chromed, they may not be as bright as other areas of chrome.

Mask all threads. In general, mask anything in which a dimensional enlargement would cause a component misfit (such as the headset lower race platform, or shoulder, or the fork crown). Chrome plating is not at all easy to file off, so do not put it where you don't want it.

Chrome plating has its disadvantages, such as the corrosive actions of the plating process (for example, rust forming on the insides of the frame tubes). Hydrogen embrittlement, another bugaboo of the plating process, is caused when hydrogen diffuses into the metal being plated during the chroming operation. Oven-baking at a prescribed temperature and time setting will relieve the hydrogen. However, some platers will not do this; they do not want to be bothered with it and simply do not care. The question is, do you? Some cyclists are very wary about riding with front forks weakened or made brittle by the plating process. The disadvantages of chroming (real, imagined, or simply exaggerated) are enough to discourge many from having any frame part plated. It is your choice.

As soon as the frame is chromed, get it back from the plater and remove the rust formed during the plating process. Do not allow the frame to remain in the plater's shop longer than necessary. If the plater becomes lazy during one of the steps of the plating process, you may easily end up with a shoddy plating job. One plater, who assured me that he had experience in plating bike frames, returned a front fork to me that actually peeled. Yes, I was able to peel much of the chrome plating off the fork (just as you would peel the the foil wrapping from a candy bar), exposing the copper base or under-plating. Collective opinion suggested that one probable cause was the plater's failure to keep the fork clean of dirt and or grease while he handled it. In any case, it was a shoddy job.

A verbal guarantee is just another way of saying "Maybe, but probably not." Get it in writing, and hang on to that payment receipt. A final consideration for chromed (as well as unchromed) frames is to coat the insides of the tubes with a rust inhibitor/preventative.

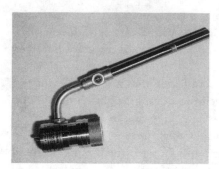

Fig. 12-21: Use this torch with Mapp gas or propane for brazing bike tubes (it does not need an oxygen tank).

Admittedly, the foregoing advice is less than complete. But with experience, you will no doubt add several tips of your own. In the meanwhile, the usual but avoidable blunders of inexperience will be minimized.

FRAME REPAIRS

If you like the idea of building your own bike frame, or brazing parts such as water-bottle cages onto your frame, a new brazing torch is for you (Fig. 12-21). The torch uses Mapp gas or propane. It does not require oxygen, thanks to a unique turbo method of using the oxygen in the room air. The torch is the Turbo-Torch, made by Victor Equipment Company, available through welding supply stores. The torch brazes or solders steel, copper, brass, and aluminum. The latest brazing rods come with flux on them. I use this torch for bike frame work, repairing small parts such as broken metal lawn chairs, and making wire sculptures.

Appendix

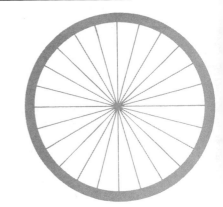

Definitions

ALIGNMENT Applies to the bicycle frame. You should have: dropouts parallel to each other; fork blades and stays parallel to the top tube; top tube centered between the stays; head tube parallel to the fork blades; fork blades parallel to each other; stays parallel to each other; seat tube parallel to the bottom-bracket sides.

BINDER BOLT Any bolt and nut that holds a part onto a bicycle, such as the binder bolt(s) for saddles, brakes, carriers, lights, generators, computers, derailleurs, cranks, and other bolted-on parts.

BOTTOM-BRACKET ASSEMBLY Spindle, bearings, cones, cups, and locknut. The crank arms are attached to the spindle.

BOTTOM-BRACKET HANGER The short round tube containing the bottom-bracket assembly and to which the down tube, seat tube, and chain stays are attached.

BRAKE BRIDGE A tube mounted between the seat stays to which the rear brake is attached. May also hold fender mount and carrier mount.

BRAKE LEVERS Handlebar-mounted levers which control the brakes.

CABLES Flexible steel cables connecting brake levers to the brakes and the shift levers to the front and rear derailleurs.

CADENCE Crank revolutions per minute, a measure of how fast the rider can spin the cranks. A good touring cadence would be 70 to 80 crank revolutions per minute for the casual touring cyclist, up to 100 or more for the trained racer.

CHAIN The articulated drive unit connecting the chainwheel gears to the freewheel gears.

CHAIN STAYS The frame tubing from the bottom bracket to the rear dropouts.

CHAINWHEELS The toothed gears attached to the bottom-bracket spindle which deliver pedal power to the freewheel gears. Chainwheels may be single, double, or triple.

COASTER BRAKES A brake mechanism contained in the rear-wheel hub, which is actuated by backpedaling.

COTTER KEY A key or pin which holds cottered cranks on the bottom-bracket spindle.

CRANK ARM The long shaft that is attached to the bottom-bracket spindle and to which the pedals are attached.

DERAILLEUR From the French, meaning "to derail" or shift. The rear derailleur shifts the chain from one freewheel cog to another; the front derailleur shifts the chain from one chainwheel to another.

DISHING Describes truing the rear wheel so the rim is centered exactly between the hub axle locknuts. Necessary because of added width of the freewheel. In dishing, the rear-wheel rim is more toward the right hub flange, whereas the front-wheel rim, which is not dished, is centered between the hub flanges.

DOWN TUBE The frame tube which is connected to the head tube and to the bottom bracket.

DROPOUTS Slotted openings into which wheel hub axles fit. Holds front and rear wheels.

FORK Consists of the fork blades, fork crown, front-wheel dropouts, and steering tube.

HEAD TUBE The short tube to which is connected the top and down tubes and which holds the fork with its associated headset bearings, cups, cones, and locknut.

HUB The front and rear wheel units that hold the wheel axle and to which are attached the spokes.

QUICK-RELEASE A cam-and-lever actuated mechanism which permits quick and easy removal and installation of a bicycle wheel.

SADDLE The seat.

SEAT POST A hollow tube sized to fit into the seat tube, designed to hold and support the saddle. Adjustable so saddle can be tilted and moved closer to or farther away from the handlebars.

SEAT STAYS Two hollow steel tubes attached at one end to the seat tube and at the other end to each of the rear wheel dropouts. With the chain stays (see above) they form the rear triangle of the bicycle frame.

Further Reading

Technical

Brandt, Jobst. *The Bicycle Wheel*. Avocet, Inc., Menlo Park, California, 1983.

Burke, Edmund. ed. *Science of Cycling*. Human Kinetics Books, Champaign, Illinois, 1986.

Hayduk, Douglas. *Bicycle Metallurgy for the Cyclist*. Douglas Hayduk, Murray, Utah, 1987.

Marr, Dick. *Bicycle Gearing: A Practical Guide*. The Mountaineers, Seattle, 1989.

Whitt, Frank Rowland, and David Gordon Wilson. *Bicycling Science*. The MIT Press, Cambridge, Massachusetts, 1988.

Catalogs

Bike Nashbar, P.O. Box 3449, Youngstown, OH 44513-0449. Phone: 1-800-627-4227. FAX: 1-800-456-1223. (Both numbers include Alaska and Hawaii.)

Palo Alto Bicycles, P.O. Box 1276, Palo Alto, CA 94302. Outside CA: 1-800-227-8900; in CA: 415-328-0128. Everything in bicycles.

Pedal Pushers, 1130 Rogero Rd., Jacksonville, FL 32211-5895. Outside FL: 1-800-874-2453; in FL: 1-800-342-7320. Good catalog, compiled by cyclists.

Performance Bicycle Shop, P.O. Box 2741, Chapel Hill, NC 27514. Phone: 1-800-334-5471. A beautifully put-together catalog of bicycles, parts, components, accessories, clothing. Very helpful in parts selection.

Recreation Equipment, Inc., P.O. Box C-88125, Seattle, WA 98188. Outside WA: 1-800-426-4840; in WA: 1-800-562-4894; for Canada, Hawaii and Alaska: 1-206-575-3287. If you join their benefits program (fee $5) you receive a membership card which, when used with orders, gives you quite a substantial discount. Catalog is free. Everything for the outdoors. Camping gear, bicycles, books—you name it, they have it.

Rhode Gear, 765 Allens Avenue, Providence, RI 02905. Phone: 1-800-HOT-GEAR. Excellent panniers and other equipment designed by this firm. Plus lots of parts, clothing, and other gear.

The Third Hand, P.O. Box 212, Mt. Shasta, CA 96067. Phone: 916-926-2600. FAX: 916-926-2663. The bike tool doesn't exist if it's not in their catalog. Plus small parts unavailable elsewhere. Prices generally lower than retail outlets.

Index